To Josue
with love and admiration
from
Angela

Between the Temple and the Cave:
The Religious Dimensions of the Poetry of E.J. Pratt

E.J. Pratt's religious beliefs have baffled literary scholars for years: critics have assigned him positions ranging from orthodoxy through agnosticism to atheism. *Between the Temple and the Cave* provides a definitive exploration of Pratt's complex relationship with Christianity, providing insight into both the man and his works.

Drawing on a wide variety of newly available source material, Angela McAuliffe examines the roots of Pratt's religious attitudes, including his strict Methodist upbringing in Newfoundland and his plans to enter the ministry. She explores Pratt's early prose and unpublished poetry, including his theses on demonology and Pauline eschatology and the unpublished poem "Clay," to trace the origins of religious ideas and motifs that occur in his later work.

McAuliffe focuses on key motifs in Pratt's poetry, such as his image of a distant and formidable God, his apocalyptic vision of the world, and his belief in determinism and fate. She concludes that the diversity of religious positions attributed to Pratt and the image of God that emerges from his poetry are facets of the ironic vision of a man of twentieth-century sensibility who wrestled with God and sought a medium of expression equal to his themes.

ANGELA T. MCAULIFFE is an independent scholar and retreat director at Loretto College in the University of Toronto.

Between the Temple and the Cave

The Religious Dimensions of the Poetry of E.J. Pratt

ANGELA T. MCAULIFFE IBVM

McGill-Queen's University Press
Montreal & Kingston · London · Ithaca

© McGill-Queen's University Press 2000
ISBN 0-7735-2057-0

Legal deposit second quarter 2000
Bibliothèque nationale du Québec

Printed in Canada on acid-free paper

This book has been published with the help of a grant from the Humanities and Social Sciences Federation of Canada, using funds provided by the Social Sciences and Humanities Research Council of Canada.

McGill-Queen's University Press acknowledges the financial support of the Government of Canada through the Book Publishing Industry Development Program (BPIDP) for its activities. We also acknowledge the support of the Canada Council for the Arts for our publishing program.

Excerpts from E.J. Pratt's poetry are taken from *E.J. Pratt: Complete Poems*, 2 vols, edited by Sandra Djwa and R.G. Moyles (Toronto: University of Toronto Press, 1989). Reprinted by permission of University of Toronto Press.
Excerpts from "Little Gidding" in *Four Quartets*, copyright 1943 by T.S. Eliot and renewed 1971 by Esme Valerie Eliot, reprinted by permission of Harcourt Brace & Company.

Canadian Cataloguing in Publication Data

McAuliffe, Angela T. C.
   Between the temple and the cave : the religious dimensions of the poetry of E.J. Pratt

   Includes bibliographical references and index.
   ISBN 0-7735-2057-0

   1. Pratt E.J. (Edwin John), 1882–1964—Criticism and interpretation. 2. Pratt E.J. (Edwin John), 1882–1964—Religion. 3. Christianity in literature. I. Title.

PS8531.R23Z72 2000   C811'.52   C99-901606-7
PR9199.3.P7Z72 2000

Typeset in 10/12 Baskerville by True to Type

Contents

Preface   vii

Acknowledgments   xi

Abbreviations   xiii

1 "Up from Newfoundland":
  The Preacher in Search of the Poet   3

2 "The Good Lord" with "a Glittering Monocle":
  The Problem of God   39

3 "Ghosts of the Apocalypse"   65

4 "A Tendency to ... Fatalism Tempered with
  Humanity"   123

5 The Wheel Comes Full Circle: The Atoning Christ   157

  Conclusion   199

  Notes   205

  Bibliography   227

  Index   245

Preface

Any careful study of the writings of E.J. Pratt, one of Canada's most distinguished and consistently productive poets of the twentieth century, cannot but help lay bare a question of major importance that emerges from the heart of his work – his attitude towards religion in general, and towards Christianity in particular. The few books and many articles which constitute Pratt criticism serve to confirm the significance of this question, embracing within their range a wide spectrum of interpretation. For example, Northrop Frye and A.J.M. Smith indicate Pratt's debt to Christian ideas and attitudes, but leave the reader wishing that with their degree of perception they had pursued the matter further. John Sutherland is so determined to find Christian themes and images that he wrests them out of the most unlikely contexts. Sandra Djwa struggles with what she perceives to be the "dualisms" in Pratt's religious thought as she finds them reflected in the poetry. Frank Davey assumes Pratt's denial of all but the natural order, while other critics such as Vincent Sharman and Glenn Clever seem bent on proving Pratt's rejection of traditional Christianity.

Complicating the issue are certain attitudes on the part of Pratt himself – his ironic vision of humanity and of the world around him; his relentless effort, particularly as a narrative poet, to achieve "dramatic objectivity"; and his self-deprecatory comments about his work. Significantly, no one, to this date, with the exception of David Pitt in his authoritative biography, appears to have looked very far beyond the general or vague information provided by Pratt in private conversations or in public interviews to what must surely be the foundation of his attitude towards religion or of his reaction against it – his upbringing in a family and a community of strict Methodist affiliation, his schooling under religious auspices, and the years he spent in preparation for the Methodist ministry to which he was ordained.

It should prove rewarding, then, to explore Pratt's poetry in the light of the religious and cultural atmosphere of Newfoundland in which he was raised, the early education and the pastoral initiation which he received there, and the studies in formal theology and psychology which he undertook in Toronto in the early years of the twentieth century. His two theses, written in partial requirement for graduate degrees in philosophy at Victoria University, and copies of his lectures as a professor in the Department of English, introductions to readings of his poetry, and occasional talks and papers which he delivered throughout Canada and the United States, together with the texts of posthumously published and little-known poems and collections of correspondence, provide insights into Pratt the man and into those of his works that have appeared, even in part, to be problematic.

Within the context of this study, several questions of significance must be posed or reformulated. For example, what was the nature and the extent of the religious crisis that Pratt is said to have undergone? When did it occur? Was it the reason for his decision to forego the ministry for an academic career? Did it lead him to a total renunciation of religious belief and to the severance of all connections with organized religion? How much was he influenced by the scientific, philosophic and theological works of the nineteenth and early twentieth centuries? To what degree are his biblical and theological studies reflected, consciously or not, in his poetry? What is the image of God that emerges most consistently from his work? Can it be clearly formulated? Similar questions must be asked about Pratt's image of Jesus Christ: is Jesus anything more than the epitome of human nature? What is his relationship to God, to humankind, to time, and to history?

Any doubts that I might have entertained about the value of this task in view of the many and extreme interpretations that have been read into Pratt's poetry in the past have been relieved by three sources. The first is information that I gathered between 1972 and 1999 in interviews and conversations with those who knew Pratt closely or intimately. The second is the abundance of barely tapped source material mentioned above. The third is a letter Pratt wrote in 1957 in reply to Dorothy Doyle, who had asked his opinion of her proposal to write a study of the relationship between nature and grace as it is reflected in his poetry. Pratt's response was surprisingly enthusiastic. After pointing out both the positive insights and the limitations contained in John Sutherland's book, he remarked, "leafing through *Collected Poems* recently, I was astonished at the numerous references to Christ, the Cross, and to the symbol of grace." In addition to the narrative poems that raise questions of a religious nature, Pratt then suggested nine lyrics which he felt should be considered in such a study as "they contain undercurrents of my convictions." This personal letter, appended to one copy of a doctoral thesis, came to light only after much of this study was completed, and served to confirm the validity of such an approach and to indicate Pratt's general attitude during his later years towards a religious or Christian interpretation of his work.

Acknowledgments

I acknowledge with gratitude the patient encouragement and the advice of Dr Malcolm M. Ross, Professor Emeritus in the Department of English, Dalhousie University, Halifax, Nova Scotia. I am most thankful, too, to the late Viola and Claire Pratt, Northrop Frye, Allan R. Bevan, E.J. McCorkell, CSB, and J.S. McGivern, SJ; to M.G. Parks, Dalhousie University, Halifax; to David Pitt, Gwenyth Puddester, and Arthur Kewley, St John's, Newfoundland; to Lorna Fraser, Donald Finlay, CSB, and to Robert Brandeis, Anne Black, and the librarians at Dalhousie, Victoria, St Michael's and Queen's Universities, the Thomas Fisher Rare Book Library, Toronto, and the Atlantic School of Theology, Halifax; to Boyd Hiscock and Glenn Lucas, United Church Archives, St John's and Toronto; to Dr John Griffin, professor emeritus, Queen Street Mental Health Centre; to the members of the English-Speaking Canadian Province of the Society of Jesus; to McGill-Queen's University Press, particularly Judy Williams and Joan McGilvray; and to the members of the faculty and staff of Regis College, Toronto School of Theology, to the teachers who introduced me to the poetry of Pratt, and to the students with whom I was later privileged to share it. I am especially indebted to the leadership and to the members of the North American Branch of the Institute of the Blessed Virgin Mary, to the members of my family, and to all my friends for their interest, encouragement, and loving support over the years.

Abbreviations

The following abbreviations are used in parentheses in the text.

1. *E.J. Pratt: Complete Poems*, Parts 1 and 2. Toronto:
2. University of Toronto Press, 1989 (followed by appropriate page numbers)

DS   E.J. Pratt. "The Demonology of the [New Testament] Synoptics in [Its] Relation to Earlier Developments and to the Mind of Christ." MA thesis, University of Toronto 1912

EL   "An Experience of Life." Typescript of a Radio Interview with Ronald Hambleton. *CBC Times*. Part 1, 6 March 1953: 3; Part 2, 20 March 1953: 3–4

MS   Pratt Collection of Manuscripts, Victoria University Library, Toronto (followed by appropriate box, folder, and item or page numbers where applicable)

PE   E.J. Pratt. *Studies in Pauline Eschatology and Its Background.* Toronto: William Briggs 1917

PLP   *E.J. Pratt on His Life and Poetry.* Edited by Susan Gingell. Toronto: University of Toronto Press, 1983

PPAA   *E.J. Pratt: Pursuits Amateur and Academic.* Edited by Susan Gingell. Toronto: University of Toronto Press, 1995

Abbreviated titles of secondary sources and works by other authors cited will be identified in endnotes.

Between the Temple and the Cave

1 "Up from Newfoundland": The Preacher in Search of the Poet

HOME IN THE CLEFT OF THE ROCK

This exploration, like many others, might well have begun *in medias res* rather than *in principio*, yet it seems that to attempt to bring into focus the religious and theological dimensions implicit in the poetry of E.J. Pratt without reference to the early years of his life would be to invite further misunderstanding of the man, and greater misinterpretation of his work. The atmosphere of his family and home, the natural and social environment in which he grew up, and the particular orientation of his education all contributed to the way in which Pratt envisioned both his own immediate world and the universe beyond it.

E.J. Pratt was born in Western Bay, Newfoundland, on 4 February 1882, the third son of "fiery John Pratt,"[1] an evangelist who had emigrated from England just as British Methodism in the enthusiastic wake of its centenary was expanding its missions abroad.[2] Little is known of John Pratt's early life, except that he was born on 28 August 1839 in the market town of Barnard Castle, Durham, where John Wesley once preached;[3] he worked in the lead mines near Gunnerside and Kettlewell, Yorkshire, and as a youth he "gave his heart to the Lord."[4] The basic education that made him a literate and eloquent man he probably received under Methodist auspices, if not at the school at Headingly, Yorkshire, at the academy at Wharfedale founded by Joseph Lawrence, a wealthy merchant, to recruit probationers for Newfoundland and Nova Scotia.[5] John Pratt then spent several years as town missionary on the Blackburn and Rochdale Wesleyan circuits, at the centre of Lancashire's textile industry with all the social and environmental ills that it spawned.[6] It was, perhaps, in part to escape from these "dark Satanic mills" that in 1873, at the age of thirty-four, he left his country. One year after his arrival in Newfoundland, the Methodist Church of Canada was founded with a Newfoundland Conference,[7] and provisions were made for the education of a native clergy.[8] On 17 June 1877, after having served the usual three years' probation in Catalina and St John's, John Pratt was "received into Full Connection, and ordained a minister of the Methodist Church of Canada."[9]

The strain of Methodism that John Pratt brought with him was charged with the primitive missionary zeal preserved in the northern counties of England since the days of the Wesleys and Whitefield.[10] Conservative and apolitical, unlike other versions of Methodism, it was generally regarded both at home and abroad as a wholesome influence against radicalism.[11] During John Pratt's thirty years of travelling the circuits of Newfoundland, from Bonavista around the Avalon Peninsula to Grand Bank, he was credited with great religious awakenings.[12] When John Pratt preached at a revival, Charles Lench, a contemporary, recalls, "one would have to go to church at five o'clock to secure seats." On such occasions, Lench adds, "Boanerges," as Pratt was known, "took his hearers to Sinai ... then led them to Calvary."[13] It was regarded as a tribute to his preaching that during his last visit to England in 1902 John Pratt was invited by Charles Haddon Spurgeon, the Baptist preacher whom he had long admired and supported, to address the congregation at the Metropolitan Tabernacle in London.[14] E.J. Pratt later remarked that his father seemed rather moderate in his views in a community with a strong Calvinist tradition, but he admitted the influence of the kind of sermon to which he had been exposed from early childhood:

Oh, the preaching I listened to as a boy! ... The preachers in my day, whether local preachers or ordained clergymen, could lift their congregations out of their pews by the most gorgeous descriptions of heaven, or else shake them under the planks by painting hell with colours never seen on land or sea. [When a preacher really got going on the Apocalypse] we, as youngsters, would creep under the seats until the time came for the benediction. We would come out from our hidings when we were sure that the colours were dry. One might dispute the Gospel truth of the message, but no one could deny the power. It was a real heaven and a real hell we saw. The cinders were in our eyes on Sunday night. Only the morning put out the nightmare fires and not always then. (MS 9.68:1–2)

In a Christian denomination in which church buildings were plain and unadorned, and in which ritual and liturgy were underplayed, the emphasis fell quite naturally upon the hymns and the sermon whose texts were taken frequently from the Old Testament and the Apocalypse.[15] The impression these sermons made upon the imagination of a sensitive child would have been great. There was no need of concrete visual imagery, other than that provided by the world around him, to reinforce it. Listening to sermons, moreover, gave him a sense of the power of the spoken word. The rhetorical techniques of the preacher and those of the narrative poet are not mutually exclusive.[16] E.J. Pratt later found no difficulty in exchanging one role for the other.

In 1901 John Pratt, then serving at Grand Bank, was elected president of the Newfoundland Conference Sessions to be held at St John's,[17] although at that time his health was already failing. By the time of the Conference of 1904, he was dead, and the delegates remembered him as another John the Baptist, "a burning and a shining light" (Jn 5:35), by which "many were enabled to find their way to the Cross, and to the City of God."[18] His mystical zeal and dedication were evident in the last letter he dictated to his son James, which was read posthumously to his congregation.[19] He wanted his flock to be confident that he died "in sure and certain hope."[20] The circumstances surrounding his death and burial were the stuff from which another son's poems were later to be made: the coldest March on record – so cold that the ice did not break on Placentia Bay; the steamer to St John's stuck three miles from shore for twelve days with John Pratt's body on board; and the shortage of food, and the mounting fear among the passengers which drove at least one person overboard.[21] The Centennial Conference of 1916 placed a memorial plaque at Grand Bank commemorating John Pratt, who "alone was destined to fall at his post during the first century of Methodism in Newfoundland."[22] There is little doubt that the compassionate service of the minister in E.J. Pratt's *Rachel*, and the heroic and single-minded zeal of his Brébeuf, reflect facets of John Pratt's character which his son could, if not not wholly emulate, still admire.

Towards the end of his probation, John Pratt had asked for and received from Captain William Knight, skipper of a sealing vessel, permission to marry his daughter, Fanny.[23] The wedding took place on 4 July 1877 shortly after Pratt's ordination. John Pratt's vocation would mean an itinerant life for his family, as they moved with him every three years from circuit to circuit and from outport to city during the course of his ministry.[24] His wife's untiring and affectionate presence, however, meant it was not an unstable one. Theirs was a close-knit family whose role in Methodist society was clearly defined and accepted.

John Pratt, as head of the family, was charged with the responsibility of providing for the needs of its members. As husband, he was expected to be faithful and constant, to treat his wife with delicacy and tenderness, to forgive her human failures and shortcomings, and to look to her welfare, support, and protection. He was exhorted to be pious, moral, and abstemious, to implement the tenets of religion, and to avoid unjust business practices and litigation against other Methodists. He presided at family prayers, read and explained scriptures to the members of his household, and led the Sunday hymn-singing. It was hoped that as an ordained minister, he and his family would set for others a pattern of the Christian life that was marked by wisdom, charity, and order.[25]

For her part, Fanny Pratt might take as model the virtuous woman of Proverbs 9:10–31. As the social rank and education of the minister's wife were not expected to be as high as those of her husband, it was assumed that she would defer to his authority, and be faithful and modest as wife and mother, frugal as a housekeeper, and just and kind to servants. Like Susanna Annesley, the mother of John and Samuel Wesley, Anne Taylor, the mother of Nathanael Burwash, and Anna Vincent, matriarch of the Massey clan, she was meant to be the spiritual heart of the family, instructing the children in their prayers, in Christian doctrine, and in moral conduct, encouraging in them the formation of conscience and helping them to discern between genuine and spurious religious experience. She would console them when their prayers seemed to go unanswered, and witness their first and foundational experience of conversion when it occurred.[26]

As the Methodist congregation or the class meeting was the social context in which adults could find support for their faith, it was assumed that children with their limited understanding and judgment would find theirs within the embrace of family and home. Hence, parents were enjoined (albeit with moderation, love, and good example) to break the inherently rebellious will and tame the natural tendencies of their children, who were assumed to share from birth the natural depravity of fallen humankind.[27]

It is not difficult to imagine how Will, the first-born child of John Pratt and Fanny Knight – a sensitive and gifted boy – must have chafed under the discipline meted out by his father to the first of the Pratts of Newfoundland. As a young man, he left home after a bitter quarrel with his parents, and his name was never mentioned again in the parental home.[28] He acquired a position first in St John's as journalist with a local newspaper, then in New York as editor of an encyclopedia. He married, led an unhappy life, and eventually ended it by suicide. One wonders if much the attempt to break the will of the oldest son did, in fact, "break Will," and how much of it was witnessed and internalized by his younger brothers and sisters.

Such a life imposed on the children responsibilities and restrictions which might not have weighed so heavily had their father not been a minister. In their home the sabbath was observed strictly, most of the day being devoted to church services and Sunday School. Since the children were not permitted to play, they might spend the rest of the day learning scriptural texts, singing hymns or reading religious or edifying material such as that provided by the children's pages of available Methodist publications. Religious observances, however, were not confined to Sundays. The weeks were marked by family prayer, preparation for the observance of the major religious festivals, revivals, class and testimony meetings, love feasts, and covenant services, in all of which the children, having undergone the evangelical experience of conversion, were expected to participate. The Methodist church forbade the "worldly pleasures" of drinking, smoking, dancing, card-playing, betting, gambling, participating in lotteries, and attending entertainments such as theatrical performances, circuses, horse races, or exhibitions of dancing.[29]

If such an atmosphere did not wholly stifle the imagination, it tended to produce a type of mind in which the sense of beauty or the aesthetic judgment and emotion were imperfectly developed. Nevertheless, John Pratt's children all gave evidence of one or more artistic talents, and all of them, like E.J. Pratt's "Truant," were blessed with what could rightly be called the saving grace of an irrepressible sense of humour.[30] Looking back on that stage in his life, Pratt the poet could later say that those years provided him with a wealth of experience which, never exhausted, cropped out in his work "in the most unexpected places, in subjects which might at first glance appear to be outside the area" (MS 9:68.1).

E.J. Pratt's reaction, at the age of four, to a streptococcus infection resulted in rheumatic fever.[31] In its acute stage it kept him in bed for the best part of a year, delaying his entrance to school and making him extremely susceptible to pneumonia, bronchitis, and other childhood diseases and thus more dependent for care on his mother than he would normally have been. The after-effects of this illness were to haunt Pratt for the rest of his life in one form or another – damage to the heart, neuritis, weakness, aches and pains, swelling of the joints, tremors, lack of co-ordination, emotional hypersensitivity, and depression. His parents impressed upon him early in life that, as a consequence, he had to be very careful about himself and about what he did. Rough and tumble play, tag, contact sports, track and field, soccer, and football, except in the role of spectator, were all forbidden to him.

It was probably as a concession to his condition that he was allowed to read *Boys' Own Annual* and *Chums*. Pratt's enthusiasm, later in life, for boxing matches together with the stag parties for which he became famous gave rise to unfounded speculation on the part of some that Pratt was a homosexual.[32]

E.J. Pratt did find some compensation for the activities of a normal boyhood that were denied to him by his fragile health. His awareness of a fundamental relationship with the natural environment and with his fellow human beings, of the lore and the language of ships and seafaring, of fishing, whaling, and sealing, and of the demanding daily lives of Newfoundland's ordinary people formed the background and foil for his experience of such intensely dramatic moments as the great fire of 1892, when John Pratt was minister of Cochrane Street Church in St John's; the return of the sealer *Greenland* in April 1898, with its cargo of pelts and frozen human bodies; and Marconi's first transatlantic message of 1901.[33] It became characteristic of E.J. Pratt that, like his father, he saw such events in terms of their human demands or implications.

As a minister, John Pratt may have been spared the fear of unemployment, but he and his family shared the hardships and the poverty of the people he served. Although he was always supplied with a furnished parsonage and a horse, his yearly income, which must have reached $1000 at its maximum during the years in St John's,[34] was scarcely enough to allow him to support and to educate eight children. His gratitude to the relatively well-to-do congregation of Cochrane Street Church for their Christmas gifts for his family and home was heartfelt, and he was obviously moved by the generosity of the young men who stayed in the church after the watchnight service to present him with "a very fine overcoat."[35] Yet in spite of financial constraints, John Pratt made every effort to ensure that his children could attend, for as long as possible, the Methodist College in St John's. They stayed, when the family residence was not in the city, at the Boarding Home for Ministers' Children. John Pratt's letters to his children at school[36] reveal a knowledge of their individual interests and abilities, and a very real affection for them.

E.J. Pratt's formal education began in the small outport schools at Cupid's, Brigus, and Blackhead (MS 9:68.2) maintained by the Methodist Board.[37] By the time that he was fifteen, however, his indifferent progress and apparent lack of interest in further education had qualified his parents' ambition for him, so rather than go to college he left home and school to begin an even less successful apprenticeship of three years in the shop of W.A. Sclater, a draper, in St John's.[38] But the Methodist emphasis on reading as a means of self-improvement and on education in general was strong in Newfoundland, and there is little doubt that Pratt was encouraged to read and study independently.[39]

If John Pratt were typical of Methodist ministers of his time, his library would have included, in addition to the Bible and the standard commentaries on it, the complete works of John Wesley, the sermons of noted evangelical preachers such as Moody, Spurgeon, Talmadge, and Banks, the devotional works of à Kempis, William Law, and Jeremy Taylor, Foxe's *Book of Martyrs,* and other classics included in the fifty volumes of Wesley's *Christian Library.* These did not include the works of Luther and Calvin, but they did include the works of five French and two Spanish mystics whose names had been associated with Quietism, namely Pascal, Brother Lawrence, Fénelon, Mme Guyon, Mme Bourignon, John of Avila, and Molinos.[40] Such books might not have tempted E.J. Pratt, but he would likely have found, in addition to them, the plays of Shakespeare, the works of Milton, Bunyan, Carlyle, and Macaulay, standard histories, and the approved English works of poetry and prose which the Methodist publishing houses, in their work of teaching and evangelization, made available in inexpensive editions.[41]

E.J. Pratt would have discovered in his father's library, or in that of the uncle with whom he stayed, little or no fiction. In June 1895 an editorial in the *Methodist Monthly Greeting,* to which John Pratt was an occasional contributor, carried a dire warning against reading novels. Such literature, it was held, would have a delusive effect on mind and character. The reader would lose his "relish for history and science, and all that requires manly thought, and live only in the land of romance and day-dreams."[42] This opinion brings together two nineteenth-century attitudes, the evangelical notion that fiction is composed of lies and the utilitarian belief that it is a waste of time.[43]

The emphasis on history and science implied in this editorial was borne out by the curriculum of the Methodist College in St John's. Pratt's enrolment there in 1900, after his three years of business experience, was, no doubt, facilitated by John Pratt in return for his son's promise to present himself as a candidate for the ministry. At that time, the principal of the college was R.A. Holloway, BA, FRCS (London), a specialist in science, whose instruction Pratt was never to forget (MS 9:68.1) and under whose tutelage he first encountered the theory of evolution and probably read Darwin, Huxley, and Spencer.[44] As early as 1888 the college boasted of having, in addition to a museum, a laboratory "fully equipped with chemical, electrical and other physical apparatus."[45] It offered courses in "all the physical sciences including practical mineralogy and analysis, heat, light, electricity, physics, chemistry and mechanics,"[46] in addition to scripture, history, mathematics, French, music and art, physical education, and manual training.[47] Classes in English were confined, for the greater part, to grammar, composition, and the history of English literature. The well-qualified faculty, many of whom were recruited from British universities including London, Durham, and Edinburgh, prepared students for the London Matriculation examinations in Latin and Greek, mathematics, science, and English.[48] Courses in pedagogy and school management offered at the college in association with its model school qualified students for certificates to teach in the Newfoundland schools supported by the Methodist Board.[49]

Having completed his matriculation and satisfied himself with a second-class teaching certificate, E.J. Pratt spent the years from 1902 to 1904 as a teacher and local preacher in Moreton's Harbour[50], an isolated island community about eight miles from Twillingate. While, according to some accounts, he was eventually to be fairly successful in the classroom, he did not, at first, find the work congenial and was lonely, discouraged, and anxious about the welfare of his family. In the summer of 1903, conscious of his father's rapidly deteriorating health, E.J. Pratt returned home and, confronted with his brothers' unwillingness to take up their father's profession, renewed his promise to prepare for the ministry.[51] There is no doubt that his desire for further education and for an eventual escape from the confinement of Newfoundland made him more sensitive to pressure from the family than he might otherwise have been. In 1904, having satisfied the requirements set down by the General Conference of the Church – matriculation with Greek option into a Canadian or British university, examination on Wesley's *Sermons* 1 to 20, the catechism of the Methodist church, and the New Testament with accurate quoting from a large number of texts[52] – E.J. Pratt was accepted as a candidate for the ministry of the Methodist church only months after his father's death.

E.J. Pratt's three years as a probationer on circuit, the first stage in his training, took him, as assistant to the Reverend William Harris, to Clarke's Beach and to Cupid's[53] on Conception Bay where he had lived as a child. The fifteen-mile hike, in fair weather or foul, every Sunday, in the course of which he was expected to preach three times and to conduct Sunday School twice, in addition to weekly prayer meetings and other obligations, took its toll on his fragile health. In the second year he was moved to Portugal Cove and Bell Island, an iron-mining district twelve miles north-west of St John's. His yearly salary there as a single probationer was $350,[54] small enough to discourage any candidate whose motivation was not strong. From 1904 to 1907, in addition to his pastoral duties, Pratt was required to complete the course of private study for probationers set down by the General Conference of 1902, and to sit for examinations in five subjects at the end of each year.[55]

Included in the curriculum for the three years of probation were English Bible study, Old Testament history or church history, Greek Testament, theology (chiefly the works of John Wesley and the doctrines of Methodism), homiletics, and practical theology.[56] Standing in the examinations was reported at the district ministerial sessions each year, when probationers were given the opportunity to display their preaching ability to the assembly. During the ministerial sessions of 1905, E.J. Pratt was appointed to preach in Gower Street and George Street churches,[57] two of the oldest and largest in St John's.

In 1907, at the end of his three years on the circuit, Pratt and two of his friends and fellow probationers, W.H. Pike and S.H. Soper, requested that they be permitted to attend the theologically liberal Wesleyan College affiliated with McGill University in Montreal. However, the Newfoundland Conference, which had spent much of its time denouncing the extremes of the new theology, had resolved that Wesleyan College be declared "out of bounds to all further candidates from Newfoundland." Therefore, the stationing committee recommended that Brothers Pratt, Pike, and Soper be sent instead to Mount Allison University, Sackville, New Brunswick,[58] the usual institution of higher learning for Methodist students from the eastern provinces and Newfoundland. Bridling at the arbitrariness of such a decision, the trio risked the ire of the Conference and the possibility that it would withdraw its financial support and betook themselves instead to Ontario. There, having exhibited the proper signs of contrition, they were eventually to be reinstated. The *Minutes* of the 25th Sessions of the Newfoundland Conference record the fact that, by then, Pratt and his friends had successfully completed one year of studies at Victoria College at the University of Toronto.

When E.J. Pratt left Newfoundland for Toronto, he did not go with any disadvantage. He was twenty-five years old and ready to benefit from his maturity. The education that he had received at the Methodist College in St John's was equivalent to, if not better than, what his contemporaries had enjoyed in Ontario. The early adolescent years out of school had whetted his appetite for learning, while his reading then, and later on the circuit, had taught him independence and intellectual discipline. He knew what it meant to be poor, to have limited physical stamina, and to have to work hard for a living. When he approached theology, he did so with a wide knowledge of the scriptures and with pastoral experience. There was no overt sign, then, of rebellion against religion, even against life as a minister. There were simply no other options open to him. While he had received little exposure to systematic theology, or to modern biblical criticism as such, it is probable that Pratt had faced, both in Holloway's science classes and within the framework of apologetics, controversial issues such as the Darwinian theory of evolution, and that these constituted no shock to what might have been then his fundamentalist sensibilities[59]. Ironically enough, what Toronto was to offer him more than anything else was room to expand his vision, and eventually to indulge the imagination that Newfoundland had formed.

ON THE OLD ONTARIO STRAND: VICTORIA COLLEGE

By 1907, when Pratt arrived in Toronto, the Methodist church, then just over twenty years old, was the largest Protestant body in Canada.[60] While the strain of Methodism in which Pratt had been raised was still, because of both its origin and Newfoundland's isolation, fundamentally Wesleyan and conservative, what he found in Ontario was a hybrid variety, at times and in some respects more American than British in flavour, and more socio-politically oriented as a result of its past role as an agent of reform in Upper Canada.[61] As expectation and controversy were growing over the proposed union with the Presbyterians and the Congregationalists there was the sense – and on the part of some, the fear – that Methodism in its more sectarian expressions was passing away. Others welcomed the prospect of union with enthusiasm.

Victoria University, which appeared to have survived its move from Cobourg, Ontario, and its federation with the University of Toronto without either losing its religious identity or becoming engulfed by the larger and more challenging urban environment, helped its students through a similar process of adjustment. Unlike the Methodist College at St John's, which had looked to Britain for its orientation as well as for many of its senior faculty, Victoria had looked to the American universities for its model and for some members of its faculty, until it was able to call upon its own graduates whom it had encouraged to go abroad for further studies.[62] In its search for a way to bridge what appeared to be the widening rift between faith and reason, it had adopted in 1841 the highly structured college curriculum proposed by the Yale Report of 1828.[63]

Like the school at St John's, Victoria had from the outset placed great emphasis upon the sciences. This stress was due, in part, to the pragmatic approach to education of its first principal, Egerton Ryerson, who as superintendent of education for the province in the late 1860s had introduced evolutionary science into the classrooms of elementary and secondary schools of Canada West.[64] But it also reflects that early nineteenth-century view which saw religion and science as supporting each other (see p.9, above). The belief, perhaps best expressed by Paley's *View of the Evidences of Christianity* (1805), which was still used as a text in some classes in apologetics at Victoria in 1905, that science had established a realm of facts illustrative of the ways of God, was reflected in the early emphasis on geology and mineralogy. It was, ironically enough, in this field that the rift between science and religion first became evident with Lyell's *Principles of Geology* (1830) and *The Geological Evidences of the Antiquity of Man* (1833).

When Pratt enrolled at Victoria College, the atmosphere was by contemporary standards relatively liberal. After 1908, attendance at classes and lectures in "religious knowledge" and at chapel services was encouraged, but not enforced. Students were urged to frequent city churches, and to engage as volunteers in religious and social work, especially in providing for the needs of suburban congregations.[65] E.J. Pratt assisted on Sundays in rural areas around Toronto, and during vacations on the mission circuit in Saskatchewan and Alberta.[66] His life and conduct were under somewhat closer scrutiny than those of the average student, since he was answerable to the College Meeting, a supervisory body of faculty members, and as his progress through college and his standing as a probationer were recorded in the *Minutes* of the Newfoundland Annual Conference. His tuition and board were financed with loans from the educational society of the Newfoundland Conference that were to be repaid within seven years after ordination.[67] While he enjoyed a certain degree of independence, he had neither the time nor the money to indulge himself. He worked hard, still finding time to tutor, to read for a blind student, and on occasion to submit an essay or poem to the college magazine. As a graduate student he was to become a local editor (1909–10) and then literary editor (1910–11) of *Acta Victoriana*, to which Pelham Edgar acted as faculty advisor.[68] During those years Pratt became a regular contributor to that journal, and later to the *Rebel* (1917–20), the precursor of the *Canadian Forum*.

It was in the honours course in philosophy that Pratt registered as an undergraduate. Long before Victoria College had moved from Cobourg to Toronto in 1892, Hegelian idealism, hailed by some as the antidote to materialism and naturalism, was replacing the empirical "common-sense" philosophy of the Scottish school of William Hamilton, Dugald Stewart, and Thomas Reid, and by 1905 it had become fairly well established as the predominant school of philosophy there.[69] To some persons of faith, it seemed to offer a new understanding of the universe which could embrace evolutionary theory without compromising the moral nature of human beings or their essential freedom. As early as 1870, Samuel Nelles, then president of Victoria College, introduced the works of Kant to his classes in philosophy,[70] and as time went on courses and special lectures were offered in the thought of Hegel, Schleiermacher, and Ritschl, as well as in the "objective idealism" of Josiah Royce and the "spiritual philosophy" of T.H. Green and John and Edward Caird.[71] The philosophy of Schleiermacher, which stressed the subjective nature of religion as well as the feeling of utter dependence, seemed to hold the greatest affinity with the essential spirit of Methodism.[72] It is unlikely, then, that Pratt meant literally what he said later in a frequently quoted remark that at Victoria he "scarcely got a whiff of idealism" (EL 1.3). It would have been very difficult for him to have escaped it. It is possible, though, that he found the thought of Hegel and his followers to be deterministic in that it regarded the historical process as automatic, directed only by pure spirit, or by certain leaders, the key to whose appearance in world history was a secret of the spirit,[73] or in that it made the standard or end of morality lie not in a personal and loving God but in a fallen humanity.[74]

New developments in the field of psychology, until then considered a branch of philosophy, were looked upon with fear and suspicion by many evangelicals of the day, for they seemed to explain away religious experience and undermine the trust in spiritual intuition in which their faith was rooted. Victoria College met this challenge as it had met others, head on, and hoped to display to its students and to the world at large that any opposition between science and religion was there in appearance only. Ironically, the psychology of the day was the structuralist tradition of experimental psychology represented by William Wundt of the University of Leipzig, whose disciples, including E.B. Titchener of Cornell, were establishing laboratories at leading universities throughout the world. Experiments in Wundtian psychology aimed at examining the mind in terms of its structural parts, their interplay, and the relationship of these to physiological changes in the body. At its worst, such an approach could lead to a mechanistic and materialistic view of human nature, or to psychological determinism. The faculty of Victoria College considered it fortunate that August Kirschmann, an evangelical Lutheran, was chosen in 1893 to head the laboratory at the University of Toronto. Kirschmann believed that the religious consciousness was the integrating factor in human nature, and directed the attention of students, among them George Blewett, towards the higher activities of the mind, such as literary and aesthetic consciousness.[75]

It is also possible that the real "determinism" that Pratt implied he disliked was his own temperamental inclination towards fatalism, fostered by the environment and experience of his childhood and youth and strongly reinforced by the determinism inherent in the psychology that he studied, in the applications to which it was being put, and in the works of Thomas Hardy, which he read and enjoyed. Whatever the explanation, the aversion to determinism was not strong enough then to turn Pratt away from philosophy. In 1909 he merited, in addition to the Bede Prize in Church History, the John Macdonald Scholarship in Philosophy. In 1911 he was awarded his Bachelor of Arts degree with the S.H. Janes Silver Medal in Philosophy.[76]

Traditionally the two criteria applied in determining fitness for the Methodist ministry had been evangelical fervour and the ability to preach. Until the 1870s the storm raised by the conflict between religion and science had not hit Canada with sufficient force to make higher education for the ministry appear to be necessary or even desirable. Then, in 1873, an endowment made possible the founding of a faculty of theology at Victoria, and it is significant that Nathanael Burwash, who was named first head of the faculty, resigned from the chair of natural science to take that position.[77]

A graduate of Victoria University in 1859, the year of the publication of Darwin's *On the Origin of Species* and a year before the appearance of *Essays and Reviews*, Burwash had spent six years in pastoral charges, during which time he had witnessed the impact of these works on the faith of members of his congregations and experienced their challenge to his own. Invited to join the faculty of the college as a member of the department of science, he became a steady presence there from 1867, studying in his spare time to qualify for the degree of Doctor of Sacred Theology from Garrett Biblical Institute in Evanston, Illinois. Deeply convinced of the compatibility between reason and faith and of the university's reponsibility to demonstrate this compatibility, he found himself able to accept the Darwinian theory of evolution without, however, subscribing to the theory of natural selection.[78] After reading the text of the Bampton Lecture of 1885, Canon Farrar's *The History of Interpretation*, Burwash further demonstrated a remarkable if selective openness to the "higher criticism,"[79] believing that the divine truth contained in scripture could not be prejudiced by the application of sound historical and linguistic methods of criticism. His quiet insistence as head of the faculty of theology and as president and chancellor from 1887 to 1913 that evolutionary thought and contemporary biblical criticism be taught and discussed at Victoria brought him into inevitable conflict with Albert Carman, the general superintendent of the Methodist church, as well as with some wealthy lay supporters of the college and of the Methodist church.

Burwash's influence over Canadian Methodism did not end there. With the support and help of Samuel Nelles he had negotiated and engineered the agreement that had brought Victoria, a small denominational college, into the mainstream of the University of Toronto. In addition, as secretary of the educational society of the Methodist church, he was for fifty years responsible for and directly involved in the training of ministers whether on probation on the circuit or in the colleges.[80] In a series of textbooks in theology which he wrote between 1881 and 1900 he tried to bring to Wesley's teachings on the witness of the Spirit and on Christian perfection the support, not of Hegelian idealism, but of inductive reasoning.[81]

From the beginning, Burwash was an enthusiastic supporter of church union, proposed by the Presbyterians in 1902, and acted as chairman of the joint committee's subcommittee on doctrine. He was convinced that by entering into union, the Methodist church in Canada was both remaining true to its Wesleyan heritage and confronting the challenges held out to Christianity by twentieth-century Canadian and North American culture.[82]

Like Burwash himself, and like Pratt, who was to follow later, the Methodist colleges in Canada, with their strong commitment to science, embraced within themselves both sides of the debate between the doctrine of creationism and the Darwinian theory of evolution, between fidelity to Methodist "experience" and the need for a systematic theology, and between Hegelian idealism and Baconian inductive reasoning, and it is largely thanks to them that the Methodist church in Canada survived as well as it did the heated controversies that were bound to occur in the realm of biblical criticism.

By the end of the century at Victoria, the application of historical and critical methods to biblical studies, while it challenged the traditional Methodist view of the inerrancy of the scriptures, was advancing slowly but surely. By insisting on the study of Hebrew and Greek and of exegesis, and by grounding the curriculum in the work of the Cambridge scholars B.F. Westcott, J.B. Lightfoot, and F.J. Hort, men of faith who had actually welcomed the challenge thrown to theology by nineteenth-century science and philosophy, the faculty of theology at Victoria College believed that it could be sure of sound scholarship and of a strong historical and linguistic approach to the Bible.[83] While this methodology was not without its limitations, it constituted a move away from fundamentalism and provided a solid foundation from which to explore the higher criticism. When Pratt read Strauss's *The Life of Jesus* (1835–6; translated 1848), he was well prepared, and read it in the light of the seventy-five years of scholarship that had followed its first publication.

Two dramatic cases that occurred close to the turn of the century serve as indicators of the progress of theology at Victoria College. In 1891, Dr George Workman, who had recently returned from studies in Germany, was dismissed from the faculty after a lecture on Messianic prophecy which he delivered before the college theological union and which was subsequently published in the *Canadian Methodist Quarterly*.[84] This dismissal did not ensure the ultimate victory of his opponents, since Burwash pointed out to Workman's critics that the historical method of scholarship was then almost universally recognized as legitimate, and the historical method continued to gain ground. Then, in 1909, shortly after E.J. Pratt arrived in Toronto, the Reverend George Jackson, who had come from Edinburgh to be minister of Sherbourne Street Church, was condemned without a hearing by Dr Albert Carman, the general superintendent of the Methodist church. Jackson's offence was his confession before a Bible class of his inability to accept either the Mosaic authorship of the Pentateuch or the book of Genesis as "an anticipation of the findings of modern science."[85] Jackson was vindicated as a result of the support that he received from Burwash, who, like Wesley, insisted that the right of private judgment was fundamental to Protestantism,[86] and who offered Jackson the chair of English Bible at Victoria. With this incident, liberty in biblical interpretation was established at Victoria, and the principle of academic freedom in theology was reasserted by the General Conference of 1910.[87]

What was equally influential on Pratt, though certainly less dramatic, was the appointment in 1906 to the chair of Ethics and Apologetics of George John Blewett, a young graduate of Victoria College who had begun his teaching ministry in philosophy at Wesley College in Winnipeg. Blewett had studied abroad, first at Wurtzburg under Oscar Kulpe, a former pupil of Wundt, then at Harvard in a department of philosophy whose faculty included, at the time, William James, George Palmer, George Santayana, and Josiah Royce. His doctoral dissertation, "The Metaphysical Basis of Preceptive Ethics" (1900), had won him a scholarship to Oxford, where he studied moral philosophy and social ethics under Edward Caird and A.M. Fairbairn before moving on to the University of Berlin and to sociology with George Semmel.[88]

While, like others at Victoria, Blewett hoped to find in psychology the meeting place of science and religion, in his own highly original work he left behind the Wundtian experiments in sensation and apperception for ethics and metaphysics. His "oecumenical" and "catholic" world view sees the history of civilization as a process of becoming more human as it moves upward through the Incarnation and the Cross to its full realization in the heavenly "civitas Dei."[89] While grounded in the reality of sin and suffering, Blewett's thought, which prefigures that of Teilhard de Chardin, is poetical and mystical in its expression, and in its evolutionary synthesis and its approach to scripture moves fearlessly beyond the framework of apologetics and beyond the apparent threats posed by modern science and the higher criticism.[90] His suggestions for reorganizing the department of philosophy so that it would provide a better foundation for lay students and probationary ministers alike were respected, and his serene and scholarly pursuit of the truth inspired his students with hope and courage.

It was within this heady atmosphere that E.J. Pratt embarked on a program of graduate studies in philosophy complemented by courses in systematic and historical theology, hermeneutics, and homiletics. He had the opportunity to take the required Hebrew, Greek testament, apologetics, logic, and ethics as an undergraduate.[91] In 1912, after a year's work, he was granted the degree of Master of Arts in philosophy with honours standing. His thesis, "The Demonology of the Synoptics in Its Relation to Earlier Developments and to the Mind of Christ," reflects the fairly liberal outlook that he found then at Victoria. It seems almost inconceivable that within thirty pages a writer could even outline such a subject. The appearance of the manuscript may belie the author's impatience, at this stage, with the stringent demands of scholarly writing, yet in a style that is lucid and free from pedantry, Pratt indicates concisely his insight into the nature of the problem, and his grasp of the complex factors that contributed to it. He surveys the anthropological and historical background, and the literary sources, scriptural evidence, and theological attitudes, before arriving at his own conjectural yet rhetorically effective conclusion. Since access to the complete thesis is limited and since it remains an interesting literary essay, a synopsis may prove helpful to a clearer understanding of Pratt, the poet.

At the beginning of "The Demonology of the Synoptics in Its Relation to Earlier Developments and to the Mind of Christ,"[92] Pratt notes that an examination of the religious life of primitive races today reveals the universal belief that both physical nature and human life are under supernatural control. In the majority of savage tribes, he observes, it is the evil spirit that figures most prominently in the imagination (1). While illness and "incidents of a prejudicial nature" are directly attributed to the action of such a spirit, or even to the ghosts of the departed, the cessation of the injury is rarely ascribed to the positive action of a beneficent one. Hence the development of the belief in the action of evil spirits has generally been accompanied by many and various rites of exorcism (2).

We should not be surprised then, Pratt suggests, to find similar beliefs in the civilizations of antiquity. The works of Hesiod and of Homer indicate that the Greeks placed the blame for human afflictions upon a hierarchy of evil spirits, and exercised protective rites to ward them off (3). The Book of the Dead reveals the Egyptian belief that the deceased possessed power to heal maladies caused presumably by the presence of demons. Reliance on the efficacy of certain words and magic formulae led to the Egyptians' burying with the dead texts concerned with reincarnation (4). With the political union of the Babylonians under Hammurabi and the systematization of local cults there came about a reduction of the pantheon and the organization into a hierarchy of thousands of lesser spirits, each class of which had its proper domain in the natural world. Deformed or abnormal human beings were believed to possess demonic powers (6). In such a setting there quickly grew up a well-established class of professional exorcists (7).

In tracing the development of demonology through the Old Testament, Pratt states that it is difficult to determine the boundary line between foreign influence upon Hebrew thought and the native tendency to attribute natural changes to unseen powers. After the Exile, a rapid demonological development occurred (8). As the concept of the absolute transcendence of God with the exclusive nature of his righteousness grew, the origin of evil was ascribed to an intermediate hierarchy of evil agencies. The image of Satan as the arch-demon was reached only as the result of a long process. In early books of the Old Testament he was both the messenger of the Lord and the Adversary. Later, he accused human beings before God and attempted to work their destruction. Gradually the latter function gave Satan his pre-eminence. With the influence of Zoroastrian dualism, Satan, by analogy with Ahriman, was given lordship over the powers of darkness. In this early part of the thesis, Pratt draws upon a wide variety of sources ranging from the Encyclopedia Britannica to the classics and Frazer's *Golden Bough* to sketch in broad strokes the historical and cultural development of demonism.

The universality in the primitive religious consciousness of belief in the power of evil spirits, especially as experienced in dreams, gives Pratt a point of departure for the study of demoniacal phenomena as presented in the Gospels (10).[93] He states his intention "to show by an historical method what relationship the current Jewish views in New Testament times, the views of the evangelists, and those of Christ had with reference to the developments already traced" (11).

In the Gospel accounts of demonic possession, Pratt finds remarkable similarity to earlier developments. The Gospels attribute physical and moral disorders of peculiar and exaggerated types to demonic or Satanic power (11). The demons, though intangible and invisible, have a marked aversion to a disembodied condition, a partiality to unclean habitation after expulsion from a human being, a fondness for the desert and the graveyard, and a behaviour characterized by unusual exhibitions of strength, by convulsions, and by the grinding of teeth. It is clear, however, that certain phases of the phenomena as reported in the Gospels appear to have no analogue in previous development. The Gospels show little sympathy for the multiplication of formulae of exorcism chanted by a priest over the sufferer. The paraphernalia of the professional exorcist becomes unnecessary as authority is vested in Christ, whose word alone is sufficient (12). There is in the Gospels a studied attempt "to avoid the gaping curiosity of the crowd, to exclude the startling accompaniments,[94] and to screen all actions as much as possible within the shadow of a reticent humility" (13).

The first critical question which Pratt raises is that of the authenticity of the facts of healing, and of the causes assigned to them (13). He suggests that any conclusion made in this respect must be largely a matter of conjecture (14). He points out the differences that exist in the synoptic accounts of the incident of the Gadarene swine (Mt 8:28; Mk 5:1–17; Lk 8:6–40), of the healing of the dumb demoniac (Mt 12:22–8; Mk 3:22–7; Lk 11: 14–22), and of the cure of the daughter of the Syro-Phoenician woman (Mt 15:21–8; Mk 7:24–30). After examining the mythological interpretations of critics such as Strauss, and the allegorical ones of Baur and Volkmar, he concludes that the explanation is not a simple one (14). The incidents have a historical basis, but they are coloured by subjective prepossessions and are reported through the medium of a crude popular vocabulary (15).

Pratt next explores the nature of healing according to the Gospel accounts. There is no assurance, he notes, of the impossibility of a return of the same disease, but neither is there indication that any individual went to Jesus a second time (18). The reality of the healings appears to rest on substantial grounds. Citing examples from modern medical history of the treatment of alleged demonic possession, Pratt indicates the value placed by medical experts on a sympathetic insight into the background of the individual, and on a proper religious atmosphere: "whatever efficacy there may be experimentally proved to reside in a calm, self-possessed, and authoritative personality over the mental and moral aberrations must have been supreme in Christ"(20). Reflecting on the attitude of society and of religious sects towards the afflicted, Pratt remarks that Christ's approach, "not with the authority of the scribes, but rather with the authority of a kindly touch and a genuinely human treatment"(20), must have been unusual. Even the attitude of Christ's enemies is evidence of the reality of his cures (21).

The problem fundamental to theological implications remains, namely the relationship of Jesus to the current belief as outlined above. It must be remembered that the incidents of healing under consideration were described by those who were confirmed believers in demonic possession. Pratt finds no evidence either to support or to contradict the theory of accommodation: "Christ makes no claim here either to supernatural knowledge, or to any adaptation to popular needs"(24). As to the view that regards Jesus merely as an inheritor of beliefs from the past, Pratt points out that if Christ did believe in the activity of Satan and his vast confederacy of demons, its most complete expression was to be found in the cultured circles of the Pharisees. Yet Jesus spurned such a point of view and showed that the seed of corruption, where evil was doing its most finished work, lay in the hearts of his official antagonists. That fact alone is sufficient to place Jesus outside the line of traditional succession regarding the belief in demoniacal agency.

Pratt concludes that the lack of direct evidence that Jesus shared this belief may best be explained by the fact that his life was concerned with affairs of weightier significance.[95] He was too intensely earnest in dealing with individual concrete cases of sin and suffering to speculate on the abstract nature of sin. He frequently refused to respond categorically to points of scribal dispute, and would suggest that the solution lay outside the reach of the argument: "if some Pharisaic dialectician had inquired of Jesus the reasons why these unfortunate persons afflicted with fever, epilepsy and mental derangement had been brought so completely within the grasp of Satan and his legion of demons, he would in all likelihood have replied that such affliction was no more due to demonic power than the blind man's infirmity was due to his parents' sin and his own" (31).

The conclusion of this thesis would appear to be at best elusive, since Pratt avoids stating precisely what, in his opinion, Jesus did believe about demonic possession. From another angle, however, the work may be seen as Pratt's first exercise in the ironic mode. Pratt's detachment from the theological arguments he has examined, whether it is intentional or unconscious, is an ironic reflection of the attitude which he attributes to Christ with regard to the abstract disputation of the scribes and Pharisees (30). After he has marshalled all the evidence, and after he has weighed all the learned hypotheses,

Pratt dismisses the theories of the critics and exegetes as inconclusive and even insignificant. Consequently, the image of Christ which emerges at the end of the thesis is shrouded with greater mystery than it was at the beginning.

This thesis is a "five-finger exercise" in modern biblical criticism, at the end of which Pratt remains, if evasive, still open. Although he has demonstrated his understanding of contemporary scholars, including Strauss, whose fundamental hypothesis, he indicates (14–15), is already outdated,[96] Pratt's unmasked distrust of theological speculation would, at this point, seem to reflect more of the stance of the theologically sophisticated Canadian Methodist than that of the twentieth-century sceptic. If his notion of Christ appears to be insecure, even verging on the unorthodox,[97] Pratt's thesis does not seem to have caused so much as a stir at Victoria College. On the title page is the evaluation, "Passed with Honours."

By 1912, the year in which he was granted his Master of Arts degree, Pratt had fallen in love with Lydia Trimble, who had come to Victoria College from Red Deer, Alberta, but his petition to marry before ordination was rejected.[98] He then asked to be transferred from the Newfoundland Conference of the Methodist Church to the newly founded Alberta Conference. The opening up of the west with its prospect of new mission fields had already attracted a number of volunteers from Newfoundland, which was abundantly supplied with Methodist preachers. Pratt's summers had given him a chance to see the west, and to consider the prospect of life there, but his request, which was granted, according to the *Minutes of the 29th Newfoundland Conference Sessions* (8), suggests perhaps more than anything else a determination not to return to Newfoundland for ordination. For reasons nowhere indicated, Pratt's three years as a probationer in Newfoundland were discounted, while the probationary periods of those who transferred with him were allowed. His ministry is listed in Alberta records as beginning in 1907 rather than in 1904.[99] It is possible, however, that this arrangement enabled him to qualify for the loans that he would need to continue his education. Although their engagement is said to have been broken off months earlier, the tragic death of Lydia Trimble only four days before both were to be granted degrees at Victoria, and the death of George Blewett later that summer, cloaked Pratt's achievements with a pall.[100]

In 1913, E.J. Pratt received his Bachelor of Divinity degree with the Sanford Gold Medal for General Proficiency.[101] On 13 June, he was received *in absentia* into full connection with the Alberta Conference of the Methodist Church, and two days later was ordained a minister in Toronto. Assigned to the Red Deer District, Penhold Circuit, he was to be left for one year without a station, at his request.[102] Encouraged to continue his studies, he assisted with pastoral work around Toronto, and kept himself by tutoring and part-time teaching in psychology. By 1917 he had fulfilled the requirements for the degree of Doctor of Philosophy, among them a thesis which, while reflecting attitudes and approaches established in his earlier work, is a much more prodigious feat of scholarship.

In his doctoral dissertation, *Studies in Pauline Eschatology and Its Background*,[103] Pratt examines the development of Jewish eschatological thought and its bearing on the outlook of Paul (6). Describing his approach to the topic in the introduction to the thesis, he expresses even more strongly than he did in "The Demonology of the Synoptics" his antidogmatic bias:

This, then, is the task of the thesis. It is not a case of what might be called the "objective truth" of the beliefs registered in the literature, not a case of the discovery of criteria by which certain religious views might be rejected as simply "subjective fancy", and others sustained because of their supposed "absolute validity" but rather a question of determining by critical analysis how various controlling ideas which regulated and inspired the action and thought of a people emerged out of antecedent ideas into distinctness, and how, in their turn, these again were formative in producing the thought-content of a succeeding age. (8–9)

Pratt considers this approach to the subject "a psychological study" since "the question is as to the nature of the interaction between the processes of imagination, belief and reflection, and the political events of a nation, or of a group of individuals, as this interaction is reflected in the transmitted symbols which we call their literature"(9).

Pratt then details in tabular form the key concepts of eschatology as they appear in the major texts of the prophetic and apocalyptic ages (10a–c). He thus enters into his exploration of Pauline eschatology through an examination of earlier traditions, just as in his first thesis he approached the question of Christ's attitude towards demonic possession through a survey of the beliefs of previous ages and other civilizations. Characteristic of the biblical and apocryphal texts of the pre-exilic or prophetic age, Pratt notes in his summary of the tables (11–22), are the appeals of the great teachers for national repentance, the fundamental insistence upon the righteousness of Yahweh involving in turn the demand for the righteousness of his people, the certainty of judgment upon wrongdoers, the assurance of the favour of Yahweh resulting from obedience, and almost universally the promise of a coming era of blessedness for the kingdom of Israel contingent upon its preparation in human hearts. This kingdom was to be one wherein all forms of oppression would cease, whether of the character of civic injustice or of foreign despotism (11–12).

In turning to the writings of the post-exilic age, Pratt assumes on the part of his reader an understanding of the term *apocalypse*, the transliteration of the Greek word for revelation. Pratt uses this word in two senses in his thesis. On the literal level *apocalypse* is used to designate experiences such as that which Paul underwent on the road to Damascus, or on the occasion of his moments of mystical insight into the nature of Christ and the significance of his message (92). But Pratt also uses the term *apocalypse* in a broader sense to denote a particular literary genre popular in Israel in the centuries after the exile and the great prophets. Having discussed the characteristics of the apocalyptic form, which will be considered in greater detail in relation to his poetry (see chapter 3, below), and having illustrated the way in which it differs from the works of the prophetic age, Pratt traces the growth of Paul's Christocentric eschatology, and his gradual shift of emphasis from the traditional accompaniments of the apocalypse (196) to the all-important return of Christ (192).

Once he has drawn up a conjectural outline of Paul's life, and a chronological order of the epistles according to theological authorities such as Weiss, Sabatier, Harnack and Turner (24), Pratt turns to a consideration of Paul's general use of the terms "spirit" (*psyche*), "soul" (*pneuma*), "flesh" (*sarx*), and "body" (*soma*) in the light of the teaching of the Old Testament (29). In the development of his topic he shows how these concepts used in relationship to the various meanings of "life and death" are fraught with an irony which Paul had perceived through experience, and upon which he could freely draw (76–7). Pratt concludes, however, that any attempt to find rigid categories in the thought of Paul must meet with failure (40). While Paul did differentiate between body and spirit, the evidence of the epistles is against the view that he took over as a finished metaphysical product the dualism of the Alexandrian school (59). Nor can it be proved that Paul was an exponent of asceticism in either the Stoic or the Essenic sense (62). His "glorying" did not lie in adherence to ascetical practices, but rather in the fact that through the "crucifixion" in which he participated, the Spirit of God by its indwelling in the temple of his body made it an instrument for the fulfilment of the law of Christ (67).

Pratt states that Paul is the heir of Palestinian Judaism in its depreciation of the present evil world, which is to have a cataclysmic ending. The traditional views of angelology and demonology are reflected in the epistles from the first to the last. But the references to such agencies, while they indicate to some extent Paul's acceptance of the rabbinical tradition, reveal not so much the apostle's interest in cosmological inquiry as a deeply practical appeal to converts in terms that they understood. Pratt thus finds it more appropriate to apply the "theory of accommodation" to Paul than to Jesus (DS 24). He concludes that Paul's notion of immortality is the continuation of a similar conception seen in the Psalms and the prophets, and transfused with new life in the teachings of Jesus (*PE* 77).

In many aspects of eschatology, Pratt observes, Paul's attitude was one of characteristic independence. He accepted a tradition whenever he felt convinced of its harmony with his special message, and rejected it if it appeared to be contradictory (80). By placing the condition of resurrection upon moral rather than ethnic grounds, Paul freely allowed the Gentile the same right as the Jew. This fact constitutes, throughout the epistles, Paul's leading departure from the inherited standpoint (80).

There is evidence within the epistles to indicate that Paul, in line with both Greek and Judaistic traditions, believed that it was possible to attain in this life some comprehension of the nature of the heavenly or pneumatic world.[104] The vision or apocalypse became a source of Paul's insight into the gospel of Christ, and into his eschatological character. Paul does not make it clear whether such revelations came in the form of dreams in the waking state, or in trances, or whether the language used in their description is highly symbolical of overwhelming convictions regarding the significance of Christ for the salvation of all. At any rate, they revolve around Christ, especially in his eschatological capacity as the important centre (92–3).

Pratt points out that the fluid and popular usage of language is characteristic of Paul. Nowhere is there any indication that Paul possesses the technical equipment of scientific vocabulary. It must be remembered that the apostle, versed as he was in the prophetic development of his age, and in rabbinical argumentation, quotes from the Old Testament in the language of the Septuagint, and this brings to the formulation of his religious thought a mode of expression unknown to those who shaped Hebrew theology (112–113). Pratt states that Paul's methods are not those of a theorist who wished to construct a view of the universe that might satisfy a logical test, but those of a missionary who brought a practical ingenuity to bear upon the multifarious moral and social needs that grew in proportion to the expansion of the churches, and that often demanded immediate adjustments. Pratt's Paul, no more than his Christ (DS 31), could give solutions *in abstracto*.

When Paul set himself the task of making known what he designated as "the riches of God in Christ" to the heterogeneous population of his time, Pratt shows that he stated his case definitely and clearly (115). To this end, he adopted modes of thought and phraseology native to the peoples concerned. His language had more in common with the current vernacular than with the terms of the academies and eclectic circles. Figures of speech, similes, and illustrations reveal not only his skill in communication but also the scope of his intellectual insight and practical sagacity. He ranges the whole field of Jewish, Roman, and Greek metaphor. His images are drawn from agriculture, astronomy, architecture, the stadium, the race-meet, the gymnasium, the garrison and the barracks, the parade ground, and the pageant in honour of a conqueror. He was no more in need of a clear system of concepts than the Hebrew prophets. The difficulties arose later when exegetes began to operate on problems of analysis (115). Pratt's discussion here shows his aversion, not for religion, but for any narrow system of theology.

It is important, Pratt remarks, to determine how much of the speculation of the preceding centuries Paul took over as fixed tradition, how much he rejected, and to what extent events in his life, especially contact with the teachings of Jesus, led him to modify it. Starting with the early epistles, Pratt indicates Paul's main divergence from the contemporary apocalyptic. The apostle introduces Jesus as the Messiah or Christ, and makes his Parousia coincide with the end of the age that now is (123). Nowhere in Jewish literature so far is there a record of a Messiah whose career is cut short by a death so loaded with calumny as the Crucifixion. This event, the persecution of Jesus' followers, and the rooted antagonism of the Jews to the idea of universal salvation constituted grand apostasy on their part. While Paul handles traditional imagery freely in the early epistles, he abandons most of it later. He identifies the Parousia with the Day of Judgment on which the final consummation of the kingdom takes place. Pratt sees in the missionary journeys the history of Paul's success in breaking down the wall of partition in Christ, so that the sifting which would occur at the Parousia would be based upon moral rather than ethnic grounds (148).

Pratt shows that most of the functions ascribed to the Messiah in the contemporary apocalyptic are in the Pauline epistles assigned to Jesus (153). At times Jesus' official duties are distinguished from the work which God alone has to perform, while at other times both are regarded in the same eschatological capacity (153). The Parousia is invariably that of Jesus, who is to appear from heaven with the angels of his power, but the deliverance which the believer obtains is always from the retributive judgment of God. Pratt does not attempt to deal with Paul's reconciliation of the exalted position of Christ with Jewish monotheism. He shows that Paul surpassed all apocalyptic precedents in declaring the authoritative functions of the Messiah. In the later epistles, all eschatological interests centre in Christ and in humankind's relationship to him (159).

Pratt then sets about examining the factors that led to this culmination in Paul's view. He outlines the complex character of the problems confronting the apostle at the outset of his missionary activity. The political, cultural, and intellectual influences of Hellenism had been fostered rather than disturbed by Latin civilization, and the common speech of the Graeco-Roman world was Greek. The decline of the city-states opened up a vision of brotherhood transcending the limits of city or tribe, while Stoic philosophy transformed the principle of universalism into a system of ethics (162). As many powerful currents with Eastern sources streamed into the West, Tarsus became the best example of the union of the oriental with the occidental. Hellenistic Judaism produced a great literary achievement in the Septuagint. Religious life seemed to have found its most distinct expression in syncretism grounded in the mystery cults of the East (165). One feature of those religions emerged in the foreground, namely the exercise of mysticism as the remedy *par excellence* against the power of fate (169). This Graeco-Roman world with its vast amalgam of religious beliefs constituted the environment in which Paul lived, breathed, and thought.

In the light of this background Pratt considers some of the problems of Christology that arise in the later epistles. He inquires to what degree the high Christology of the imprisonment epistles may have been shaped by the reaction of Paul's thought to the religious movements of his time. He suggests that the Alexandrian acquainted with his own literature received from Paul emphatic declaration about the earthly history of Jesus, while the Jew was impressed with the fact that all Palestinian speculation about the Messiah fell short of the real glory of Christ.

Pratt also attempts to establish to what extent Paul attributed divinity to Christ. Having pointed out that Paul uses the title *theos* with reference to Christ only once (Rom 9:5), Pratt remarks that "there are no other examples of such a direct appellation in any of the letters ... The data which might be brought to corroborate this theistic interpretation is of an indirect character"(177). Nevertheless, he reminds the reader, Paul's failure to use the term *theos* frequently with reference to Christ does not indicate that he did not believe that Christ shared the divine nature (177).[105] Paul applies constantly to Christ the title *kyrios*, a term used in the Septuagint to translate the Hebrew designation of Yahweh. The phrase "the day of Yahweh" becomes in the language of

Paul "the day of the Lord" (177). While it cannot be decisively ascertained whether Paul uses the title "Son of God" as an official Messianic appellation or as something more, it is quite clear, even in the early epistles, that Paul's all-consuming concern is to proclaim the Lordship of Christ (178). In the later epistles Paul transcends the Jewish notion of the Messiah by ascribing to Christ the functions of pre-existence and creative power belonging to abstract Wisdom in Alexandrian literature.

Pratt concludes that Paul's twenty years of profound reflection upon the scenes of his missionary labours in countries which exhibited the most heterogeneous types of religious belief, and contact with the mystery cults practised in every large city of his time, must have affected the apostle deeply (180). To say this is not to imply that any leading phases of his teachings were derived from the mysteries. The gods in whose names the rites were performed had little affinity with the Christ that Paul preached (180). Whenever Paul alludes to the believer's relationship to Christ he implies an ethical transformation of the heart, namely the death to sin and the life to righteousness (182). The more he stresses the Parousia, the more weight he lends to the position that the forces of death and resurrection are already at work producing, in part, the very transformation which the advent of Christ will accomplish in its completion. The Parousia will then initiate on a cosmic scale what is already in process in the lives of Christians (183). Some critics have attributed to Paul the *ex opere operato* notion of the sacraments (181). If a sacramental theory is implicit in his teaching, the point is never for a moment forgotten that the hidden life of Christ in the believer, which reaches full bloom at the Parousia, is one of intense moral obligation for which no magical process can ever be held as a substitute (184).

It is not impossible, Pratt remarks, that Paul's message may have been interpreted by the Asian churches as just such another cult as existed everywhere in their midst (185). The universal craving for salvation which Paul found on his journeys must have awakened in his heart a reaction which demanded an appropriate adjustment of his message. In the later epistles we have the mature reflection of the apostle upon the character of Christ, and upon his capacity as saviour. The earlier standpoint of his Messianic functions as deliverer from the coming wrath (1 Thess 5) and of his subordination to the Father (1 Cor 15:24–8) is transcended, and the central theme becomes the exaltation of Christ, the summing up of the totality of creation in him who is "*all in all*" (186).

Without making any claim for the extensive derivation of Paul's teaching from the mysteries, Pratt suggests that Paul's employment of many of their concepts showed how sympathetically he felt towards the "groping after God" which the mystic process in all its complexity of apparatus expressed. The gospel which he had to offer was a *mysterion* "hidden for all ages"(187). In fact Paul had attained, in its non-eschatological sense, the *soteria* which was the one goal of the ardent votary of a mystery god (185). The exact nature of the process through which he reached it is not known. While he laid great stress on his conversion experience on the road to Damascus, still further knowledge of Christ and his Gospel came to him with the expansion of his own missionary work throughout the world. Whatever may be the complete analysis of the experience expressed by the term *soteria*, from the standpoint of Paul it lay hidden in the *apocalypsis* of Christ (188).

Just as Paul's bold originality often changed in context concepts current in the Judaistic language, so terms in use in the religious formulations of his churches – *mysterion, apocalypsis, sophia, gnosis* – though still retained, were charged with a new content (189). Paul would never have held to a syncretism in which a rival to Christ might claim equal standing. Paul shows the supreme lordship of Christ so explicitly that he exhausts his vocabulary in picturing the dominion over which Christ reigns (189). The pageant that signalized the conquest of Osiris over death is surpassed in its splendour by the triumph of Christ (190).[106]

Pratt concludes that it was Paul's tendency to establish the supremacy of Christ over against that of every deity or archon worshipped in his day that caused him to make use of the bold predicates he employed. If the terms that he used do not admit of the predication of deity, they express such an approximation thereto that we cannot think that Paul applied them to any other being. When clear-cut concepts failed him, he could still say that God had given to Christ "a name that is above every other name (Phil 2:9–11)."

While on the one hand it is true that Paul attributes certain functions exclusively to God – for example, that of raising Jesus from the dead, giving him his exalted name, placing him at his right hand – on the other hand all knowledge, salvation, wisdom, and creative capacity are summed up in Christ. Even if the most searching analysis of Paul's thought, carried out by the aid of exegesis, historical criticism, and theology, fails to reach a unanimous verdict upon the significance of the predicates applied, one path of development might easily lie in the direction of the Christological dogmas of the third and subsequent centuries (192).[107]

After summarizing the use which Paul has made of the terms *psyche, kardia, sarx,* and *pneuma* (193–6),[108] Pratt notes the growing tendency within the epistles to ignore the lurid accompaniments of the Parousia, to express the whole apocalyptic change by a single phrase, "the day," or "the Day of the Lord," and to focus attention upon the conformity of the new life and organism of the Christian to that of Christ in his supra-earthly existence.[109] Belief in the imminence of the Parousia loses some of its conviction with the passage of time (196). The Messianic kingdom, according to Paul, is a transcendent and pneumatic one in which the only ground of citizenship lies in the union of humankind with Christ.

Pratt states that the Messianic concept not only emerged out of the hopes of a given society (199), but also became the ground of reinvigorated faith amidst long stretches of misfortune and disaster. The analysis of the interplay between great religious beliefs and customs, and their underlying conditions in the social and political experiences of the Jewish people, may properly be called the psychology of their religion. The changing connotations of certain words and phrases as they were carried over from the prophetic age into the apocalyptic, and were exchanged in turn for Greek terms, is an important factor in the growth of all concepts, religious and otherwise (200).

Reflecting as he did in "The Demonology of the Synoptics" the influence of neo-Hegelian dialectic in the development of the topic under consideration, Pratt observes that the process of concept formation in the early Judaeo-Christian tradition took place along two general lines.[110] The first is a process of attenuation by means of which a given concept (*thesis*) could lose much of its original content by normal refinement in the history of the Jewish religion (*antithesis*). The second line of development from the original concept, which Pratt calls *synthesis* (*PE* 201), tends towards a general enrichment of the concept by the introduction of new properties contingent upon the critical periods through which the nation was passing. The former process is evident in the prophetic age with the gradual abandonment of earthly concerns as a result of the developing pessimism of the Jewish outlook for a national future. The synthetic process may be seen in the combination of generalities to form a concept such as that of the resurrected *soma* with the properties of eternal life, felicity, and glory (201).

How this analytic-synthetic method was perpetuated amidst the new scenes and interests of the first century AD may be seen in the foregoing treatment of the thought of Paul, Pratt states. But it must be remembered, he warns, that technical formulation was not Paul's purpose. Most of the terms he used were current in the vocabulary of his time, and were so little fixed in connotation that they were often used in fluid substitution. Hence the concepts which they covered would lack the precision of scientific definition, although in Paul's preaching and writing they readily lent themselves to proper interpretation (203).

Studies in Pauline Eschatology and Its Background is a work of exact and dedicated scholarship applied to a problem of considerable difficulty which had awakened contemporary theological interest. In bringing together and balancing the views of a wide range of critical opinion from the scholarly and moderate linguistic approach of the Cambridge theologians and Fairbairn through the French modernists Renan and Loisy, to the German idealists from Baur to Harnack and Albert Schweitzer, Pratt was performing an invaluable work for himself as he grappled with the question. Persuaded by faculty advisors at Victoria that his work might be of value for other theological students, Pratt allowed the thesis to be published by William Briggs, the Methodist printing establishment in Toronto. When the publisher failed to display the book, its sales were minimal and Pratt later found himself having to pay for it.[111]

In his study of one aspect of Pauline theology, Pratt shows how Paul's eschatology comes to focus on Christ, and on the Christian's relationship to him. As this occurs, the traditional accompaniments of the apocalypse diminish in importance until they are no longer of concern. In "The Demonology of the Synoptics in Its Relation to Earlier Developments and to the Mind of Christ," Pratt dwells on the humanity of Jesus as expressed by and experienced in his works of healing during his public life. In *Studies in Pauline Eschatology and Its Background*, he concerns himself with Paul's knowledge of the Christ who has undergone death and resurrection and who is to come again. In his transcendent state Christ is known and experienced by faith. The pattern comprehended by both theses reflects something of the typical nineteenth-century attempt to get behind both the Church's theology and Paul's, to the Jesus of the synoptic Gospels. While Pratt treats Paul and the synoptics separately, there is no real evidence that he was trying to make the distinction between Harnack's "religion of Jesus" and "religion about Jesus" which the German theologian attributed to "the gloomy Paul," or that he subscribed to the unnatural divorce between the "Jesus of history" and the "Christ of faith" of the post-Hegelian school.[112]

Pratt's methodology in both theses is strikingly similar. In approaching the demonology of the synoptics and Pauline eschatology through an exploration of the cultures out of which they grew, Pratt reflects the historical and evolutionary approach to theology which antedates both Darwin and the liberal Protestant theologians, and which may be seen as early as 1848 in works such as Newman's *Essay on the Development of Christian Doctrine*, or as late as 1911 in

Blewett's *The Christian View of the World*. From this viewpoint, ideas or events can be seen in their true significance only in the light of the great unfolding process of which they are a part. Whether this process is envisioned as linear or cyclical, as *chronos* or *kairos*, Pratt's vision is essentially a teleological one. His evolutionary concept of time, which may owe something to the Hegelians such as Reville or Sabatier, as well as to Spengler, and to Toynbee and Blewett, may with struggle usher in a higher degree of civilization, or it may, with human collusion, bring about a regression to barbarism.

The suffering or crucified Christ, who constitutes Paul's point of divergence from the contemporary apocalyptic (*PE* 148), and who was the focal point of Wesleyan evangelism, reappears in Pratt's poetry, as he does in Blewett's prose, as the crux of the evolutionary process and, at times, as the only source of hope for the human race. For, Pratt suggests, it is only by a change of heart whose expression may have to be as radical as the *kenosis* of Jesus (Phil 2:7) that twentieth-century men and women, religious or secular, may be able to recognize and embrace, rather than destroy, their sisters and brothers.

Both theses are studies in the psychology of religion. Pratt traces the interplay among imagination, belief, and reflection on actual events that led to the development of a highly systematized demonology and eschatology and their effects upon a given culture. As far as evidence allows, he studies the minds of Jesus and Paul in their reaction to certain traditional beliefs. Both works concern themselves with the relationship between the primitive and the civilized in religion, the nature of belief, the phenomenon of healing, mystical experience as a means of insight or liberation from the power of fate, and the origin of dreams and visions. John Wesley himself was interested in the psychology of religion. Pratt's interest was deepened by the subjective philosophies of Schleiermacher and Ritschl, and confirmed by the observations of Wundt and William James. It is significant that Pratt decided to explore a topic in theology in which, despite his ingrained prejudice, he had a genuine interest. His continued concern with the psychology of religion is evident in the themes and in the imagery of his poetry.

Pratt sees Jesus and Paul respectively in relationship to the culture and the religious traditions of which they were a part. Both were affected and influenced by the worlds which they knew, yet both were prophetic, even revolutionary figures, the dynamism of whose message had to break through the accretions of the past. Pratt held that Jesus neither affirmed nor denied the existence and power of demons. His sole concern was to relieve the suffering of afflicted persons and restore them to society. While Paul at first used traditional eschatological language and imagery to portray the Parousia, he gradually shifted emphasis from the accidental phenomena to the central mystery, the coming of Jesus as Lord and Saviour. Just as Jesus was too much concerned with the plight of suffering human beings to indulge in abstract speculation on the nature of evil, Paul, the active missionary, felt called to respond to the practical and immediate needs of specific churches rather than to develop a clearly systematized theology.

This observation of Pratt's reveals a distrust of ideas and a preference for action over contemplation that are typically evangelical.[113] But these attitudes had been reinforced by a healthy transfusion from the thought of the liberal Protestant theologians with whose works Pratt had been acquainted. Their aversion to precise dogmatic formulation (see DS 28–9), and to the institutional church together with their high moral tone, when reflected in Pratt's poetry, has caused some critics to label him an anti-intellectual.[114]

It might be possible, after reading Pratt's first thesis, to concede to Vincent Sharman[115] the point that Pratt raised the question of Christ's divine authority (DS 20), but it would be equally possible after studying the second to conclude that he accepted it. In all fairness to Pratt it must be remembered that the theses are academic exercises. Thus it is possible to absolve him of both inconsistency and hypocrisy. Soteriology and eschatology were key concepts in both Wesleyan evangelism[116] and nineteenth-century and early twentieth-century criticism.

Pratt's theses are, in one sense or the other, exercises in demythologization and, as such, would scarcely have caused a stir at Victoria. While Pratt explores the implications of both questions, and the variety of critical attitudes surrounding them, he denies neither the divinity of Christ nor the possibility of his second coming. We may safely conclude that Pratt's own attitudes to demonology and to eschatology reflect those he attributed to Jesus and to Paul. The value of the topics that he chose lay not so much in their originality as in the opportunity which they must have afforded him to clarify for himself, and to come to terms with, the key issues of traditional teaching and of turn-of-the-century criticism. Although this approach shows his attempt to be "objective," it is not inconceivable that he found in the course of this study the occasion to evaluate and determine his personal attitude towards his own religious inheritance.

While Pratt is interested in the humanity of Jesus and Paul, he is moved, in turn, by their compassion for human beings. Paul's obsession with the universal nature of salvation is a reflection of Jesus' compassion, which extended to the most wretched and alienated of sufferers. Both reached out to what Pratt saw as the "deep malaise in the communal heart of the world" ("A Prayer-Medley," 1.297).

In these works, too, Pratt broods over the mystery of good and evil. In his first thesis he observes the human tendency to blame suffering, sin, and death on the intervention of evil spirits, and society's desire to exclude the evil or imperfection that it fears. But he notes that Jesus teaches that sin is due not so much to the intervention of the demon as to the perversion of the heart. While he does not try to explain why persons suffer from illness and deformity, he asserts that sin is not necessarily the immediate cause.

In his study of the epistles, Pratt examines Paul's treatment of life after death, the nature of judgment, sin and righteousness, heaven and hell, and Satan and the angels. He states that, according to Paul, justice lies not in adherence to the law, but in conformity of the heart to the risen life of Jesus. The strong emphasis in both theses upon Christian action and conduct is again a reflection of what had come to be the traditional Methodist attitude, verging at times upon semi-Pelagianism and reinforced by the ethical imperative of Schleiermacher and his followers.[117] Pratt's exploration of the Pauline letters did not provide him with an explanation for innocent suffering or for natural evil any more than his study of the synoptic Gospels did. In his poetry, as in his life, he confronted the mystery again and again.

Pratt's theses reveal his childhood interest in language and communication, which had been fostered by the linguistic approach of the Cambridge scholars to biblical criticism and by his own studies in psychology. In Pratt's approach to the Synoptics he illustrates the fact that the primitive belief in the power of the written or spoken word over the world of spirits gave rise to elaborate rites of exorcism. After examining the Gospel accounts Pratt suggests that Jesus ignored the traditional formulae, and by a simple word and gentle touch motivated by deep compassion brought healing and reconciliation to the sufferer. In the doctoral dissertation, Pratt traces, by a study of key words and phrases, the evolution of eschatology through the prophetic and apocalyptic ages into the thought of Paul. He notes with interest the difficulty inherent in translating words and concepts into another language, as he sees Paul's mission as that of communicating the gospel of salvation to people of heterogeneous cultures. The apostle's genius, Pratt concluded, lay in his ability to speak to each community in terms and in images with which it was familiar.

The source of the compassion that motivates human beings to risk or to give their lives for the salvation of others, even those unknown to them; the nature of good and evil; the possibility of life after death; the use of power whether divine or natural; the implications, scientific and humanitarian, of the multifarious means of communication – all the important questions raised and explored in Pratt's theses, precisely because they possess metaphysical dimensions, remain as themes for further contemplation in the poetry. Both works, searching, inquisitive, and open-ended rather than conclusive, imply in their approach in their handling of many points of view that Pratt considered that no sole authority, or even all of them together, can claim a monopoly on the truth. This approach was later refined and polished until it reflected "the convergence of the manifold" (EL 1.3), Pratt's characteristic point of view, his own particular brand of irony. In its relationship to paradox, this is perhaps closer to the Christian form of the revelation of truth than are Pratt's themes in themselves.

LIFE PROFESSIONAL, DOMESTIC, AND CREATIVE

When his doctoral dissertation was completed, Pratt spent the years from 1917 to 1920 much as he had passed the five preceding ones, assisting in pastoral work in the suburbs of the city, working as a demonstrator in psychology at the University of Toronto, administering psychological testing for the psychiatric clinic at the Toronto General Hospital, writing occasional reviews and articles on matters of psychological interest,[118] and collaborating with his friends and colleagues Clare Hincks and C.F. Clarke in the establishment of the Canadian National Committee for Mental Hygiene.[119] But the structuralism of Wundt and Titchener, which could be illustrated by demonstrations in the laboratory, and the functionalism of Dewey and James, which he found far more congenial, were giving way to the psychoanalytic approach of Freud, who, while he left his mark on Pratt's thought and imagination, did not wholly claim his sympathy. In addition, he chafed under the rule of W.G. Smith, chief instructor in psychology, who had supervised his doctoral thesis.[120] Moreover, the premature death of Blewett had deprived him of a mentor who might have helped him to put into less gloomy perspective his personal grief at the loss of contemporaries and his horror at the widespread suffering and devastation wrought by the First World War.

The fact that Pratt did not take up a full-time ministerial charge can hardly be interpreted as evidence of a crisis of faith. While it was a departure from the custom of early Methodism, where preaching was considered the primary role and function of the ministry, it was not at all extraordinary at the colleges sponsored by the Methodist church in Canada, least of all at Victoria College. Records indicate that between

1870 and 1890, of fifty-three graduates of Victoria who were ordained to the Methodist ministry, nine were "employed full-time by the church in her educational work in the colleges."[121] In 1904 alone, several men were ordained (among them George Blewett) who "not feeling the call of the pulpit, went into education."[122]

By 1917, Pratt's own experience in the pulpit had convinced him that his talents did not lie there. From the time of Burwash, however, English literature, languages, and psychology were considered important in moral and spiritual formation at Victoria.[123] After Pratt married Viola Whitney on 20 August 1918 he had more than his own welfare to consider. The west had lost its lure with the death of Lydia Trimble, and there is evidence that his physical and psychic strength was limited.[124] Pratt would not have objected to the church union proposed for 1925 – all the evidence is to the contrary – but the Methodism which his father had lived and which his mother had hoped he would preach was passing away. By 1919 a new trend became evident in theological circles: "the institutional church as distinct from the strictly evangelical church was on the move,"[125] and with this trend, temperamentally and by training, Pratt could have had little sympathy.

Thus, it was probably a combination of personal and practical reasons that led Pratt either to propose for himself or to accept Pelham Edgar's fortuitous offer of a position in the Department of English in 1920. In the records of Victoria College, Pratt is listed as a lecturer until 1925, when he was appointed associate professor. In 1933, he was made professor of English and retained that position until 1950, when he was named professor emeritus and special lecturer.[126] In addition to the regular obligations of a teaching professor, Pratt found time during his tenure to write poetry, conduct summer courses at the universities of British Columbia and Toronto and Dalhousie and Queen's universities, edit *Canadian Poetry Magazine* from 1935 to 1942, produce regular columns and occasional book reviews, go on reading and speaking tours, conduct a voluminous correspondence, and entertain and encourage Canadian and American writers and artists.

Nowhere is there any evidence of the one proverbial and decisive "crisis of faith" from which Pratt is believed to have emerged as an atheist or, at best, an agnostic. It was only to be expected, however, that given his experience of life and his sensitive and reflective nature, there should have been a steady and more subtle development in Pratt's religious attitudes, as Desmond Pacey suggested,[127] or "a gradual modification of religious views," as Pratt himself described the process (EL 1.3). After the Act of Union was officially put into effect in 1925, Pratt became a member of the United Church of Canada, attending first Timothy Eaton Memorial and then St George's United Church in Toronto. As late as 1960, four years before his death, the Alberta Conference of the United Church still listed him as a member of the Red Deer Presbytery, "engaged as a professor at Victoria College, Toronto."[128]

In the summer of 1960, against the idyllic backdrop of Edwards Gardens, Toronto, ironic in its contrast with the view of nature which seems predominant in his poetry, the Canadian Broadcasting Corporation televised an interview with Pratt conducted by the late J. Frank Willis. In the course of this conversation, which was broadcast across Canada on 7 February 1961, a few days before his seventy-eighth birthday, Pratt admitted (as he had done in an earlier radio interview) that he had "never felt at home in the pulpit."[129] Some colleagues and church officials seem to have interpreted this as an expression of his wish to be relieved of the ministry. In the 1961 Meeting of the Alberta Conference of the United Church of Canada *Minutes* (37), the Settlement Committee recorded the resolution "that the name of Rev. E.J. Pratt be removed from the roll of the Red Deer Presbytery at his own request."[130] However, there is no notation, as there is after the names of other ministers listed with him, "due to his resignation from the ministry of the United Church of Canada."

In the three years of failing health that remained to him, Pratt was not attached, as a minister, to another conference of the United Church. Apart from the file maintained by the Church Pension Fund, from which Pratt had found it necessary to withdraw in 1940,[131] no personal record of ministers of the United Church was kept until 1968, by which time many details pertaining to those ordained before 1925 had been lost. The personal record sheet now at the Division of Ministry, Personnel and Education, United Church of Canada, lists Pratt as a retired minister of the Alberta Conference from 1953 until 26 April 1964, the day of his death. His funeral in Convocation Hall, University of Toronto, attended by many friends, students, colleagues, and admirers, was a religious service conducted by Dr Arthur Moore, president of Victoria University and a minister of the United Church.[132]

It does not appear, then, that Pratt forgot that he had been ordained a minister and simply failed to resign. After 1953, there was no reason to remain in the ministry in order to retain position or pension. The opportunity to withdraw had presented itself on more than one occasion, and had his lack of pastoral activity in earlier years disturbed his conscience, he would have acted. Pratt felt no compulsion to resign from the ministry, and this attitude more than anything else suggests that whatever religious questions may have made their appearance in his poetry, they do not constitute a complete and personal rejection of Christianity. They do, however, remain mysteries to which Christianity must address itself afresh in each succeeding generation.

Whatever Pratt's private convictions eventually led him to believe, he simply could not put aside the religious orientation that had been a formative influence in his life for so long. As Northrop Frye remarked in his introduction to the second edition of *Collected Poems*, "Pratt's religious views are never obtrusive, but they organize all his poetry" from *Rachel*, the Newfoundland mother (and Mother Newfoundland) who mourns for her children and "refuses to be comforted because they are not" (Jer 31:15), to "The Highway" or *Towards the Last Spike*, where the construction of a road through the desert (Is 2:3; 35:8) or across the mountains (Is 49:11) or the government of a dominion "from sea to sea" (Ps 72) is seen ultimately as the fulfilment of prophetic vision, sacred or secular. While it would be wrong to interpret Pratt's religious upbringing and his theological works as indicative of the degree of his mature personal faith, it is, nevertheless, rewarding to consider them as an introduction to his poetry. If they are approached from this angle, they shed light upon the poet's characteristic ways of perceiving and conceiving.

2 "The Good Lord" with "a Glittering Monocle": The Problem of God

THE THEOLOGICAL AND PHILOSOPHICAL PROBLEM

Unbeliever, agnostic, humanist, Christian – the fact that the most vocal critics of E.J. Pratt's poetry have been able to attribute to him such a diversity of religious positions[1] indicates one of the major sources of ambiguity and irony in his work. Although such labels are often applied indiscriminately and without adequate definition, few readers, however they choose to designate Pratt, would deny the presence of religious concerns in his poetry, or claim that the spiritual tradition which he inherited and the philosophical and theological studies which he later undertook left no mark on his imagination.

It may be assumed that "The Demonology of the Synoptics in Its Relation to Earlier Developments and to the Mind of Christ" and *Studies in Pauline Eschatology and Its Background* presuppose on the part of the author, at least during the years of his preparation for the ministry, a fundamental belief in God. If, as it is sometimes claimed, the first thesis, with its focus upon the humanity of Jesus, might raise the question of Pratt's acceptance of Christ's share in the divine nature,[2] the second might just as easily be said to correct the balance, as Pratt shows how Paul, in the course of his travels and letters to the churches, came gradually to predicate of Christ the power and the privilege attributed to God alone. Since both theses are limited to particular aspects of theology under discussion at the turn of the century, the more fundamental issues of the existence of God and of God's nature are simply taken for granted. Pratt approached the specific theological question posed in each thesis with much of the dramatic objectivity which he later strove to attain in his poetry. He examined Christ's treatment of the demoniacs as reported by the synoptic authors and traditional eschatology as it was interpreted and developed by Paul.

If we are to find the source of the religious dilemma which appears to be reflected in Pratt's later work, we are less likely to discover it stated explicitly in his theses than to find it suggested in his poetry. The dilemma was inherent in the religious and cultural atmosphere in which Pratt was raised, in the particular spiritual tradition which he inherited, and in the theological school in which he was trained. Viewed in this perspective, the "problem of God" as it appears in Pratt's poetry is not simply a personal one, and clearly deserves to be seen in less simplistic terms than as the Freudian rejection of a harsh father-figure. While the expression of the dilemma may owe much to the liberal Protestantism of the nineteenth and twentieth centuries, its roots lie deep within the philosophical and theological controversies underlying the Reformation, and in certain consequent dislocations inherent in the Protestant tradition.

In the art and literature of earlier centuries, what seems to be Pratt's essential difficulty, the reconciliation of the power and the justice attributed to God with divine love and mercy, was often presented allegorically, as in the traditional debate of the Four Daughters of God.[3] Later, divorced from its wider context in the total scheme of the redemption, the Atonement, in the sense of the reconciliation of God with a fallen humankind through Jesus Christ, became the focal point of Reformation theology[4] at a time when the imagination, deprived of much of its earlier freedom, was forced to look for new forms in which to express the human longing for assurance of salvation. The paradoxical relationship between divine providence and the evil present in the world continued to loom large. By the nineteenth century, however, belief in eternal punishment and in the substitutionary penal view of the Atonement were regarded by many as incompatible with any intelligible conception of the benevolence of God, and were important factors in the reshaping of theology at the time when Pratt was undertaking his formal studies.[5]

In later years, E.J. Pratt referred to the influence of Calvinism upon the religion of his childhood (EL 1.2), and the abstract and remote, apparently disinterested deity which appears from time to time in his poetry may be, in part, a caricature or an oversimplification of the Calvinist image of God to which Methodism often turned in the course of popular preaching, if not in its doctrine and discipline. The God of Calvin is primarily the God of Sinai[6] into whose presence John Pratt, the evangelist, first led the members of his congregation at a revival.[7]

This God, who makes himself manifest in splendour and majesty, who reveals himself in glory in the Mosaic theophanies (e.g., Ex 3:3–6), but whose ways remain inscrutable, is the essential agent and also the sole and final end of all creation.[8] He is holy and absolutely transcendent, acting in all things for his own glory. To be fair, it must be remembered that Calvin did not intend his emphasis on the omnipotence and the sovereignty of God to result in the oppression of humankind, but rather in a sense of freedom and growth that he believed would come from total dependence on the free gift of salvation.[9]

However, such a doctrine of the sovereignty of God is fraught with difficulties. If pushed to its furthest limits, it opens an unbridgeable chasm between grace and nature on all planes of existence from the personal to the cosmic. A God without power is no God at all, but while the God of revelation is known primarily as a saving God who manifests power and greatness by snatching a chosen people from annihilation (Ex 14:30–1; Dt 33:29; Is 35:4), a deity such as that described in theological terms by Calvin can keep all his sovereignty only if his creatures, especially human beings, are reduced to nothingness.

The outcome of such thinking is the image of a God forbidden to communicate himself to his creatures, of humanity cast into overwhelming solitude, of a world and a God "inexorably condemned to the most utter extrinsicism."[10] Although John Wesley reacted against the excesses of Calvinism, this universe was to be a significant part of the inheritance of the founder of Methodism, and still later of John Pratt and his son, the poet.

A sense of separation between God and his creatures such as that outlined above tends to throw into bolder relief the role of Christ in the work of the Atonement. While the life, death, and resurrection of Jesus Christ are intrinsically related in the true biblical meaning of sacrifice, they become unnaturally separated in the late scholastic theories with their debates on how much value should be assigned to his life, and how much to his death. This rigid and one-sided interpretation of sacrifice probably derives from the distorted view of an angry God looking about for a creature on whom to be revenged, and then being appeased by the killing of a passive and subservient victim.[11] In such an interpretation, the Father becomes known chiefly for his power and his just wrath, while the Son, his divinity concealed, is associated with mercy and with love.

The legacy of Pratt and his generation included other difficulties arising from the unsolved problems of seventeenth-century Protestantism which had gradually exchanged its reliance upon Aristotelian logic for dependence upon Cartesian intuition. It is significant that, as early as the seventeenth century, Protestantism had shown not only a consciousness of history,[12] but also an open-mindedness to new ideas and a respect for science.[13] By the eighteenth century, however, the rationalism which had brought about the break with traditional philosophy and the embrace of a thoroughly scientific world view had led to the machine-like universe of Locke and Newton, in which all events were to be explained as parts of a network of natural causes, and in which the laws of God all too soon came to be identified with the laws of nature.[14]

This rationalism led, too, to the concept of the Supreme Being of deism which bore a superficial resemblance to Calvin's image of God, but whose function was merely to start in motion the machine of the universe, guarantee the validity of the moral laws, and ensure the rewards of the righteous.[15] In time, deism was to lead to the rise of the "higher criticism," to the study of comparative religions, and to the development of the philosophy of religion. Meanwhile, natural theology, with its emphasis on God as the First Cause, tended to reinforce the impersonal image of the deity. Ironically, natural theology was to become an essential part of the curriculum of the nonconformist academies, including the Methodist college at St John's attended by E.J. Pratt.[16]

The pietist and evangelical revivals of the eighteenth century, suspicious of both scholasticism and rationalism, unfortunately bypassed the critical questions being posed by philosophy and science, and in doing so, further prepared the way for the total breach between reason and faith. This dichotomy is evident in certain features of Pratt's poetry no less than in the artistic achievements of many of his contemporaries. In the popular imagination, certain features of Calvin's image of God were associated with some aspects of the Great Clockmaker of the deists and with the First Cause of natural theology, to the neglect of important attributes of the God of revelation. On the whole, science and religion parted company, science becoming more mechanistic and quantitative, and evangelical religion insisting on the sufficiency of faith alone, and on the literal truth of the Bible.[17] The relationship between reason and faith and between nature and the supernatural was first seen to be obscured, then broken altogether.

One effect of the deflation of philosophy was that religion turned for support from speculative argument to scripture and experience. In the course of the rationalistic and deistic movements of the eighteenth century, the Methodism of which E.J. Pratt was also the heir appeared within the established Church of England as a popular movement of return to God through an ardent devotion to the person of Christ. Accommodating itself, at first, to Anglican theology and liturgy, it rejected Calvinist predestination while combining the Puritan sense of the degenerate state of human nature with the Arminian insistence on personal responsibility, free will, and good works.[18] It asked of its adherents only a "desire to flee from the wrath to come, and to be saved from their sins."[19] E.J. Pratt himself remarked on the influence of his parents' religion:

My father was a Methodist clergyman, and he seemed rather moderate in his views in a community with a strong Calvinistic affinity ... (*PLP* 42)[20] There was no predestination as the Calvinists believed. They insisted you were doomed at birth, damned without hope of redemption. But the Methodists had a relieving philosophy – there was [the] possibility of repentance. We grew up in this atmosphere. My father often quoted the line, I remember it so well: "When the lamp holds out to burn / The vilest sinner may return." "Vilest," you see. Sin was a *malaise* to be cured in all forms. When the fishermen came back from Labrador they backslid, of course. Had to go to the penitent form outside the church. Ask God publicly for repentance. (EL 2)

Saving philosophy notwithstanding, there is in Methodism, as one authority comments, "still a lot of Calvinism left when you take away predestination and church polity."[21]

John Wesley spoke of the divine Being with all the wealth of Augustan terminology.[22] For him, no less than for Calvin, God was "awful," "adorable," "sovereign," and "omnipotent," "the All wise," "the Governor of the world," "the Lord of Nature," and "the Almighty Power."[23] But evangelical religion, though it rarely used the unadorned name of God, was wary of the abstract connotations attached to many of the divine titles by association with deism.[24] So Wesley spoke of God, too, in the more familiar and concrete terms of the New Testament, as well as in titles which he coined himself or borrowed from the culture and occupations of his congregations. God was not only the "Great Judge" (15:103) but also "the Shepherd of Souls," "the Great Physician" (5:53), "the Lord of the Harvest," "the Great Captain," and "our Father" (6:333).

John Wesley saw the whole natural world as an organic system, marvellously constructed and maintained by God, but of itself unevangelical, corrupt, and somnolent, in a state of utter darkness (1:25). Thus he shared with Calvin a sense of the separation between the Creator and his universe and a Neoplatonic suspicion of all that was not purely spiritual. Yet he still took pains to emphasize that the whole of creation would have a true share in the redemption (60:248). More significantly, he stressed the Pauline teaching that all – the poor, the social outcasts, even the most sinful and downtrodden – were called to salvation. In addition to this universalism, Wesley stated his belief that Christianity is a religion with social dimensions and that to interpret it as a private concern only is to destroy it (24:296). The very organization of Methodism expressed the belief that, as instruments of God's providence, men and women are responsible for each other's physical and moral welfare.

But Wesley also believed that to be encouraged to seek the salvation offered freely to all, one had first "to face the 'terror of the Lord' (2 Cor 5:11),"[25] to recognize one's status as a sinner before a justly offended God and to be confronted with the total depravity of one's fallen human nature (7:82; 6:72) and with the fate that one deserved if one did not repent. With this self-knowledge one then might flee to the foot of the Cross (6:75)[26] and find in the redeeming blood of Christ the only remedy for "the loathsome leprosy of sin" (21:252).[27] It was his compassion and concern for humanity, as well as his interest in psychology and his distrust of human nature, that persuaded Wesley to appeal first to the motive of fear (15:226).

Thus for John Wesley, too, the Atonement became the very focus of faith. But, unlike Calvin, he bypassed the historical theories of the Atonement and constructed his doctrine straight from scripture. He did not set this element of his teaching inside a legal framework in which God is made subject to an eternal, unalterable law of justice, but rather stressed the biblical emphasis on propitiation as appeasement for the divine wrath, and on the covenant between God and humankind. Concentrating on the death of Christ as the essence of the message of salvation, Wesley held that reconciliation consists equally and indeed almost primarily in a change of attitude on the part of God, a change from wrath to kindness, from condemnation to pardon, from rejection to acceptance for the sake of his Son (9:197; 20:237).[28] As God turns to the creature in grace, the latter with a free will is enabled to turn back to the Creator, first in repentance, then in the faith by which he or she is justified (5:53), and finally in hope and love. As the creature is justified by God and regenerated, he or she experiences in a personal manner not only the forgiveness of sins but also the indwelling of the Holy Spirit. This assurance of salvation manifests itself in a life of good works (41:259). Methodists did not expect the one experience to endure and bear fruit for a lifetime. Conversion was a continual turning back to God through grace. If one were to persevere, the will needed to be strengthened frequently through the renewal of one's covenant with God.

Although throughout his lifetime John Wesley assiduously avoided theological debate and precise formulation,[29] Wesleyan faith presupposes in the most explicit fashion the two doctrines of the divinity of Christ and of the unique redemptive value of his sufferings and death (7:85). However, the relationship between these doctrines constitutes a dichotomy inherent in Methodism from the time of its separation from the Anglican communion: "the weakness of the 'revival' and of the whole Methodist movement comes from the failure to incorporate these two truths into a harmonious theology."[30]

It is possible to see something of this weakness reflected in the official sermon of the Theological Union delivered by the Reverend John Pratt at the Newfoundland Conference Sessions of the Methodist Church held in St John's in 1890. Taking as his text John 20:17, Pratt preached on "The Fatherhood of God." "God was first known as the Creator, the Preserver, and the Destroyer," he said.[31] In the Old Testament, he pointed out, any concept of God as a father was understood in reference to the Jews alone. Not until the time of Christ were all people everywhere taught to say "Our Father." Having indicated that fatherhood implies love, care, and discipline, Pratt went on to the theological implications of the text. All believers, he stated, were "sons of God" by adoption, but Christ was the "Son of God" by procession, of one substance with the Father. With the exception of the dualism implicit in the first quotation, what Pratt said here is fairly consistent both with scripture and with the Nicene Creed. He continued, however, that Christ "never says 'Our Father' as regarding himself and his followers, but 'My Father and your Father.'"

It would be unfair to draw conclusions from one sermon, but it is nevertheless possible to see implied within it some of the theological difficulties which John Pratt and his generation of preachers inherited and passed on to their sons. Many of John Pratt's homilies, typical of Methodist sermons of their time, were based on texts drawn from the Old Testament books of the post-exilic period, influenced by Hellenistic dualism and interpreted in such a way that God is indeed seen as both Creator and Destroyer (a philosophical as well as a theological dilemma). Again the relationship between the God of the Old Testament and the Father from whom Christ proceeds is not made clear. In this context the filial relationship between the Father and the Son, and between God and humankind through Christ, is certainly not "incorporated within a harmonious theology."[32]

If, at times, critics have sensed in the poetry of E.J. Pratt an inconsistency in his attitude towards God, an inability to reconcile the glorified divinity of the Father with the suffering humanity of Jesus, it may be a reflection, in part, not only of one of the key paradoxes of Christianity become a central theological problem of Protestantism, but also of the doctrinal fluidity inherent in the preaching and the teaching of John Wesley and his followers.

This lack of dogmatism is not surprising in a denomination in which scripture became the supreme authority, and the sole rule of faith and practice. The theological atmosphere of Canadian Methodism at Victoria College shortly before E.J. Pratt's arrival in Toronto was reflected in the Workman and Jackson episodes (see 17, above), which the Church considered critical, not merely because they challenged the literal interpretation of the Bible, but because they were precipitated by ordained ministers of the church whose responsibility it was to safeguard the pure preaching of the Word of God. Apart from this, the doctrinal flexibility appropriate to Methodism in Canada at the turn of the century is indicated in the preface to the *Digest of the Doctrinal Standards of the Methodist Church*, a harmony of John Wesley's *Sermons, Notes,* and *Articles*[33] drawn up in 1895 for probationers and students for the ministry by Dr W.I. Shaw, then principal of Wesleyan Theological College in Montreal:

It is sometimes said in pleasantry that the Methodists have the largest creed in Christendom in the *Sermons, Notes* and *Articles* hereafter analyzed. There are certainly some advantages in such a mode of declaring our faith. First, it is more easily understood because of explicit statement; and second, it is more free from shibboleths, and is not so likely to create a blind narrow prejudice for a human form of words. The meaning is explained rather than condensed. The *Standards* under consideration, it is to be remembered, are of authority only for the ministry. *A member's relation to the Church is determined only by spiritual life and character. As to creed he may be a Calvinist, or Baptist, or a pre-millennial Adventist without imperilling his membership. But for agreement of faith on the part of the ministry these standards are authorized.*[34]

Once cut off, in this sense, from any consistent theological or philosophical underpinning, Methodism, at least in Canada, had unwittingly left itself open to many features of nineteenth-century and early twentieth-century liberal Protestant thought which its founder could only have viewed with alarm. Although John Wesley was a literalist in his interpretation of the Bible, he had been greatly indebted to Bengel, the Lutheran scholar whose edition of the New Testament had marked the beginning of a scientific approach to exegesis. By the end of the nineteenth century, however, the very respect for science fostered in the nonconformist schools had led to a too rigid and unimaginative application of the scientific method to biblical studies.[35] In addition, the native evangelical impatience with theological formulation and with institutional religion which was to be E.J. Pratt's birthright was strengthened by the metaphysical scepticism of the Kantian school of philosophy and by certain elements in the thought of Hegel.[36]

The publication of Darwin's theory of evolution precipitated what is generally recognized as the great Victorian dilemma in that it challenged the literal interpretation of the biblical account of creation. How should Genesis then be understood, especially in the light of the historical methods exemplified in Jowett's *Essays and Reviews*, which followed shortly after? Further, the theory underlined the difficulties inherent in theism by directing attention to those aspects of nature that are hard to reconcile with the existence of an omniscient and loving God. How could an intelligent and beneficent creator allow nature to grope its way forward as if it were subject to blind chance? Finally, the theory of evolution seemed to deny humanity's unique place in creation and the superiority given to it in Genesis. Was there anything to guarantee the existence of an immortal soul or life hereafter? The tendency was to oversimplify Darwinism and to apply it uncritically to everything.[37]

The reaction was varied. Among intellectual believers a subtle accommodation began almost immediately, together with the conviction that theology must recognize and come to terms with new knowledge or Christianity would be doomed. Conservative Christians were outraged and held fast to the literal interpretation of Genesis because they were afraid that to consider the possibility of another would endanger the truth of creation. For many of the general public, however, Darwinism heralded a loss of faith which any religion, including Methodism, seemed powerless to restore; for others it pointed to an optimistic belief in human progress, and for others still to the hopelessness appropriate to the victims of blind chance.[38] On the whole the challenges to faith which Methodism as an evangelical denomination confronted by the turn of the century were greater than they had been in Wesley's day.

The particular stress on the inward experience of conversion expressing itself in a life of Christian morality, which had once given Methodism its distinctive character, led in later generations either to an extreme subjectivism or to a legal moralism in which the larger background of Wesley's spirit and teaching was often forgotten. In addition, the subjective aspect of Methodism prepared the way for Schleiermacher, who, with his interest in psychology, would relegate the religious attitude to the realm of the emotions.[39] Awareness, insight, intuition, feeling, and response – all, incidentally, significant characteristics of Methodist enthusiasm – became in general the virtues that helped to make a person a Christian whose salvation was to be found within the social dimensions of an organic community of people constituted by the awareness of God.[40]

Gradually, Christian experience replaced revelation and grace as the basis of authority, while the Methodist stress on universal salvation corresponded with a liberal tendency to consider denominational differences insignificant. As salvation appeared to be more generally accessible, there was less concentration on the wrath of God, the depths of sin and the isolation of the experience of justification.[41] The ethical emphasis in Wesley's thought, always a corollary or a consequence of justification and sanctification, became separated from its foundation in religious response and was considered independently. The will of the individual, his or her capabilities and responsibilities, often took the place of the earlier witness to God's freedom, sovereignty and gift of salvation.[42]

As liberalism placed greater stress upon the natural, the life of grace or the supernatural declined in significance. The centrality of the person of Christ in its immanence and humanity to which John Wesley had redirected attention was still underscored, but Jesus came to be spoken of as the pre-eminent teacher or model, and no longer as the unique crux of the divine plan for salvation.[43] As this happened, a distinction was gradually made between the Christ of theology and the Jesus of history. It became fashionable to drive a wedge between the supposedly simple religion of Jesus and the complex theology of Paul and to claim for the apostle a larger share than his master in the development of the institutional element in Christianity.[44]

At the time when these liberalizing tendencies had scarcely touched the ordinary adherents of Methodism in Newfoundland, they were making themselves felt in Toronto. They tended to blur the distinguishing features of Methodism, seeming to alter as they did so the role of minister and sacrament, and helping to ease the way for the compromise that constituted the foundation of the United Church of Canada in 1925. But whatever the effect of liberalism on the evangelical faith of E.J. Pratt, he, no more than James Joyce, could jettison the whole of his religious inheritance. The tensions between the just exercise of divine power and the mediating effects of mercy and love, between faith and reason, between science and religion, between nature and grace, and between God's providence and the presence of evil in the world – all from time to time viewed apart from a consistently unifying foundation in philosophy and theology – haunted Pratt for the rest of his life. The hopeful synthesis offered in George Blewett's *The Christian View of the World* came too late to have a permanent effect on his thought.

The Calvinist orientation of his early childhood, his Methodist upbringing, and the liberal Protestant tendencies present in theology during the period of his formal studies are all strains that find their echoes in Pratt's poetry. There are moments when they seem to sound in unison. At other times they pull apart, leaving the reader with either a feeling of discord emanating from a problem with which Pratt struggled in vain, or with a sense of tentative harmony or ironic balance in the face of what he realized must remain forever a mystery.

THE PROBLEM OF GOD IN THE POETRY

Notwithstanding Pratt's religious and theological background, indeed perhaps because of it, the image of God as it appears from time to time in his poetic works constitutes what is generally agreed upon by critics to be a problem. Its frequent negative associations tend to overshadow any positive connotations, and thus to reinforce the belief that early in his career Pratt underwent a severe "crisis of faith" from which he never entirely recovered. The undue stress on this "crisis," which cannot in any way be documented, draws attention away from the image of God as a loving father or as a benevolent creator when it does appear, or is even implied in Pratt's work. For example, the banquet in "The Depression Ends" is provided under the auspices of the "Lord of Love ... Lord of Light" (1.266). Although Pratt states that the banquet is subject to "the logic of a dream" (1.261) whose fulfilment has, incidentally, been guaranteed (1.266), he does not suggest that the feast is merely an illusion. It is a free gift to the dispossessed, participating in both time and eternity. In *Brébeuf and His Brethren*, to be discussed later in detail, the events of the narrative are invested with value and meaning only in so far as they are seen to be embraced by the will of a loving God. It is in the darkest moments of the drama that the "God of all comfort" (1.235) reveals himself (2.70, 71, 80, 93, 95–6).

In other poems the heart of God is envisioned as the source of mercy and compassion for desperate men and women. In *The "Titanic"* the thought of the fourteen hundred passengers, half of them immigrants trapped in the liner's steerage compartments, elicits from Smith, the captain – and, one senses, from the narrator too – an almost automatic or spontaneous appeal to the only possible source of salvation (1.324). Again, in "Dunkirk," the soldiers floundering desperately off the beaches find the touch of a spar or a halyard "like a hold on the latch of the heart of God" (2.123).

More frequently in Pratt's poetry, however, God's action or presence is symbolized by the hand, a traditional sign of divinely creative power. In the context of a poem whose irony springs from the contrast between the subject, a dog which has exhibited extraordinary life-saving skills, and the mock theological argument to which Pratt allows the poem to give rise, he suggests that an animal such as Carlo could have sprung only from "a dam, / Shaped to this hour by God's own hand" (1.49). In "The Highway" Pratt pictures humanity seeking to "grasp again" the creative hand which appears to have led the evolving universe to the culmination of its beauty and perfection in the "Son of Man" (1.257). In "The Depression Ends" the hand which wrought "the planets and the suns" (1.267) is associated with the "Lord of love,

... Lord of light" (1.266) in a "towering fantasy" that suggests, though in less sublime context, something of Dante's vision of the love "that moves the sun in heaven and all the stars" (*Paradiso*, 33. 130–4).

Pratt's moral vision is rooted in what he saw to be the necessary connection, in human conduct, between the heart, in the Pauline sense of *kardia* (*PE* 35, 182), the responsive and emotional source of intelligent motivation, and the brain or the hand that should translate the motivation of the heart into action. This vision, bequeathed to him in part by John Wesley, informs or controls the content and structure of many of the poems from "Silences" and *Magic in Everything* to *The "Roosevelt" and the "Antinoe"* and *Behind the Log*. While this association has suggested to some critics "the heroic and muscular Christianity" of Kingsley and Henley, or Pratt's familiarity with the Wundtian theory of apperception[45] – and there may be some correspondence with the latter – it is probable that its foundation lies elsewhere, in his firm belief that charity must be translated into action and in his hatred of the type of hypocrisy or Pharisaism (*PE* 56) harshly condemned by the prophets of the Old Testament (Is 29:13), and just as harshly denounced by Jesus in the Gospels (Mt 15:7; Mk 8:15; Lk 12:1).[46]

With this in mind, it is interesting to note that while in poems such as "The Highway" and "The Depression Ends" God's mighty deeds are seen as expressions of benevolence, Pratt does not always depict the works of the divine hand as if it were informed by the *kardia* that should animate Christian action. In "Clay" the divine hands represent the force in nature which Julian, in his romantic posturing, tries to identify with the destructive and repressive power of God. He testily inquires:

> What jealous hands
> Are these, that ever closing in their grasp
> On bird and brute, must henceforth seek to hurl
> Hell's jungle-statutes on the race of men? (2.333)

The narrator in *The Iron Door* dreams that "a giant hand" has fashioned the cruciform gate as an impenetrable barrier between this world and the next (1.205).

On several occasions Pratt uses the phrase "the hollow of God's hand,"[47] an image of biblical origin suggesting divine providence or protection (1 Chron 21:13; Is 40:12). But he usually employs it to convey humanity's sense of God's lack of concern, or failure to use power in a positive or meaningful way. For example, in *The Iron Door* it appears that "every wind that raged upon the land / Had fled the nescient hollow of God's hand" (1.211). There is, in addition, a suggestion in Pratt's poetry that as history moves on, and as civilization becomes more complex, God's power may be in decline. The questioning of his providence, once evoked chiefly by natural disasters such as that which befell the crew of the *Roosevelt* (1.236), now arises from more subtle but no less sinister circumstances. But "the hollow of God's hand" seems to offer little protection as the battle moves from macrocosm to microcosm. Humanity's concern is not so much with the storm, not even with the war without as in "Come Away, Death" (2.111–13), but with the battle between "the silent and invisible" leucocytes and microbes in "the little world of man":

> Once it was flood and drought, lightning and storm and earthquake,
> Those hoary executors of the will of God,
> That planned the monuments for human faith.
> Now, rather, it is the silent and invisible ministers,
> Teasing the ear of Providence
> And levelling out the hollows of His hands
> That pose the queries for His moral government.
> ("Under the Lens," 2.27)

It is by this means, too, that the query is posed in "The Doctor in the Boat" (2.301–2).

Many of the early short lyrics reflect God's apparent indifference to human beings, who consequently feel that they have been abandoned in a hostile universe. In "The Ground Swell" the low, insistent voice of the sea caused by a distant gale or seismic disturbance expresses "some dull pang," perhaps of appetite, "that grew / Out of the void" before creation. Set against it in ironic contrast is the sharp "edge for human grief" fashioned by eternity and now reawakened by the fear born of experience that conscious and sentient human beings may be no more than "harvest sweepings" strewn casually on a winter sea by the winds of God, "To feed the primal hungers of a reef" (1.63). In "The Toll of the Bells," a pair of sonnets commemorating the tragedy that befell the crew of the sealer *Greenland*, the enormity of the loss of human life is so overwhelming that no Christian ritual for the dead, it seems, can give it adequate expression. While "cathedral voices" sing of "God's Tomorrow," the survivors can only feel that today, "Sorrow / Has raked up faith and burned it like a pile / Of driftwood" (1.68). The melancholy tone and the vision of the harshness of nature conveyed in these poems outdoes that of Old English elegiac laments such as *The Seafarer* or *The Wanderer*. Humankind is bereft of all earthly comfort and left weary of heart, and much less sure than the Wanderer of "the Father in Heaven" as the only stronghold.[48]

At other times, it seems that God, instead of merely showing indifference in the work of creation, has deliberately constructed an obstacle course for his creatures. In *Towards the Last Spike* the predominant view of nature (2.216, 227–32, 239–40), that of the planners and builders of the railroad, is that of Calvin, although it bears a close affinity also to Wesley's vision of the natural world as "unevangelical, corrupt and somnolent" (1:25). The western mountains which the railroad had to cross or penetrate were "barriers built of God" (2.213). But men had to contend, too, with a wilderness complicated by bogs and sloughs, "And that most cursèd diabase which God / Had left from the explosions of his wrath" (2.238). The building of the line proceeded not quickly, smoothly, and logically, as reasonable human beings would have it, but "Across the prairies in God's own good time, / His plodding, patient, planetary time" (2.214). George Stephen, instead of turning to God for help, looked upon Van Horne as the better-than-divine architect presiding over the creation of a new and improved world (2.222–32). So skilfully does Pratt "put on the mind" of his heroes in *Towards the Last Spike* that the reader must frequently recall the poet's quest for dramatic objectivity. It would be a mistake to equate Pratt's vision of nature with that of the nation-builders, however closely they may correspond from time to time.

On occasion throughout Pratt's poetry the ruler of the universe, who combines features of the God of Calvin, the Clockmaker of the deists, and the First Cause of natural theology, appears as an unskilled architect, or as the principle of a universal order which is alien to humankind. Like the "great Panjandrum" in "The Truant" (2.125), he is usually an abstraction. He is "the Master of the Skies" who with "a mighty baton took command / Of perfect orchestration" in a dance in which individual and imperfect human performers do not belong ("Out of Step," 1.284). Elsewhere he appears as "master mason" ("The Radio in the Ivory Tower," 2.44), "the Lord of Hosts" ("Cycles," 2.196), "the Referee" whose arbitrary calls deserve to be challenged ("The Decision," 1.67), the "gambler" ("Clay," 2.319; *Behind the Log*, 2.164), or "the good Lord" with "a glittering monocle" ("The Parable of Puffsky," 1.285–6). Sometimes his role is seen as that of servant rather than master of the historical process or of the universal design of things. In *The Iron Door* (1.208) he does duty as "the eternal steward," and in "The Highway" (1.256) as the "cosmic seneschal." Frequently he is deaf or inattentive (*The Iron Door*, 1.210; *The "Roosevelt" and the "Antinoe"*, 1.235–8; "Jock o'the Links," 1.290).

These occasional but accumulated images, drawn largely from the pages of the first edition of *Complete Poems*, suggest something of the nature of the problem of God as it appears in Pratt's work. To determine the true dimensions of the point at issue it would be wise to examine more closely three poems often cited as expressing Pratt's concept of God.

The questions of the existence and the nature of God arise in Pratt's poetry for the first time, and are stated most explicitly, in "Clay" (2.305–56), the lengthy, posthumously published closet drama written probably some time between 1917, when Pratt finished *Studies in Pauline Eschatology*, and 1920, when he joined the staff of the Department of English at Victoria College. Belonging quite clearly to the literary tradition of the nineteenth century, this three-act dialogue with choruses and lyric interludes undoubtedly owes something of its structure to works such as Shelley's *Prometheus Unbound* and *Julian and Maddalo* and Hardy's *The Dynasts*. But "Clay" so reverberates with echoes from the Bible, particularly Job and Ezekiel, from Shakespeare's *King Lear* and *Macbeth*, and from the works of the Romantic and Victorian poets that there often seems little opportunity left for Pratt's own voice to make itself heard. In its more than forty pages "Clay" is lacking in unity, uneven in style, and quite obviously unfinished, yet it is worth careful consideration for the insight that it affords into both Pratt's ideas and his craftsmanship. It embraces not only the dialectical structure of his theological theses, which, translated into poetical form, became in time an important source of paradox and irony[49] in Pratt's work, but also the major themes and images which recur in the later poetry. Furthermore, it contains two modes of poetic language and expression, one of which Pratt was eventually to set aside in favour of the other.[50]

It is easy to be distracted by Pratt's own statements about his poetry. There is evidence that the title, "Clay," whose meaning is clarified in the poem but whose full significance can be realized only in the light of Julian's last speech (2.354–5), was chosen deliberately rather than accidentally, as Pratt later suggested.[51] While it may first call to mind the image of the potter and his wheel in Fitzgerald's 1868 translation of *The Rubaiyat of Omar Khayyam* or in Browning's "Rabbi Ben Ezra" and "Caliban Upon Setebos," it is important to note that Pratt uses the symbol here, as in *The Iron Door* (1.213), in a slightly different sense from these poets.[52] Through the persona of Julian in "Clay," Pratt attempts to work out the fundamental and universal questions of the nature of God, the immortality of the soul, and the reconciliation of divine providence with the apparent injustice of unmerited human suffering. Since Julian feels compelled to set aside as meaningless any appeal to revelation, arguments must be made in terms of philosophy or natural theology.

The questions, although they are couched in late nineteenth-century terms, are nonetheless those of Oedipus or Job or King Lear. Julian and his companions can no more be called "characters" than

Job and his friends. They are mouthpieces for three different philosophies of life or religious attitudes: Julian, that of the would-be apostate; Thaddeus, that of the visionary prophet or idealist; and Merrivale, that of the legalistic traditionalist. Their points of view, not always consistently delineated or equally well developed, are meant to play against each other and to contribute to Julian's final position. They are interpreted, augmented or objectified, at times, by Penrose and Donaldson, visitors to the island, and are echoed or counterpointed in the lyric sections of the verse drama by the comments and conversations of unnamed persons (2.311–15), and by the voices of the wind and the waves (2.310–11).

The dialogue between Penrose and Donaldson which introduces the first act of "Clay" (2.305–9) exposes Julian's fundamental philosophical and religious dilemma. Like Job, he has been overcome to the point of illness or despair by the problem of evil, although it appears to have touched his person only indirectly.[53] Nevertheless, it has driven him, like Prospero, into self-imposed exile on an island in the Atlantic. Evil, as Julian is aware of it in the first act of "Clay" (2.305–25), is evident in the imperfection or the cruelty of nature, especially in the evolutionary process, which seems to ensure the survival of the fittest only. Julian's kindness, his singleness of heart, his sensitivity to another's pain, and his prophetic, almost Christlike gift of healing, all the marks of an idealist, have made him an easy prey for cynicism:

> he looked obliquely on the world
> He lived in; everywhere that human feet
> Had trod he saw the Satyr's hoof; a core
> Malevolent inhered in life; the ape
> Was grinning through men's eyes and teeth, and this
> Marked all his utterance with a tragic note. (2.307–8)[54]

However, the quest for the nature and the existence of evil is inseparable from the quest for the existence of God.[55] Having felt obliged to deny the possibility of a God who could permit evil such as he has witnessed, Julian has consequently abandoned "all that men call faith / In human goals" (2.308). Like Shelley's Julian he has found no refuge from the world's ills in stoicism, and would if he could, like King Lear (3.6.76), "anatomize" humanity to discover the secrets of the heart (2.308, 319).[56] Unwilling to allow for any degree of freedom on the part of either the creator or the creature, Julian leaves himself open to a type of modern atheism described by theologian John Courtney Murray:

At the bottom of an atheism whose matrix is the problem of evil, there lies a moral absolute. It asserts not only that evil has no right to exist, but that its existence is intolerable. This is a problem of such absoluteness that the God of the Bible does not admit it as an imperative on his governance of the world. He judges evil to be evil, but he does not regard it as intolerable. He shows towards it the "forbearance" of which Paul speaks (Rom 3:25). This now becomes the charge against him. He who is God – so runs the indictment – ought not to tolerate evil. Since the God of the Bible does tolerate it, he is not God. God is rejected in the name of God himself. This is the purest and the most passionate form of atheism, when man rejects God in the name of his own more God-like morality. It towers high above the petty biblical atheisms and above the shallow monism of philosophy.[57]

The apparent cosmic indifference, or the rift between God and nature, is objectified in the second scene of "Clay" (2.309) by the violent storm. This tempest does not correspond to the traditional biblical setting for a theophany such as that which Job experiences (38:1; 40:6), nor does it become a school of personal suffering such as that in which Lear (act 3) must learn what it means to be truly human.[58] Julian, nevertheless, does find some parallel between the storm without and "the little world of man" within (*King Lear*, 3.1.10), concluding with lines characteristic of the view of nature presented by Pratt in his earliest poetry: "And so does man's existence find its form / Envisaged in the ocean's eyeless face / Swept by the besom of the winds" (2.310).

Using the destruction wrought by the storm as a bulwark for his preconceived notions of good and evil, Julian turns a deaf ear to what the chorus suggests about the paradoxical nature of reality[59] – that while the human cry is often lost in the fury of the storm (2.310–12),[60] human hands and nature herself will rebuild (2.313). He also rejects Merrivale's reminder that the works of nature are governed by divine providence. As far as Julian is concerned, "there is no power / Above the winds," and "there is found / No eye to pity and no will to save" (2.324). It is as if "a gambler's been at work upon this job, / Or else a journeyman that did not learn / His trade too well" (2.319). Fatalistically he concludes, "the gambler's leaded throw" rules all (2.320).

Although he balances precariously on the verge of atheism, or at least of agnosticism, Julian does not consistently reject the notion of a Supreme Being. But he does ask, if there is such a one, what human beings should call him, since God's apparent indifference seems to belie his traditional New Testament titles (2.324). As Julian attempts to reconcile the notion of a deity of power and wrath with that of a God of love and mercy, he is caught on the horns of a dilemma. C.S. Lewis outlines it quite simply:

If God were good, He would wish to make his creatures perfectly happy, and if God were almighty He would be able to do what he wished. But the creatures are not happy. Therefore God lacks either goodness, or power, or both.'[61]

It is in this context that Julian's most anguished questioning pours forth:

> Who calls him Father; hears his Shepherd's voice;
> Knows him as Friend, Physician, Master, King?[62]
> The subject's head falls crushed within the wheels
> Of some immaculate law. The sower swings
> A tiring arm on arid soil bestrewn
> With thorns and stones. [Lk 8:5] A sufferer calls in pain
> In the lone watches of his couch, and hears
> No answer save the leaden brush of wings
> Against the window-pane. The son's last right
> To heirship, to inheritance of love
> Is spurned upon the doorstep of his home,
> His kinship cancelled, and his brother's ties
> Dissolved in mutual blood. Named you him Father?
> God? No. Rather a Potter with some clay. (2.324–5)

Scandalized by the presence of evil in the world of nature, Pratt's Julian finds himself unable to adopt either the attitude of stoicism[63] or that of blind, unquestioning faith. He looks for an answer in terms of human justice and cannot accept the paradox and the irony which confront him on every side. For the names used in the New Testament to express the close relationship between God and humanity, Julian feels compelled to substitute the less personal title of the potter commonly used in the Old Testament. C.S. Lewis suggests that the figure of the potter is an analogy of the "lowest type of love, that of the artist for an artifact":

The limitation of such an analogy is of course, that in the symbol the patient is not sentient, and that certain questions of justice and mercy which arise when the clay is really "living" remain unrepresented.[64]

The problem of reconciling human suffering with the existence of a God who loves is insoluble as long as Julian attaches a limited meaning to the word "love" and looks upon the universal scheme as if humankind rather than God were the centre of it. God cannot exist purely for the sake of creatures, as Julian seems to think.[65]

57   The Problem of God

Act 2 of "Clay" (2.325–50), set in 1915 after an interval of two years, is introduced by a chorus of representative voices which include those of an old man from a harbour town, young men on the battlefield, and members of the medical staff at an army base. Like the voices in Wilfred Owen's "Last Words" or "A Terre,"[66] or in Thomas Hardy's *War Poems*,[67] they reflect attitudes to the First World War ranging from patriotism and parental pride thrown into relief by irony, through personal fear and melancholy, to pity and clinical detachment (2.325–8). These speeches are fragmented, but the language, in contrast to the stilted philosophizing of Julian and his friends, is colloquial and refreshingly natural. The chorus of "Cries Afar Off" (2.328) relates the death of humankind to that of nature, and the image of snow falling over the battlefield has something of the universal levelling effect of the snowfall in James Joyce's story "The Dead."[68] These lines of the Chorus represent one of Pratt's first known attempts in the lyric mode, and here, as in the fragments of dialogue earlier in the scene, we feel that he may be speaking for the first time in his natural voice and idiom.

While the storm of act 1 served as an objective correlative for the cosmic indifference of nature, the war in act 2 of "Clay" represents the problem of moral evil in both its personal and social dimensions. However, since Julian still lives as a recluse on his island, and since the war makes no demands on him personally as it does on MacLeish's hero J.B., the anguish in his response to the horrors described by his friends (2.331–6) is less than convincing. Julian may represent Pratt's earliest attempt to work out for himself the proper relationship between the imagination and reality, and the reflection of that relationship in art – in other words, Pratt's portrait of the artist or the poet in his quest for objectivity. In terms of the poem itself, while it is also possible to see Julian as the type of person who must try to reconcile the problem of natural and moral evil with the existence of a loving and providential God, his total detachment from the world, and from the ugly reality that it frequently presents, reduces his spiritual and intellectual efforts to vague theorizing.

Julian's friend Thaddeus paints the horrors of the battlefield (2.331) in the colours of Armageddon (Rev 16), the strewn bodies (2.332) recalling Milton's fallen leaves in Vallombrosa. As he tries to recreate for Julian something of the shocking experience of war, Thaddeus stresses the senseless waste of young life:

> Young lads of growing years,
> Who pain or weariness had never known,

> Lay in strange sleep upon the fields, alone,
> Or huddled up in ghastly heaps where death
> Had flung them. Night winds gambolled with their hair,
> Golden and brown and dark – they heeded not. (2.332)

Over the carnage the harvest moon shines in its fullness on a field in which men, once ranged as enemies in life, are now revealed as brothers in death (2.332–3).

This description merely rekindles Julian's spirit of rebellion earlier directed against the devastation in nature (2.318–25). Even though he is removed from the experience and hears of the war as he heard of the storm, at second hand, Julian feels compelled to reject any remaining belief in the justice and providence of God:

> O Thaddeus! there is an iron in the will
> Of Him who shapes the times. His power is seen
> Within the flash that cleaves the oak; it germs
> Within the hidden matrix of the earth,
> When cities rock before convulsing fires
> Prepare their tombs; it lurks within the fang
> Of shrike and puma, in the slanted stroke
> Of the vulture's beak upon the escarpment's flint,
> In every coil and spring and furtive eye
> Watching a desert pool. What jealous hands
> Are these, that ever closing in their grasp
> On bird and brute, must henceforth seek to hurl
> Hell's jungle-statutes on the race of men. (2.333)

Again, Julian does not openly deny the existence of God, but as he equates the divine power with the primitive and destructive force in nature, his vision becomes pantheistic. The God that he portrays is little more than Schopenhauer's "Will," a blind, non-rational force, lacking in transcendence, and condemning humankind to an eternal round of torment and misery. "These never-breaking cycles yield no faith / To him who blindly trusts," Julian wearily complains (2.334). When, in the past, man's misplaced zeal led him, in the person of Abraham, to attempt human sacrifice (2.334), God intervened to prevent it, but has been strangely silent since:

>   The heavens close
> Against the suppliant's cries. The long slow climb
> Of all our vaunted progress leads to shame,
> And Moloch's fires light up the spiral stairs

> Which, being scaled, yet no alternative shows,
> But horrid regress lurid with the flames ... (2.334)

As far as Julian is concerned, Calvary, "on which the world / Had built the warrant of a grander faith, / A hope more excellent" (2.335), is a scandal. The sufferings of humankind still mount "until they twist and sag / The rivets on the bolted doors of God" (2.335). Julian denies neither the historicity of Christ nor the nobility of his sacrifice, but like the dreamer in *The Iron Door* (1.211) he questions the source of authority that promised him victory over death:

> Power to act,
> To back the Cross with sovereign energy,
> To mould a world as fits a monarch, fell
> Most tragically in far arrear of claims.

If Christ failed to save the world he loved,

> The charge, not his,
> Must elsewhere lie. If God's then sovereignty
> Is as a sorry fable – shells of words
> Without a kernel. (2.338)

In Julian's opinion, a God who would remain unmoved by Christ's sacrifice, or who would even permit it, is a dying God, the impersonal ruler of the Lucretian or Newtonian universe whose power, like that of the Panjandrum in "The Truant" (2.130), is in decline.

Once he has rejected divine revelation as grounds for faith (2.335, 338, 343), Julian must face the fact that the only remaining evidence for the existence of God lies in nature – a nature that he knows to be imperfect. He is torn between the notion of a God wholly extrinsic to the universe (2.323–4), and that of one wholly immanent in nature (2.333), either of which is unsatisfying and even, at times, repugnant to him. Thaddeus points out that Julian, in his search for an alternative image of God, tends to pursue absolutes.[69] Julian is attempting to make a God conformable to the dictates of his own imagination, one of power alone – but power to be used as he, Julian, judges fit. This could only be an idol or a false god totally lacking in freedom:

> Were this the end,
> That one might take the overplus of might,
> Transmute it into something handled, seen,
> Bow down before its image, whether stone,

> Iron or gold and say – "Let this be Good,
> Or God," call it what name you please, "the Law,
> The Natural Statute, That by which the race
> Is ruled, by which it comes to be". Were this
> The sum of all advantage that a slip
> On ground unequal gives the victor right
> To wear his laurel, while the soul of contest
> Is pushed aside by rude arbitrament
> Of power, or blackened so that greed alone
> Is common by acknowledgement, the Earth
> Might justly say to all her seedlings – "Grow!" (2.342)

Unable to find an image of God which will satisfy his demands, Julian feels compelled, in the end, to abandon religious faith. As he does so, hope and patience, true to the Pauline relationship of the virtues (Rom 8:24–5; 2 Tim 3:10; *PE* 35–6, 66, 95–7),[70] depart too, and Julian is overcome by psychological depression (2.347–8). While he continues the search, throughout the rest of the drama, for the source of evil, and while the degree of recovery that he achieves is based upon his tenacious belief in the immortality of the soul (2.354–5), Julian never reaffirms, even in terms of natural theology, any belief in God.

Although there may be evidence in the poem of a religious "groping" (Acts 17:27; *PE* 186) that could never be satisfied by the limited notions that Julian rejects, there is, after all, no answer to the problem of God in "Clay." Rather, the work affords Pratt, like Jacob wrestling with his assailant in the dark (Gen 32:24–32), the opportunity to question persistently the divine nature. At the end there are signs in Pratt as in Julian of a new maturity that is marked by a tolerance of the ambiguity and mystery of life.

It is possible to see in "Clay" an alternative approach to that of *Rachel* as Pratt tries to find, in philosophic terms, the answers to some of the questions raised by events in the narrative, but *Rachel* was too much like Wordsworth's *Michael*. By 1917 the language and expression were artificial and outdated, and Pratt had not yet learned to combine the narrative mode with unobtrusive reflection on the significance of the action involved. "Clay" was unsatisfactory for another reason. Pratt wrote about it later:

> I re-read the poem ... like a stranger with a cold critical eye ... I came around to the conviction that philosophical and ethical insights, wherever they find their way into poetry, should be emotional renderings of experiences actually lived, or imaginatively grasped. (MS 9:69.4)

61 The Problem of God

It was this transformation of experience that he tried to achieve in his later poem, *The Iron Door* (1927).

The vision of *The Iron Door* (1.204–13) may be seen at the beginning of the poem in the light of Julian's image of "the bolted doors of God" ("Clay," 2.335). But while Julian's mind remains for the most part closed to other possibilities suggested to him, the imagination of the dreamer possesses a freedom which enables him to see alternatives to his own limited concepts. The door first appears to be an impenetrable barrier between two worlds. All the evidence available to the dreamer suggests that its creator is a powerful smith, capable of "ironic jest" (1.205), and in his regard for human beings, unhearing and nescient (1.211).

But each person to appear before the door performs, within the context of the dream, a function similar to that of Thaddeus and Merrivale in "Clay," presenting the dreamer with a concept of God's nature complementary to his own. The little boy with an "unvoiced appeal" looks for a Father who he hopes can restore life just as he gave it (1.206). The master-mariner who has lost three sons in a work of rescue calls upon "the unknown admiral of the unknown ocean," demanding to know the "ground rule" of his realm (1.207). Having given his life in an apparently fruitless attempt to save another, the young man questions how the "eternal steward" reckons the true value of "the mutual sacrifice" (1.208–9), while the artist or aesthete, contrasting the beauty humanity has wrought with "the grave-stone and the iron monument" that confronts him, questions the Creator's purposeful use of divine power (1.209). Finally, the importunate woman bearing an almost insupportable burden of hereditary guilt[71] pours out her "miserere" before what might seem to be "the unhearing ears of God" (1.210–11). Only the face of the dreamer's mother, devoid of any "trace of doubt or consternation," reflects the "serene belief" (1.208) that was hers during life. Since, unlike the others, she has no need to cry out for help, there is no hint of how she sees God.

The dreamer is not sure which prayer may have been answered, or what source of "supreme authority" (1.211) lies behind the miraculous opening of the door. He is privileged with no direct vision of God. Nevertheless, the fact that he sees the door open suggests that the God to whom each of the dream characters cried out is neither unhearing nor powerless over death, and that in association with "the fountain of that light and life inside" (1.212) this God transcends all humanly limited or false concepts. What the dreamer hears from beyond the door and what he sees reflected in the faces of those who pass through are all attributes of the God who, Paul says, "only hath immortality, dwelling in the light which no one can approach unto, whom no one hath seen nor can see" (1 Tim 6:15–16).

The Iron Door is probably the most personal of Pratt's poems. After the philosophical and ethical peregrinations of "Clay," it is more successful in its treatment of similar themes. In a letter to W.A. Deacon, then literary critic for *Saturday Night,* Pratt wrote:

The theme came to me at the time of my mother's death last December. It originated in a dream ... From a particular experience I tried to universalize the idea ... I do not aim at solutions. I only wanted to give an imaginative and emotional interpretation of what I feel myself, because I have never done anything which put the same compulsion on me for expression. I do not know if I thoroughly succeeded. I only wrote as I felt.[72]

But whatever the opportunity he may have found in *The Iron Door* for the probing of personal emotions, Pratt, even less content with this approach to reality, set out on his quest for objectivity.

These references to various of Pratt's poems illustrate the human relationship with God as the poet often depicts the experience of it. They are frequently charged with irony springing from a view of the puny stature of the human when seen in the light of a particular but limited image of the Divine. While there is some evidence that Pratt felt little affinity for the anthropomorphized and sometimes harsh image of God presented in the Pentateuch, he was obviously drawn by emotional attachment, if not by faith, to the God of his favourite prophets. Nevertheless, his later poem "The Truant" (1942) has often been misinterpreted as an expression of either the poet's distorted notion of God or his complete rejection of the orthodox concept of the Deity.

Truant humanity stands to be judged before a God whose chief attribute is absolute and arbitrary power. This "deity" is a blind and impersonal force, the governor of the materialistic Lucretian and Newtonian systems. As he is the symbol and the mouthpiece of all forms of tyranny and oppression,[73] his "shrillest tenor" (2.127) was familiar to those living in the atmosphere of the Second World War. His titles are indicative of his nature: "Right Reverend, most adored / And forcibly acknowledged Lord" (2.125), "the great Panjandrum" (2.126), "your Imperial Majesty" (2.126), "the Awful Presence," and "the ALL HIGH" (2.127). With one or two exceptions, the biblical diction and imagery that Pratt uses ironically within the secular context of other poems such as *Towards the Last Spike* (2.201–50) are absent from "The Truant." In the abstract terms in which he is described in the poem, there seems to be little connection between the "ALL HIGH" and the God of Revelation, even the anthropomorphized God of the Old Testament, whose just wrath and judgment are balanced by enduring love and mercy, and by fidelity to the covenant with humankind (Ps 103).

The logic of the "two-edged sword" with which the Panjandrum tries to compel humanity to acknowledge his mastery is not like the word of the Lord of Revelation, which penetrates the spirit in such a way that, being paradoxical, it can be comprehended only by faith (Heb 4:12).

While the Panjandrum claims to preside over the evolutionary process that has brought genus *homo* from the "pollywogs and earwigs in the slime" (2.127), his pride lies in annihilation rather than in creation, in his power to kill, to send his adversary hurtling back through old age and death to dust (2.127–8) to join the "spiral festival of fire" (2.128). Here, the Panjandrum's work corresponds with the reversal of the biblical days of creation (Gen 1:1–2:3) brought about in *Dunkirk* (2.123) by Death, "sweating at his lathe." When the Panjandrum is informed by his lackey, "the Master of the Revels" (2.125), his "sergeant-major, Fate" (2.130), of the indestructible and immaterial "precipitate" which his chemists have been unable to analyse, he proposes to play the role of scientist and examine humanity with his "cosmoscope" to find the nature of the "spark" (2.126). This is an exhibition of indifference and ignorance in sharp contrast to the God of Revelation's intimate knowledge of creatures (Ps 139).

The "bucking truant with a stiff backbone" (2.125) does not fit in with the "plan" (*The Iron Door*, 1.209) of the Panjandrum's realm. In a context totally devoid of love, and in which the concept of sin is therefore an absurdity, the race is judged to be guilty of the very attributes that make it human – consciousness, the capacity for self-affirmation, lack of conformity to the ordered "atomic patterns," and the ability to use reason and will to challenge the Panjandrum's destructive power. Courageous in the face of almost certain death, humanity commits "grave contempt of court / By answering with a flinchless stare" (2.127) the curses and the vitriolic condemnation of the "ALL HIGH."

In this "conflict between human will and almighty officialdom" (MS 4:33), the dignity of "little genus *homo*, six feet high" (2.128) is emphasized by its sense of the preposterousness of the situation. Although the Panjandrum's language is "formal, erudite and in accordance with court etiquette" (MS 4:33), his opponent emerges as his superior in the cursing match. Accusing the "Almighty" of lacking the very qualities for which it itself stands indicted, it points out that since it has been able to name, chart, and harness the energy that the Panjandrum personifies, it, the human race, must be in essence the greater. The "ALL HIGH" might have merited a place in some Neoplatonic or abstract concept of heaven, but such a deity cannot experience or reply to the immediate human problems of pain, fear, and death. He is no saving God. Since he answers in some respects to the Lucretian description of the gods, he may be conceded speed, power, and fire, but his end will come, "not with a bang but a whimper."[74]

What the Truant rejects is not God, but a god, one who is a philosophical and a theological absurdity, created by human beings in that subconscious desire for absolutes[75] for which Thaddeus criticizes Julian in "Clay" (2.342). To submit to such a being would be not the virtue of religion but the sin of idolatry which only nullifies the worshipper (Ps 115:2–8; Is 44:9–20). In "Clay," *The Iron Door*, and "The Truant," Pratt worked out important variations on a religious theme, yet these poems are freer from biblical echoes and references than are his more obviously secular ones. It may be said that in different ways in these three poems, as in many of the shorter lyrics discussed earlier in this chapter, Pratt depicts, not his personal rejection of God, but humankind's general obligation to reject what Pratt knew God is not, and never could be – a source of blind, impersonal power, either existing extrinsic to, or operating within, the confines of the universe.

It is not, however, the image of the Deity as "God of all comfort ... father to the fatherless" (*The "Roosevelt" and the "Antinoe"*, 1.235–6) that is the prevailing one in the poetry for which Pratt wished to be remembered. When this picture does appear, it is counterbalanced by another more disturbing one, and God often seems from the point of view of the human race to be at best a divine paradox, or at worst an autocrat grown old, forgetful, deaf, and palsied. Nowhere is there any evidence that Pratt himself denied the existence of God. According to those who knew him well, there is every reason to believe that he affirmed it.[77] He did decry the emphasis placed so frequently on what he called "the negative side of religion":

We lay stress on religion as a method of escape from something. Comparatively little concern is had for the great positive character of religion, replete with affirmatives, with I can, and I ought, and I will. (MS 1:3)

Pratt's honesty, his searching spirit, and his adherence to the religious traditions of his ancestry would not allow him to settle for any simple definition or credal statement about God. From the anguish of experience he seems to have recognized one of humanity's greatest temptations. As John Courtney Murray puts it, "The driving impulse behind all idolatry is not simply to have a god, to have something to worship; it is to have the god here, now, accessible, visibly active, disponible."[77] Apart from any glimpse of God attained through Christ, the one with whom we sense Pratt wrestled in the darkness to the end remains shrouded in mystery.

3 "Ghosts of the Apocalypse"

Whatever room the available biographical data may still allow for speculation about Pratt's religious position, critics will probably concur, as they have in the past, that the vision of existence reflected in his poetry is an "apocalyptic" one.[1] If they intend to make more than a general observation, and if they proceed any further in their application of this adjective to Pratt's work, they are likely to explain their use of it in terms related to the literary genre which most are unaware the poet explored in detail in *Studies in Pauline Eschatology and Its Background* (10a, 11–22).[2] The language, imagery, and symbolism through which Pratt conveys his particular view of the origins of the world and its government and, in many cases, the poetic forms that he chooses, all echo warnings, literal or metaphorical, about the imminence of the Parousia (*PE* 135), and about the signs and wonders to accompany it. The apocalypse, as Pratt well knew and as this chapter will attempt to show, is a conventional yet highly flexible literary form which lends itself readily to the expression of eschatological concerns (*PE* 21, 68) and of cosmological perspectives (*PE* 21–2).[3] A study of the form as a vehicle for the expression of mystical experiences (*PE* 13, 88–94) will be reserved for a later chapter. A close examination of the poetry should reveal not only the extent to which Pratt's earlier studies of the apocalyptic form cast their reflection upon his work, but also the degree to which its traditional themes appealed to his imagination.

THE APOCALYPSE AS AN EXPRESSION OF ESCHATOLOGICAL CONCERNS

The kind of preaching to which E.J. Pratt listened every week as a child (see 4, above), together with the particular image of God and the consequent distrust of nature which it helped to impress upon him, composed an apocalyptic backdrop against which the harsh realities confronted daily within a seafaring community assumed dramatic proportions. Pratt later recalled the sense of being always close to death:

There was death at sea, in the terrible storms of the Atlantic. Often my father had the task of breaking the news of yet another death to a new widow in the community. I remember him saying, "How can I tell her? How can I tell her?" And my mother, she had strong faith, but she said, "Why did God allow this?" (*PLP*, 42)

Beginning with these early experiences, Pratt's lifetime spanned the greater part of a century whose psychological climate lent itself readily to apocalyptic expression. In spite of the manifestations of post-Darwinian disillusionment at the beginning of this period, there was, at first, an air of feverish expectation fanned by astounding scientific and technological advances, not the least of which was Marconi's first transatlantic cable message (see 8, above; *PLP* 45). On the other hand, social and political upheavals throughout Europe and America were no less devastating in the first half of the twentieth century than were the historical events of the post-exilic age that gave birth to the apocalypse. The Great Depression of the 1930s brought mass unemployment, poverty, hunger, destitution, and despair on a universal scale. Two world wars, neither of which proved to be the one "to end all wars," were but a prelude to a "cold war" that was even more sinister in Pratt's eyes, since it expressed "the crystallization of the hate ... in a climate of silence" ("Silences," 2.4).

Over the years it often seemed to Pratt as it did to the early writers of apocalyptic literature that history was one vast battlefield with sides and causes seen at times clearly in black and white, and at others obscurely in shades of grey. Apart from the occasional gifted leader such as Pratt considered a Saint Joan or a Churchill to be (*PLP* 126–7), where was there a prophet or a visionary left to read the signs of the times? Who was there remaining to sustain human courage in what seemed to be the latter days? There are occasions on which Pratt's poetic voice sounds as if the mantle had fallen upon him.

Pratt's early sense of the precariousness of human existence, the eschatological emphasis of contemporary biblical scholarship, and the need to bring into harmony the claims of religion and science probably all influenced the choice of topics for his theological theses. Both works are rooted in a comparative study of the apocalyptic literature of the Bible and of various early cultures, and both focus, though in different ways, on the apocalyptic relationship between life and death.

In "The Demonology of the Synoptics in Its Relation to Earlier Developments and to the Mind of Christ" Pratt comments on the tendency among primitive peoples to blame illness and misfortune on the supernatural influence of evil spirits (2), and to exclude from their presence all that is associated with death.[4] He attributes to the influence of "apocalyptic literature" on the synoptic authors the expectation of final punishment for demons, and for those whom they possess (12). In his first thesis Pratt also explores humanity's fundamental longing for grounds of belief in some degree of immortality (9). He suggests that the human propensity to sin, suffering, and death is countered, however inexplicably, by the person of Christ (30).

Later, in *Studies in Pauline Eschatology and Its Background*, Pratt attempts to determine the influence of Jewish eschatological thought upon Paul's outlook. He states that "to discover what was the apocalyptic teaching in currency when Paul was shaping the religious views of the primitive church is essential for an adequate appreciation of his position" (7). Pratt then identifies as belonging to the "apocalyptic age" those writings, biblical and apocryphal, of the last two centuries BC and of the first century AD which follow upon the works of the great prophets (12).

Continuing with a study of the apocalypse as a literary form, Pratt remarks that its writers do not usually begin their work by calling their readers to repentance as do the prophets. They concentrate their attack on the heathen oppressor and on the official priesthood as abettors in the forced hellenization of their fellow citizens. The most popular form of apocalyptic literature is the dream-vision, which embodies "all the machinery of Ezekiel rendered still more intricate" (13). The writer attempts to fix precisely the date of the coming judgment, and to associate it with the overthrow of pagan enemies and apostates, who are usually symbolized by wild animals.

The apocalyptic concept of world history, which embraces several stages, is eschatological in that the writer regards himself as living with the end in sight. He speculates about the nature of the soul, the possibility of life after death, the punishment of the wicked, and the geography of heaven and hell (21). A highly developed angelology and demonology are characteristic, too, of the apocalyptic form. At the height of its popularity the extraordinary gifts such as prophecy, the power to mystify, and the working of signs and miracles are still in evidence, but they are associated with the spirit of God (53–6). The traditional "accompaniments" of the apocalypse, which Pratt mentions frequently (14), include the disturbance of nature, lightning, thunder, fire, clouds, eclipses, light and darkness, noise, chaos, fear, and flight – all in larger-than-life proportions.[5] Pratt skilfully indicates how all these stage-props assume their proper dimensions when Paul sees them in relation to the person of Christ, who, having once died, has risen, and who is to come again.

Although the preoccupations of these theses are not reflected in any systematic fashion in Pratt's poetry, it may, nevertheless, prove helpful in illustrating his debt to his earlier studies to consider his eschatology according to the traditional schema of "the Last Things."[6] This chapter will concentrate on Pratt's vision of sin and death, judgment, and hell. The concept of heaven, or of an afterlife, which is by no means absent from his poetry, will be seen in its relation to the mystical element of the apocalypse in the last chapter.

The Warm Arts of Human Sinning

It is on occasions when Pratt, the poet, or the personas that he assumes lack Paul's Christocentric perspective or lose it even momentarily that they feel themselves threatened by the whims of an arbitrary and impersonal God or by the demands of a hostile universe. This lack of focus usually constitutes for Pratt a significant stage in the loss of integrity. If he rarely uses the word "sin" in his poetry, it is not because the reality behind it has no place in his eschatological vision, but perhaps because he knew that the word was employed too often to indicate simple and sometimes minor infractions of the moral or ethical code – an interpretation which appeared to him to be unworthy of the designation. In fact, throughout his poetry Pratt reflects an awareness of sin in its more radical and Pauline sense as inseparable from death. Sin, introduced into the history of humankind through the transgression of our first parents, brought death in its wake (Rom 5:12–20; *PE* 143–4, 148). Pratt creates, when he can, a synthesis of traditional Christian teaching with the insights provided by contemporary psychology and evolutionary thought.

According to Pratt, the possibility of undergoing a "fall" from integrity presupposes the previous ascent on the ladder of evolution to a stage which would include reason and a degree of moral responsibility. Not having attained this level of development, the fish as they are presented at the beginning of *The Witches' Brew* are amoral, but they enjoy a certain freedom which humanity appears to have lost:

> The fish transgressed no moral law,
> They had no principles, no creed,
> No prayers, no Bibles, and no Church,
> No Reason's holy light to read
> The truth and no desire to search.
> Hence from Dame Nature's ancient way
> Their fins had never learned to stray.
> ...
> As Nature had at the beginning
> Created them, so they remained –
> Fish with cold blood no skill had trained
> To the warm arts of human sinning. (1.140)

Here Pratt plays upon the inextricable Pauline connection between sin and the law (Rom 7:8–11; *PE* 76). In this case the outcome of the Satanic experiment, or the grand binge, is simply that the fish lie dead or paralysed, unable to defend themselves or to respond to Tom's challenge (1.149). Since they are not subject to the law, no account is kept of their "sin" (Rom 5:13). The fish, for all the excesses in which they indulge both before (1.140) and during the spree (1.141–5), never really fall. They remain "wet," but "cold" and amoral – in marked contrast, Pratt suggests, to sinful but "warm" human beings.

In "The Great Feud," the fish "along the Isthmian border" together with "all the stock marine" (1.169) are seen in the process of evolution. The results of the "fall" which they undergo in the course of their ascent are spelled out more specifically, and with more complex irony, than they are in *The Witches' Brew*. The "invasion of their cold / Blood by an unexplained disorder" leads to a sense of doom, or predestination (1.169). The threat of extinction fills them with unrest, prompting them to wander far from home, to indulge their senses, and, in doing so, to be drawn into "relentless snares" (1.169). The thousands of sea-creatures that survive turn their "backs upon their breed," "quaff the warm blood of their foes," or come back,

>   contemptuous to spurn
> Their parents, like the trilobite,
> With stony back and stonier heart;
> Rolled up in balls and dwelt apart
> In sulky isolation; while others,
> ...
>   came and stung
> Their little sisters and their brothers. (1.170)

In the behaviour of "the stock marine," the atavism proper to the evolutionary theme of the poem is reinforced by the Freudian concept of regression and expressed in terms of the transformation of the heart into stone, one of the most significant images of sin used by the prophets of the Old Testament (Ezek 11:19, 36:26; Zech 7:12; *PE* 27, 50).[7]

The fear of racial doom also awakens within the sea-creatures "a futile anger like a curse." But combined with their "mad desire to strike back" is

> the galling sense
> That never would the recompense
> Of battle come; that primal itch
> For vengeance would expend its force,
> According to an adverse Fate,
> Running a self-destroying course
> Down the blind alley of their hate. (1.171)

The repressed anger over a destiny from which there seems to be no redemption erupts into the dream of a "Pleiocene Armageddon" (1.168). It is interesting to note that, while "The Great Feud" is included among the extravaganzas in the first edition of *Collected Poems*, Pratt referred to it on at least one occasion as an allegory, and remarked in his introduction to a reading of the poem that, "wherever aggression takes place, there is retaliation. Life for life is exacted." (MS 1:6)

Although the elements of fantasy and humour are obvious, the underlying tone of "The Great Feud" and its psychological insight into both the personal and the social effects of sin and aggression deprive the poem of some of the spontaneous and exuberant sense of release characteristic of *The Witches' Brew*. In this context Robert Gibbs's comment about this poem seems particularly apt: "there is the matter of deliberateness which is at odds with the freedom which the poet needs to work best within the hyperbolic convention."[8] Nonetheless, in both *The Witches' Brew* and "The Great Feud" the "fall" opens the door to death, and to the universal destruction depicted in the traditional imagery of the apocalypse.

The stony trilobite of "The Great Feud" (1.170), rolled up in its ball "in sulky isolation," an image of regressive selfishness which finds parallels throughout Pratt's work, recalls Augustine's (and Luther's) concept of human nature "deeply curved in upon itself" as a result of original sin.[9] Such narcissism alienates persons from one another (*PE* 126; "To an Enemy," 1.130), causes them to forget what they have in common ("Comrades," 1.125); breaks down communication ("Silences," 2.3; *The "Titanic,"* 1.324–5), widens the range of hate ("Cycles," 2.195), deepens the divisions within the human family ("Convict Holocaust," 1.216), and leads human beings to injure and kill one another ("From Stone to Steel," 1.260; *Behind the Log*, 2.181–3).

As early as "Clay," Pratt ponders the implications of another concept of original sin derived from the prophets and from the Pauline epistles (Rom 5:12; 1 Cor 15:22) and further developed by the fathers of the church.[10] In the course of the struggle, the Julian of "Clay" is ready to admit that if humankind had only to contend with natural evil, or the pain involved in the evolutionary process, it might have the advantage. But the question is more complex:

> the fight
> With nature grows more simple every hour
> Her ways are known, but when the struggle takes
> Hell's routes and ends in bloody fratricide –
> Not once, nor twice, as though an incident
> Of casual kind had touched man's history,
> But as a baffling epidemic strikes
> A thousand times his life, failing of cure;
> How strike this foul insistent integer
> Clean from his life? The taint is in the blood.
> Try surgery there! (2.347)

Sin as a "taint in the blood" appears in other guises in "the unexplained disorder" of the cold blood in "The Great Feud" (1.169); in the "toxin in the blood" of "The Baritone" (2.5); and in "the viscous melanotic current" in the veins that leads human beings to torture one another in *Brébeuf and His Brethren* (2.67).

The dreamer of *The Iron Door* (1.210) sees the weight borne by the suffering woman in similar terms, but in this poem Pratt develops the question more fully. It seems that the woman shares with all of human nature in the consequences of original sin, which are passed on through the blood from one generation to the next:

> The same dark burden under which the race
> Reaches old age lay strapped upon her soul: –[11]
> That which collects in silence all the shame,
> Through hidden passages of time and blood,
> Then puts the open stigma of the blame
> Upon a spotless name. (1.210)

But the woman herself demands to know more particularly

> Why all the purchase of her pain,
> And all her love could not atone
> For that incalculable stain:
> Why from the tortuous stream –
> Flesh of her flesh, bone of her bone –
> Should issue forth a Cain. (1.210–11)

Her anguished questioning of the justice of the doctrine of hereditary guilt and of the redemptive value of vicarious atonement[12] leads to the "darkest moment" in the dreamer's experience, and to the dramatic crisis of the poem. Pratt claimed that this woman is the only individual in the work not drawn from someone he had known in life. She "sums up the problem, partly biological and partly environmental, of injustice and inequality in the moral order and she presents the case in its glaring enigma."[13] The surgery which both Julian ("Clay," 2.347) and King Lear (3.6.74–6) wished to use is no remedy for moral evil. It would seem that Wesley's "loathsome leprosy of sin" (21.252), or Pratt's "deep malaise in the communal heart of the world" ("A Prayer-Medley," 1.297), cannot be cured by natural medicine alone. The fact that neither the woman nor the dreamer of *The Iron Door* receives a specific answer to the question, apart from the opening of the door, suggests that any rational or materialistic explanations are inadequate.[14] As far as the dreamer is concerned, the woman personifies one of the mysteries which confound human reason but which fade into insignificance in the "light abundant" beyond the door.

Apparent, too, in Pratt's poetry is the concept of sin in the classical and Pauline sense of *hamartanein* (Rom 3:23–5; 5:12–19; Gal 3:22; *PE* 60). On the literal level this Greek translation of the Hebrew word for "to sin" means "to miss the mark," "to go astray," "to lose the road," or "to fail in plan or purpose."[15] As the great error or frailty which Paul sees springing from Adam's loss of his sense of creaturehood, it reverses the fortunes of humankind (Rom 5:12–19) and brings death in its wake. By placing the Pauline "error" in an evolutionary context, both in "Clay" and in the later poem "The Highway," Pratt probes for the fundamental reason for the race's apparent failure to develop to its full moral – and thus human – potential. In "Clay" the image conveys Julian's terrible sense of hopelessness. He expresses it as

> a slip,
> An errant step that turning from the road
> A hair-breadth, unretrieved, moves into night,

And vacancy, wherein no moon nor stars
Cast any light. (2.320)

In "The Highway" the poet, after expressing wonder at the orderly unfolding of the universe, feels compelled to demand,

But what made *our* feet miss the road that brought
The world to such a golden trove
In our so brief a span? (1.257)

The questions with which this poem ends, however, do imply some hope that the human race may rediscover the path to its true destiny. This tragic flaw, which also makes possible regression to a state of lawlessness or anomia (*PE* 132, 134) and the abdication of the qualities that distinguish a human being, Pratt sees magnified within the context of poems such as "Autopsy on a Sadist" (2.133).

The notion of hubris, which Paul also adopted from the Greeks (Acts 27:10, 21; Rom 1:30; 1 Tim 1:13; 2 Cor 12:10; 1 Thess 2:2), and which is an expression of overweening pride or of arrogant insolence,[16] also figures in Pratt's poetry as the sin which leads humanity to a frightening experience of an apocalyptic nature which it may well have set in motion but cannot control.

Behind hubris is "the Faustian clamour" ("The Good Earth," 2.193) that springs from impatience with, and misuse of, nature. The "synthetic seed" that humankind would sow, warns Pratt, can yield only "crops of carrion for the vulture." It is a form of hubris, too, that leads the sealers in "The Ice-Floes" to ignore the natural signs of the approaching storm, no longer in the necessary search for their daily bread but in the vain hope that "an added thousand or more / Would beat the count of the day before" (1.60). In "The Cachalot," "New England's pride," Martin Taylor, the skipper of the *Albatross*, has completed a successful season's fishing and has three thousand barrels of oil under the hatches (1.157). Only his decision "to try his final luck" at four thousand barrels, a bumper load, leads him to grapple with "a Titan's broken pride" (1.164). In their rash and then stubborn encounter with the giant of Nature, whose strength they underestimate, the crew of the *Albatross* appears as "a puny bunch of men," an "arrogant and impious crew" who, in the end, must follow "the Monarch to his grave" (1.165).

In the tragedy of *The "Titanic"* Pratt sees hubris in its most blatant form. Human beings exult in a "creation" of science and technology that will make them impervious to the demands of nature – especially to those of the sea – and absolve them of responsibility for their own welfare and that of others:

> The perfect ship at last – the first unsinkable,
> Proved in advance – had not the folders read so?
> ...
> And this belief had reached its climax when,
> Through wireless waves as yet unstaled by use,
> The wonder of the ether had begun
> To fold the heavens up and reinduce
> That ancient *hubris* in the dreams of men,
> Which would have slain the cattle of the sun,
> And filched the lightnings from the fist of Zeus. (1.303–4)

Even with these apparently miraculous inventions and improvements, only overweening pride would lead human beings to abandon entirely the "bone and marrow judgment of a sailor" (*The "Roosevelt" and the "Antinoe"*, 1.230), the use of their senses and the time-proven methods of navigation, and to cut off, with arrogant insolence (1.317), communication that could have averted, either for the *Titanic* or for other ships, so great a catastrophe. Through hubris humanity disrupts, seriously if not irreparably, the orderly relationship that it should enjoy with God, with nature, and with all of creation.

"Come Away Death"

While Pratt does not always picture death as the immediate consequence of sin, he frequently sees it as a stage in the common destiny of the whole of creation which participates in the effects of the fall, and which waits for the fullness of redemption (Rom 8: 19–23; 2 Cor 5:19). The inevitability of this destiny is expressed for the first time in *Rachel*, where death, while never welcome, must nevertheless be accepted as a normal, almost daily, experience in the small Newfoundland fishing community. Not content with snatching away Rachel's parents, it later takes her husband, "a gallant seaman in the prime of life" (1.21) and her only son, in whom she has found "the thrill of rediscovered life / The fond remembrance of earlier joys" (1.22).

Rachel is a fairly simple narrative poem in the style of Wordsworth's *Michael*, romantic rather than apocalyptic in form and expression. The heroine's losses, personally overwhelming as they are, are placed against the background of the shared experience and the religious faith of the society of which she is a part, and her own death, though viewed with compassion, is seen neither as a tragedy nor as a complete extinction (1.37).

75 "Ghosts of the Apocalypse"

In "Clay," Pratt adopted a more philosophic approach to the mystery of death, attempting to take on the whole burden of eschatology in a context divorced from Christian revelation. While from the beginning Julian, the hero, sees all around him "life at close grips with death" (2.320), it is death that eventually confounds his faith in God. Since he is unlike Rachel in that he is a recluse from society, Julian must rely on his friend Thaddeus to inform him of the almost universal scope of the death and destruction brought about by the storm, the symbol of "the old and deadly feud / Man's hand and nature's." The imagery that Thaddeus uses is apocalyptic in colour and scope (see 68, above).

> Everywhere on land
> Have tempests raged. The fighting's strange at times;
> The issues so confused that one mistakes
> Alignments in the quarrels. Thunders speak
> Of clashes in the clouded zones of heaven;
> Lightnings are hurtled on the hills
> ...
> Floods scoured the plains. (2.316)

In a later scene, Thaddeus combines personification with apocalyptic imagery to conjure up the unnatural atmosphere of a war in which men turn upon their brothers:

> Death – Death stalked everywhere on land and sea,
> In clouds that banked the sun, in mists that hid
> The stars, or half disclosed the swollen moon.
> No cavern sunk beneath the earth but bore
> His foot-prints. (335)

Julian's reactions to these descriptions of death suggest that loss of faith, as well as faith, may come by hearing (Rom 10:17). The extent of "the tragedy" (345), in the terms in which Thaddeus depicts it, is so great that the imagination is almost powerless to cope with it. As Julian envisions the bones of friend and foe "interlocked in mutual conquest," they become the "dry bones" of the prophet's vision (Ezek 37) stripped of their promise (cf MacLeish, *J.B.*, 81). The battlefield can only be the theatre of humanity's ultimate defeat:

> There the overlord
> Of this fair earth's the grave. Lo! triumphs there

The worm, and evolution reaches thus
Its final phrasing – "From the dust to dust." (343)

Although the excesses of language and imagery verge from time to time on the grotesque, Pratt reveals here some of the skill he later developed in juxtaposing the biblical and the Darwinian frames of reference.

Once Julian has rejected belief in God, he is unable to reconcile the concept of death as a punishment for sin (Gen 3:19; Rom 5:12), which corresponds in his imagination with the cyclical process of evolution, with the Pauline preaching of hope that is rooted in the resurrection of Christ (1 Cor 15):

So Death still keeps its ancient sting, the Grave
Its victory. Man's proud investiture
Of place and species, title, dignity
Are mock heroics playing round his name,
Whose birth is in the winds, whose death rides out
Upon the whirlwind. (2.343)

None of the arguments drawn by his friends from nature or from reason is convincing enough to restore the lost hope for immortality which Julian expresses in images that negate Ezekiel's vision:

What plan is this,
So wise and fair, as can with beauty clothe
Those bleached frames that rattle in the air,
When the winds swoop. Enswathe it as you may,
The skeleton will grin and mock the hand
That touches it. (2.345)

To this point, the apocalyptic scenes presented by Thaddeus and Julian's reactions to them have both been extreme, and since the hero has been so far removed from the storm and the war, and does not appear to have experienced the loss of anyone close to him, the result is melodrama.

In the final scene of act 2 (2.347), however, as Julian looks back to the past, he is able to reveal an experience of natural evil that touched him personally, and that from that moment became the source of the bitterness that he has nourished over the years. Once, "in the desert of life," there was one who was

A solace, a companion, one who kept
A memory green who, as he grew, became

77   "Ghosts of the Apocalypse"

A very fountain of live hope
...
I saw him dead, his face all passionless, cold.
So cloud and dust have since companioned me;
There's nothing left. (2.348)

It is not clear, at first, whether Julian has lost a son or a friend (2.348), but the references to Shakespeare's *The Winter's Tale* (1.1.33–6) in these lines, and their resemblance to the picture of the young Henry Lee (*Rachel*, 1.22–4), together with Julian's later description of himself as a male counterpart to Rachel, "a father mourning for his son" (36), clarify the relationship.

As far as Julian is concerned, however, years have intervened without the perspective that they should have lent to experience. Shocked as Julian may have been by an apparently senseless death, this scene of "Clay" lacks the dramatic immediacy of Lear's anguish over the death of Cordelia (5.3.259–308), or that of MacLeish's J.B. and Sarah over the murder of Rebecca (5, 83). Julian is unable to draw any consolation from the memory of his child, or from the knowledge that his own life would have been the poorer without him. He admits that "if this baffling life / Could give the lie to age, and prove mistrust / A whim" (349), he might still regain hope. But at this point, it is easier to believe in biological determinism than to take the risk that faith and hope require.

In a naturalistic and secular environment Julian must face both life and death without the support of that faith and hope that are rooted in the resurrection of Christ (1 Cor 15). In this confrontation Julian is not encouraged by nature's "fine contagion in the spring / For heavy hearts" (2.352). Not all his friends' talk of the Browningesque "leap as the symbol of man's daring" (2.346), or of the Coleridgean analogy of the Aeolian harp (2.354), can comfort him. He never does find in nature the "scaffolding" (308), "the groundwork" (338), the "rock from which man's hope / Might never more be swept" (353). Within a context totally divorced from revelation, what he seems to seek is not so much rational proof as that inner "assurance" that is born of evangelical faith. In his case such vain grasping can issue only in disillusionment and fatalism:

                    Belief,
A wish, a dream – where is its leverage
To raise the dead, to make those bones knit joint [Ezek 37]
To joint and leap, to pry until the mountains
Remove their base [Lk 17:20], or force the heart's wide wastes,

Where hate was sown, that love shall blossom there.
What has been, will be. Time has proved it so. (2.344)

Donaldson, who has not lost hope in humankind's natural ability to rebuild, tries to share with Julian his confidence in the inexhaustible resources of the human mind and spirit:

May not the eye
Range over those dun fields of death, and see
From vile putresence, Beauty rise in light
Unquenchable? May not the scars remind
The sufferer of his healing as of wounds? (2.344)

There is, however, far less hope of a cure for Julian's deeply engrained doubt than there was for that of the apostle Thomas (Jn 20:20, 25–8). It is noteworthy that scars become in Pratt's later poetry a sign of identity, a testimony, and a symbol, not only of past wounds and death but also of present healing and future resurrection (Lk 24:39–40). The image recurs in this sense in "To an Enemy" (1.139), *Brébeuf and His Brethren* (2.46), "The Impatient Earth" (2.29), and "Newfoundland Seamen" (2.188).

In the end, it is only the recognition of his own proximity to death and of his relationship to the "clay" of the title that stirs in Julian the longing for immortality. "Dust gathers in my mouth," he admits. He confesses that in the past he may have tried "from thistles to gather figs" (Mt 7:16), or "to pluck where the vines were dry" (Hab 3:17). Memory "ranging through the fungus years / Finds but the husks where it would take the fruit" (2.355). "And yet," Julian is forced to admit,

there is a knocking in this clay –
A restless flame – something that, if it could,
Would leap the grammared confines of slow speech,
And give the echo to your dancing words. (2.355)

Expressed in terms of Old Testament foreshadowing (Ezek 34), rather than in terms of New Testament fulfilment, Julian's wishful playing with the idea of immortality makes no specific reference to the deity, and no appeal to moral premises. Julian never affirms belief in God, and it is true to say that his desire for immortality springs from a natural rather than from a religious source.

In human terms, and in terms of the poem, Julian does achieve a certain degree of integration. As his imagination has been awakened, chiefly through the prompting of Thaddeus, he has moved beyond the fixed vision of the dead as "dust and clay, and nothing more" (Shelley, *Julian and Maddalo*, 203), to some vague personal intimation of immortality. Having rejected stoicism (2.308, 322–3), as well as a purely conventional response to the problem of evil (2.324), he is brought to the point where he is able to accept life and death as one of the fundamental ambivalences that belong to what William F. Lynch calls "the heart of the creative world," an initial step forward in the conquest of his hopelessness.[17] The danger is that apart from belief in a God who is capable of fulfilling human desires and potentialities, longing for immortality and fear of extinction can only lead back to despair.

Although, on the whole, "Clay" was not a successful work, it marks the early stages of Pratt's skill in synthesizing and balancing off against each other, in poetic form, biblical, scientific, and philosophical themes and language in the expression of eschatological questions. While it contains quotations from and references to the Pauline epistles, it remains closer in its tone and conclusions to the book of Job. Like the earlier poem *Rachel*, however, "Clay" does suggest that while death may be inevitable, it does not have an absolute claim on humanity.

While death is absent from barely a dozen of the shorter lyrics in the *Complete Poems*, it would be difficult to accuse Pratt of being morbid or death-haunted. As A.J.M. Smith has remarked, "What makes the problem of death so intensely felt for Pratt is his strong sense of life."[18] As his skill and maturity as a poet grew, his perspective became at once more simple and more complex with the added dimension of irony, and the images of death traditional in western art and literature throughout the ages took on a new light. The paradoxical relationship between life and death, a feature of apocalyptic literature adopted in a metaphorical sense by Paul (Rom 6:8–11; *PE* 78–88, 98–9, 148–9), was from the beginning one of the leitmotifs of Pratt's poetry. After his statement of it in simple terms in *Rachel*, and his exploration of it in a rambling fashion in the unfinished "Clay," Pratt infused the theme with greater subtlety and depth as he carried it over into the later lyric and narrative poems.

Although the evolutionary or psychological implications of the life-and-death relationship may in certain poems be Pratt's immediate concern, the eschatological dimension of the conflict and its outcome are often described in apocalyptic terms. Like the Paul of whom he wrote earlier, Pratt the poet finds it impossible to speak of life without considering "its antipodal contrast" (*PE* 100).[19] The elements of wind, tides, earth, and fire (Dan 7; *PE* 136), together with the natural and biblical images of the harvest (Joel 3; Rev 14:15–17), wine, oil, and water (Sir 15:16), and the bread of life (Ps 104:15; Ezek 4:16–17; Eccl 11:1; Jn 6:48–58), all key symbols in apocalyptic literature,[20] recur throughout Pratt's poetry in both their literal and their figurative senses, helping to convey the subtle relationship between life and death, and between humanity and nature, on the personal, the social, and the cosmic planes.

In one early lyric alone does Pratt attempt to convey an image of death that is two-dimensional or static. In "Come Not the Seasons Here" he presents the negation of life as it appears in the cycle of nature. Death is not marked by the changing of the seasons with their appropriate signs, by colour, or by the sound of human voices. It is not to be identified by the signs of winter, the season traditionally associated with death, only by

> the flap of a waterfowl
> In the marsh alone,
> Or the hoot of a horned owl
> On a glacial stone. (1.108)

Even as he strives to create the impression of the state of death, Pratt reaffirms life in lines of lyrical beauty.

Reinforcing the particular image of God that was Pratt's heritage, and the attitude towards creation that it tended to foster (see 43–4, above), was his experience as a Newfoundlander with the harsher side of nature. This experience led him to comment on one occasion, "A kind of war has ever gone on against the elements which never make a peace treaty with [humanity]. And it is out of that conflict mainly that the Newfoundland spirit has been forged" (*PLP* 16–17).

This conflict with the elements, especially those associated with the sea, appears often in the poetry as a fight against death, which "rides / The darkened belfries of his evening tides" (1.167). Although it is not unusual for human beings to meet death at sea, they are not called to accept it passively, and they must be ready, like the crew of the *Roosevelt*, "matching death with strategy," to take their chance "with each spent sea" (1.228), or like Fried, "to outstare Death to his salt countenance" (1.232). Later, when the *Antinoe*'s situation has become more serious, and when the storm has given no sign of abating, it soon becomes clear that

> The hour [has] called for argument more rife
> With the gambler's sacrificial bids for life,
> The final manner native to the breed

> Of men forging decision into deed –
> Of getting down again into the sea,
> And testing rowlocks in an open boat,
> Of grappling with the storm-king bodily,
> And placing Northern fingers on his throat. (1.243)

In *The "Roosevelt" and the "Antinoe"* every possible attempt is made to save life. When a number of the rescuers are lost, the human community is united, as in "The Ice-Floes," in the ritual of mourning its dead. There is, however, no time for loss of faith or hope. After the flags of both ships have been lowered to half-mast in a last salute,

> Then back to their full height the flags were run,
> To snap out like the folds of a toreador:
> With so much on the boards still to be done,
> 'Twas fitting that they should, in that same breath
> With which the storm took the salute, restore
> The colours to their stations, baiting death. (1.239)

Although in *Behind the Log* human beings must face obstacles other than those which nature provides, one of their greatest concerns is that they do not know with which side the sea will align herself. From the first she seems to express "mockery ... on face and lips and fingers." Eventually she shows her true colours

> For, after her reconnaissance, the sea,
> As urging death with a forensic fury,
> Would shed her velvet syllables, return
> With loaded fists to thunder at the gun-shields ... (2.174)

However, neither the sea nor any of the other elements always portends death. From the beginning Pratt associates with them all the ambiguity with which they are treated in the Psalms and the apocalyptic writings. From *Rachel* onwards, he depicts the sea as "jealous to exercise its right to nourish or to slay" (1.21). According to collective experience, Pratt suggests, the winds that hold "a partnership with life / Resonant with the hopes of spring, / Pungent with the airs of harvest" (1.199), are equivocal:

> Their hands are full to the overflow,
> In their right is the bread of life, [Jn 6:35]
> In their left are the waters of death. [Ps 18:4]
>   ("Newfoundland," 1.100)

The "Great Tides" (1.103) which govern the ocean but cannot save a drowning lad are also the tides which ebb and flow within the human being. As they surge through the veins of the pedant of "In Absentia" (1.52), they cause his life's "three-score years and ten" (Ps 90:4–10) to be measured by a single hour. "The Good Earth" (2.193) is good as long as persons respect her for what she is. "Fire" (1.300), "this sergeant of the executing squads," may be at times a "crimson source of human fears" (*PE* 136), blotting out, as it does in "Convict Holocaust" (1.216), the last apparent traces of human identity:

But stronger than its terror is the deep
Allurement, primary to our blood, which holds
Safety and warmth in unimpassioned folds,
Night and the candle-quietness of sleep. ("Fire," 1.300)

At other times, as in "A November Landscape" (1.288), Pratt reflects upon the relationship between humanity and nature that derives from the cyclical or the evolutionary pattern to which both must conform. This underlying awareness of life and death as part of a natural process is also characteristic of many of the writings belonging to the wisdom and the apocalyptic traditions of the Bible (e.g., Sir 14:17–19, 17:1; Job 14; Ps 103:15–16; Eccl 1:1–11, 3:19–22, 12:2–6).

Through his association of the cycle of life and death with the natural elements as they are frequently presented in the later books of the Bible (*PE* 74, 76), Pratt conveys a picture of evolving nature that is not "consistently destructive"[21] but rather, as John Wesley also had concluded,[22] imperfect and changeable and, like humankind, waiting for the fullness of redemption (Rom 8:18–23). This view is consistent with the conclusions that he makes in his study of Pauline theology (see ooo, above). It would appear that whatever degree of synthesis Pratt was able to bring about between the religious and the scientific frames of reference, it could be made only in Pauline terms. To state that Pratt suggests that "man's task is not to identify with nature, but to oppose it"[23] is surely to oversimplify his position. Again and again he reveals our kinship to nature, our need to regard it with respect, and to assume responsibility in our relationship with it.

Pratt's apocalyptic and Pauline vision of the paradoxical relationship between life and death (Rom 6:1–11) both complements and contrasts with the Darwinian view of existence as "one web of life and death" ("Fire," 1.300).[24] The paradox is expressed in varying if related terms in the later lyrics, where Pratt's reaction to the unnatural horror of war leads him to a freer use of apocalyptic language and imagery.

The poem "Still Life" (2.136–7), like "The Deed" (2.196), contrasts the romantic and the realistic visions. It is Pratt's jarring reminder to any poets who still seek to escape from the ugliness of reality to the beauty of a romantic concept of nature. In return for "still life," or the static aspect of nature that they seek as a theme for their art, he offers them the "still life" of humanity:

> We offer roses blanched of red
> In the Orient gardens,
> ...
> And time, be it said,
> For a casual hymn
> To be sung for the hundred thousand dead
> In the mud of the Yellow River. (2.136)

Even as he reminds them,

> Here are the tales to be retold,
> Here are the songs to be resung ... (2.137)

he suggests, as surely as he does in "The Truant," that as long as poets can celebrate the value of human deeds there is "still life" for humankind.

"Come Away, Death" (2.111), unlike the song in Shakespeare's *Twelfth Night* from which it takes its title, does not romantically invite death to put an end to the sorrows of life, but rather attempts to divert it. But any hope of success in this endeavour is ironic: the speaker already knows that

> However blow the winds over the pollen,
> Whatever the course of the garden variables,
> He remains the constant,
> Ever flowering from the poppy seeds. (2.111)

Death has always come out of life, and in spite of it. Only the manner of his coming and the mode of his reception have changed. The formal dignity which long ago attended his welcome release from suffering and old age and the religious ceremony which once surrounded and sanctified his advent have disappeared. While he once came "in formal dress, / Announced by Silence tapping at the panels / In deep apology" (2.111), he now arrives suddenly, announced by "the gride of his traction tread." The poem then moves from a general *memento mori* to the recollection of a specific experience of death "one September night."[25] Then, the silence that preceded it was sinister rather than deferential:

A calm condensed and lidded
As at the core of a cyclone ended breathing.
This was the monologue of Silence
Grave and unequivocal. (2.112)

In the "bolt / Outside the range and target of the thunder," and in its effects as "human speech curved back upon itself / Through Druid runways and the Piltdown scarps, / Beyond the stammers of the Java caves" (2.112–13), Pratt conveys something of his insight into the regressive nature of war, as well as his reaction against it. As speech, in the terms of Luther's description of sinful human nature, "curves back upon itself" (see 70–1, above), the evolution of the human race is reversed, and the work of creation, as well as the art of civilization, is undone. As humanity preys upon itself, the carnage and devastation that it produces are so great that, in their impression upon the human image, they eclipse all "the startling accompaniments of the Parousia" (see 68, above) foreshadowed on "the outmoded page of the Apocalypse" (2.113). In this momentary revelation of human ability to revert to the primitive, Pratt lays bare the stark horror of war.

In "The Impatient Earth" (2.29), Pratt reflects on humanity's readiness, in due time, to return to the earth from which it came (Eccl 3). But he questions why war should force death to come "out of season," in the springtime of life, "to the trumpet's unnatural summons." While the Pauline images of the race and the goal (1 Cor 9:24–6) convey the sense of life and purpose (*PE* 116), those of the harvest and the last trumpet (1 Cor 15) announce the untimely appearance of death invited by war. In this lyric, as in others, Pratt's use of the apocalyptic frame of reference suggests not opposition to nature, but opposition to what is contrary to nature.

The image of Death the Leveller is also prominent in Pratt's poetry, throwing into insignificance not only the features and the qualities that distinguish personalities but also all the causes of dissension and discord that have divided people in life. On the battlefield of "Clay," Black Watch and Brandenburger lie locked in a death embrace (2.326) while the only sound to be heard is

death's bitterest music – the low sob
Of brothers mourning brothers dead, the curse
Of fallen men that had not seen their foes ... (2.333)

In "Comrades" the enmity between human beings is seen as petty in the light of human mortality:

> Do you not know that a hemlock root
> Will enfold you together,
> Though fair be the sky
> Or foul the weather?
> To that same bed you shall come
> When the ear shall be deaf,
> And the lips shall be dumb ... (1.126)

This image of death appears too in "The Armistice Silence" (1.257), which published in *Many Moods* as a companion piece to "To an Enemy." Within the context of these poems Pratt suggests that the unity not achieved through the exercise of the Christian virtues of forgiveness and charity during life will be achieved in a more impersonal fashion in death.

In "The Convict Holocaust" Pratt depicts the bodies of the "three hundred pariahs" whose individual identities, together with the record of their crimes, have been blotted out by the flames:

> The fires consumed their numbers with their breath,
> Charred out their names; though many of the dead
> Gave proof of valour, just before their death,
> That Caesar's legions might have coveted. (1.216)

Yet the guards, apparently unable to forgive each other, try to capture (by means of thumbprints) the merely physical identity of those convicts whose true spirit was revealed in their final moments. It is clear that the law which Pratt sees applied here contravenes Paul's teaching about the freedom enjoyed by the dead (Rom 7:1), and is not the law of the spirit which gives life (Rom 8:2; *PE* 76).

The drama in *Behind the Log* is seen in the light of the sacrificial role played by the allied convoy in the salvation of a Europe torn by war and living in the shadow of death. Service in a common effort has already done much to dissolve distinctions in class and nationality. But if the ships should suffer a direct hit, an even greater levelling might take place:

> No one would mould the linotype for such
> A mass that might survive or not survive
> Their tedium of watches in the holds –
> The men with surnames blotted by their jobs

Into a scrawl of anonymity.
A body blow at the boilers would untype
All differentiations in the blood
Of pumpmen, wipers, messmen, galley boys
Who had become incorporate with the cogs
On ships that carried pulp and scrap to Europe. (2.179)

However, in the light of their common achievement, Pratt would not consider this loss of individuality or life to be in vain.

While the expenditure of human life in *Towards the Last Spike* is seen through the eyes of the politicians and the builders of the railroad as part of the cost of the "civil discipline of roads" (2.235), Pratt suggests another perspective. Sorrow, "speaking / A common mother tongue," makes no distinction between a Blackfoot tepee and a coolie's door:

Ring, ring the bells, but not the engine bells:
Today only that universal toll,
For granite, mixing dust with human lime,
Had so compounded bodies into boulders
As to untype the blood, and, then, the Fraser,
Catching the fragments from the dynamite,
Had bleached all birthmarks from her swirling dead. (2.236)

Human bodies are incorporated into the earth with as little inconvenience as oatmeal is incorporated into the bodies of the Scots who planned and financed the road across the sea of mountains (2.203), and who are willing to sacrifice all else to complete it. In this case, the bodies become a material part of the nation that stretches from sea to sea, but the irony of the context makes it clear that this is no example of what Pratt regarded as the valid laying down of a life to save another (MS 9:68.6).

In Pratt's poetry, physical infirmity is frequently used as a warning of human mortality, even as a symbol of death itself. Yet the maladies which Pratt describes are, almost without exception, the loss of sensory perception and the undefined paralysis which he calls "palsy." At times he associates these terms with personification in an ironic or humorous sense. In "Putting Winter to Bed" (1.268), the declining season is pictured as suffering because "dropsy" (Lk 14:2) has set in. As a result of the "fall" in *The Witches' Brew* the fish "lay dead or paralyzed" (1.149). In "The Great Feud," the sea-creatures, overcome by fear of racial doom, are afflicted by "consuming vertigo ... and palsy in the ventral regions" (1.170–1). In a more serious tone Pratt depicts the dying eagle as "deaf to the mighty symphony of wings" of its returning flock (2.38).

But the image of infirmity is no less effective when it is applied to foundering or sinking ships. The urgent attempt on the part of the *Roosevelt* to resume communications with the *Antinoe* is spelt out in human terms, both to preserve the tradition of personifying the ship and to make the plight of her passengers appear more precarious:

> A longer silence; and a deep suspicion.
> Destruction of the ship? or loss of power?
> Blindness was coming with the light of morning,
> Ten minutes, twenty, now a half-an-hour.
> *Where are you, "Antinoe"?* – The keys kept rapping
> But the receiving phones were dumb to space,
> And in the Pilot House there came no signal,
> The hand lay palsied on the compass face. (1.227–8)

The crew of the *Titanic*, after using signals, flare, and Morse code, make frantic but vain efforts to contact the *Californian* by radio for the help that she once, ironically, had offered. It seemed that

> No ship afloat, unless deaf, blind and dumb
> To those three sets of signals but would come. (1.336)

These images of infirmity are significantly more powerful when Pratt applies them to human beings. In poems such as "Old Age" (1.214), "Blind" (1.217), "The Lost Cause" (1.217), and "Blind from Singapore" (2.191), the extraordinary sense of empathy with sightlessness is probably a reflection of Pratt's relationship both with his aged mother, who suffered the loss of her vision, and with the blind student for whom he had once read. The fog of the poem by that title (1.70), which not only "took our sight" but also "drew the song from our throats," can almost be felt, as can the gust of snow in "The Ice-Floes," which "strangled the words in our throats" (1.61). When the Panjandrum threatens the "bucking truant" with death, he does so in terms of loss of sensory perception:

> I shall make deaf the ear, and dim the eye,
> Put palsy in your touch, make mute
> Your speech ... (2.127–8)

In "Cycles" (2.195), the speaker, weary of war and moral confusion, longs for a fair decision in the international fighting ring, even for a transfusion of new life, "before our voice is dumb, / Before our blood-shot eyes go blind" (2.196).

Although illness or infirmity may figure in Pratt's poetry as an image of death, it does not necessarily mark the end. The dreamer in *The Iron Door* sees "the frore, / Dumb faces of despair" (1.206) become "keen impassioned faces, / Transfigured" (1.213). The infirmities that recur throughout Pratt's poetry are the very ones that arouse the compassion of Christ (Lk 4:40, 8:26-36) and call forth the miracles of healing, some of which Pratt discusses in "The Demonology of the Synoptics" (see 20-1, above). They are also those which afflict humankind in general, and which set apart the guests whom Pratt would invite to the "apocalyptic dinner" in "The Depression Ends" (1.261; Lk 14:12-24; Rev 7:14-17). By portraying death, or sickness unto death, in these specific terms, Pratt does not exclude the possibility of a restoration to health, whether it be temporal or eschatological.

Pratt's awareness of the apocalyptic and later Pauline vision of "the antipodal contrast between life and death" (*PE* 100), more than his debt to Darwin, lies behind what has been called his "strange tendency" to describe death in terms of birth.[26] Nevertheless, at times Pratt achieves his characteristic irony by combining the biological terminology proper to parturition with the scriptural and liturgical frame of reference belonging to the "new birth" of baptism. Pratt's use of this imagery is suggested for the first time in *Rachel* (1.37). He shows interest in exploring its wider implications in "The Great Feud." The ambivalent nature of the power belonging to Tyrannosaurus Rex is underlined by the circumstances of his death. He is drawn by "a tidal call that beat like a pain" (1.199) to the seashore where he

> Looked into the water's face
> The rolling cradle of his race. (1.199)

For the "blind wanderer from the race marine" (1.198), the false Messiah, the womb to which he returns is truly the tomb. In *The "Roosevelt" and the "Antinoe"* when death is imminent Pratt describes the treacherous sea in imagery belonging to both birth and death. As the first lifeboat with its rescue squad is lowered, Pratt suggests the danger that it faces:

> Below, like creatures of a fabled past,
> From their deep hidings in unlighted caves,
> The long processions of great-bellied waves

> Cast forth their monstrous births which with grey fang
> Appeared upon the leeward side, ran fast
> Along the broken crests, then coiled and sprang
> For the boat impatient of its slow descent
> Into their own inviolate element. (1.233)

The relationship of these waves to the kraken of "The Cachalot" (1.153–4) is obvious.

The image of death as birth is more fully developed in the later short narrative, "The Submarine" (2.30–5). Pratt first describes the natural evolution of marine life in terms which evoke terror:

> The evolution of the sea
> Had brought forth many specimens
> Conceived in horror – denizens
> Whose vast inside economy
> Not only reproduced their broods,
> But having shot them from their wombs,
> Devoured them in their family feuds
> And passed them through their catacombs. (2.31)

But the submarine does not belong to these specimens, and her power appears to be an improvement over nature, combining "such terror with such grace":[27]

> No product she of Nature's dower,
> No casual selection wrought her
> Or gave her such mechanic power
> To breathe above or under water.

As if they are part of her mechanical fittings, she carries

> human figures caught
> At their positions, silent, taut,
> Like statues in the tungsten light. (2.32)

In contrast, the submarine's prey is described, as are the allied ships in *Behind the Log* (2.166), in warm human terms:

> The trail of smoke turned out to be
> A fat mammalian of the sea,
> Set on a course north-east by north,
> And heavy with maternity.

> Within her framework iron-walled
> A thousand bodies were installed,
> A snug and pre-lacteal brood
> Drawing from her warmth and food,
> Awaiting in two days or three
> A European delivery. (2.33)

On sighting the ship, the submarine, pregnant with death, assumes its true appearance:

> Now like
> The tiger-shark viviparous
> Who with her young grown mutinous
> Before the birth-hour with the smell
> Of blood inside the mother, will expel
> Them from her body ...
> So like the shark, the submarine
> Ejected from her magazine
> The first one of her foetal young. (2.33)

The birth of the submarine's deadly and expendable offspring, described in terms of a mechanical rather than a natural process, implies destruction for her "young" as well as for the "brood" of the "rich-ripe mammal." However, as the transport ship goes down, Pratt directs attention to "the sea's reach for a thousand souls / In the last throe of the parturition" (2.35). He does not elaborate upon any supernatural implications that may be attached to this "parturition" of souls,[28] but by his careful use of the birth-life-death imagery, and by his identification of the submarine and the transport ship with the machine or tiger-shark and the mammal respectively, he implies the values which he attaches to both sides in this "silent underwater kill." Her bloody and atavistic work accomplished, the submarine, for her own safety, retreats beneath the silent sea, away from light, "to a native lair as dark / As a kraken's grave" (2.35). Pratt's association of the submarine with the kraken of "The Cachalot" (1.153–4) leaves his readers in no doubt about how he regards it.

In varying terms throughout his poetry, not always in association with the sea, Pratt improvises upon the theme of death as birth. In "The Invaded Field" (2.110), he explores the implications of the paradox as it is perverted by Nazi doctrine:

> They brought their youth up on the lore
> Of the Phoenix and the pyre,

Of birth from death and gold from fire
And the myth of the Aryan spore. (2.110)

"The Aryan spore," like "the synthetic seed" in "The Good Earth" (2.193),

>has a way of germinating teeth
>And yielding crops of carrion for the vulture. (2.193)

The paradox is restored to its true balance with the Pauline image of the seed (1 Cor 15:36–44; *PE* 85) as it is implied at the end of *Brébeuf and His Brethren*. There, the martyrs' blood, associated throughout the poem with both life and death, is seen as the seed of a renewed faith (2.109–10).[29]

The most explicit example in Pratt's poetry of the paradoxical relationship between death and birth, in its religious sense, occurs elsewhere in *Brébeuf and His Brethren* as a masterpiece of irony. As Brébeuf watches the Hurons celebrate their "High Feast of the Dead" (2.57), he sees them "baptize into death" a captive Iroquois in a clever parody of the sacrament of initiation into life which they have observed the priests administer. At that moment, Brébeuf has a premonition of the circumstances of his own death.

As time goes on, the "hundreds of baptisms" which the priests are able to count are chiefly among the infants, the children, and the dying. The conversion of Peter, which the Jesuits might be expected to regard as a great accomplishment, is offset by the fear and suspicion suggested in the vision which the priests and the Indians have of each other (2.75). When the end does come for Brébeuf, he is quite literally baptized into death with boiling water as the Iroquois remind him of his debt of gratitude to them for sending him to eternal life (2.107).

The framework and the context of the poem as a whole throw these parallel incidents into proper perspective, and provide Pratt with the opportunity of probing into the depths of one of the fundamental mysteries of Christianity (Rom 6:3–11; Col 2:12; 1 Cor 15; *PE* 181–4). Through his use of the apocalyptic and Pauline imagery of birth and death in this poem, Pratt insists, even more strongly than elsewhere, that the ultimate victory does not belong to the grave.

The "Vapours, Sounds and Colours of the Judgment"

The traditional Christian scheme of eschatology frequently fails to draw a rigid line between the end of earthly life and the events that are expected to follow it (*PE* 139, 153–5). This is true, too, of Pratt's conception of "the last things" as reflected in his poetry. A scene of judgment, particular or apparently universal, may precede or follow death, or even be contemporaneous with it. In poems in which "the Lord" appears as judge, and in which he seems to be remote from, unconcerned with, and even ignorant of the human condition, the individual may respond either with a terror which is unworthy of human nature, or with a mixture of defiance and humour which can only dignify it.

Pratt is not incapable of treating the scene of judgment as a human, if not as a divine, comedy, or of turning a serious theological question upside down, as he noted Burns did (MS 9:66). Such is the case in "Carlo" (1.51), where after indignantly setting at nought the arguments that would exclude the dog from heaven, he offers if necessary to act as Carlo's "advocate" before the throne.

"The Parable of Puffsky" appears to be another lighthearted treatment of the particular judgment. Pratt exposes Puffsky's situation tersely: "Puffsky knew not how to live. / But only how to sell" (1.285). Never having been known to buy or to give, he is a mystery to financiers who wonder how he can multiply his wealth without parting with a dime.

Puffsky's particular judgment takes place after death when, "shambling up to God" (1.285), he tries "to dicker with his soul." But the practised salesman with his foot in the door is no match for "the Lord" with his "darkening frown" and "glittering monocle." Since there is simply no place for bartering, buying, or selling in heaven, Puffsky is sent to "try his game" in hell. But Satan, a materialist, "amazed that such a spirit could exist," appoints a commission comprising a chemist and a pessimist "to make a report on the apparition" (1.286). Since Puffsky's size and weight are "indeterminate," and he is a watered soul, "gaseous but non-inflammable when mixed with coal" (1.286), he is not, even in Gehenna currency, "worth a current damn"(1.59). Puffsky, tried according to the very values by which he has lived (*PE* 13), is found wanting. In both "Carlo" and "The Parable of Puffsky" the subjects of the poems and the treatment of the theme, together with colloquial language, a basically iambic rhythm, and a loose rhyme scheme, provide an added ironic twist to theological argument and moral exemplum, throwing into question any serious consideration, not of judgment as an ultimate reality, but of judgment in certain conventional but limited terms.

It is not difficult to see the relationship between "The Parable of Puffsky" and "Out of Step" (1.284), which appeared with it in *Many Moods* (1932), and the more mature and substantial poem "The Truant" (2.125). In the latter, the same combination of the trial scene with its judge and prosecutor, and the scientific experiment with its laboratory and technicians, constitutes the moment of judgment for "little genus *homo*" whose lack of a name, if it makes for greater impersonality, nevertheless allows him to be a representative of universal humanity. In this case, it is only in the face of the annihilation with which his judge threatens him that he discovers within himself his inner resources and reveals his ability to transcend all that a purely materialistic view of the universe implies.

Somewhat reminiscent of the trial scene in "The Truant" is Blake's uncovering of the Pacific Scandal in *Towards the Last Spike* (2.209–12). Skilled in "finding / a skeleton inside an overcoat," Blake, "each sentence regimented like a lockstep," exposes the involvement of politicians and financiers alike as if he were the Great Panjandrum himself:

> by the time
> Recess was called, he had them in the dock
> As brigands in the Ministry of Smells,
> Naked before the majesty of Heaven. (2.210–11)

Not all are as fortunate as Macdonald in surviving so merciless a judgment.

In some of the realistic or documentary poems, the occasion of death itself is seen as the moment of true judgment. In "Convict Holocaust" (1.216), the final attempt of the guards to confine the identity of the dead to their thumbprints, and to reassert society's earlier verdict, suggests the purely materialistic view of Satan in "The Parable of Puffsky," and that of the Panjandrum in "The Truant." While the last actions of the convicts may have proved them worthy of redemption, the guards are less ready than Paul to accept the fact that death has set them free.

Much of the specific imagery of the courtroom is absent from the longer narratives, yet a scene of judgment is often implicit within the context of a poem. In *The "Roosevelt" and the "Antinoe," The "Titanic,"* and *Behind the Log*, human beings facing death range themselves by their own free decisions and actions with either the sheep or the goats. In *The "Titanic"*, whose ending is marked by most of the "traditional accompaniments" of the apocalypse (*PE* 10a–c, 128), especially by chaos, fear, and flight, individuals respond on the whole as they have probably acted throughout life. There are those like the stoker (1.332), or the woman in the lifeboat (1.337), whose instinctive but uncontrolled desire for self-preservation causes them to strike out at others. On the other hand, there are also those like the men on the lifeboat, or individual passengers on deck, both the famous and the unknown, who respond with almost as instinctive a generosity (1.337). By their last actions these characters, like the members of the crew of the *Roosevelt* and of the Convoy S.C. 42, prove their mettle. Throughout his poetry Pratt presents not only death and judgment, but also life and judgment as inseparable. With the exception of moments such as that in *Brébeuf and His Brethren* (2.73–4), where the Indians attending the baptism of Peter associate

> The smoke and aromatics of the censer,
> The candles, crucifix and Latin murmurs
> With vapours, sounds and colours of the Judgment (2.74),

that event in Pratt's poetry, whether particular or universal, may be stripped of many of its traditional mythological trappings, but not of its meaning. Pratt showed as much interest in the peripheral details as did Paul.

"The Visual Affirmatives of Hell"

The apocalyptic images of hell which had their proper place in traditional Methodist preaching are reflected to some extent in Pratt's eschatological vision, but they are nowhere so clearly sketched as in his account of Brébeuf's attempt to teach the Hurons. In this incident, the basis of which he found in the *Relations* (8.4:145; 15.103–50), Pratt pictures the missionary sending to France for pictures, one

> *Only* of souls in bliss: of *âmes damnées*
> Many and various – the horned Satan,
> His mastiff jaws champing the head of Judas;
> The plummet fall of the unbaptized pursued
> By demons with their fiery forks; the lick
> Of flames upon a naked Saracen;
> Dragons with scarlet tongues and writhing serpents
> In ambush by the charcoal avenues
> Just ready at the Judgment word to wreak
> Vengeance upon the unregenerate.
> The negative unapprehended forms
> Of Heaven lost in the dim canvas oils
> Gave way to glows from brazier pitch that lit
> The visual affirmatives of Hell. (2.73)

When Pratt describes Brébeuf's pedagogical difficulties in "driving home the ethics" in minds that "let the cold abstractions fall," he certainly exposes the irony of the situation, but he also seems to speak with a certain degree of sympathy born of his own pastoral experience. A later religious writer comments upon the problem of catechesis not confined to Brébeuf's century, his culture, or his particular denomination:

> Those powerful mission and retreat sermons whose spirit was so marvellously caught up in James Joyce's *Portrait of the Artist as a Young Man*, evoking unbearable physical torments for ever and ever, could enter the bloodstream and it was not everyone who managed to overcome them with a truer sense of divine mercy. It is not difficult to see why. The rhetoric of mercy and eternal blessedness, the descriptions of paradise, were altogether more pallid and more speculative than the heightened descriptions of pains whose earthly reality was already too familiar. It was, and is easier to describe a convincing hell than a convincing heaven. Similarly, large numbers of people find it easier to believe in their sins and frailties than in their virtues, and a theology which spoke of salvation as the reward for keeping a bargain could quickly undermine hope in people painfully conscious of their sinfulness. So the rhetoric went one way – the certainty of life after death, the joys of paradise awaiting the faithful Christian – and the individual's feelings another.[30]

These words sound curiously like Pratt's own reflection on the power over the imagination of the sermons to which he listened as a child (see 4, above).

As Brébeuf had already seen in the "fiery pageant" that marked the death of the captive Iroquois (2:65–6), and as he was later to experience himself, the traditional image of hell as a place of eternal punishment for the wicked after death paled before the atrocities that his captors had power to perpetrate in life. Apart from the passages in *Brébeuf and His Brethren* discussed above, there are few references in Pratt's poetry to hell in its traditional apocalyptic setting (*PE* 136). According to orthodox theology, Carlo, despite his bravery, is "neuter" and deserves a place neither among the sheep nor among the goats (1.51), while Puffsky, the materialist, belongs neither in heaven nor in hell (1.285–6).

On the whole, Pratt seems to reflect the extreme reticence which he noted in Paul when it comes to describing the punishment of hell – a marked contrast to the apocalyptic tendency to portray it as "a continued existence in some part of Sheol or Gehenna," "an eternal dying," "a perpetual separation from God" (*PE* 96). Paul, Pratt remarks, shows little exultation over "the spectacular punishment of his foes," and on the relatively few occasions when he does refer to the misfortunes of the wicked after death, he conveys the sense of "irreparable loss" and of an existence of "tribulation and anguish" (Rom 2:9; *PE* 99).

When Pratt does draw a picture of a temporal state or experience which seems to approach the infernal, he is likely to select his images from other than the most common biblical or apocryphal ones. At times they are classical in origin. The "iron door" appears to have been brought out of "some Plutonian cave" (1.205), probably that of Virgil, while the demonic power of the "6000," the poet claims, has its source in a furnace which outshadows the fiery underworlds of mythology:

> In his vast belly was a pit
> Which even Homer would admit,
> Or Dante, searching earth and hell,
> Possessed no perfect parallel. (1.258–9)

Probably the most convincing image of hell in Pratt's poetry is that of the almost primeval chaos to which the world is reduced as a consequence of ill-considered or malicious human actions, or of the unpredictability of nature. In "The Ice-Floes," the failure of the sealers to pay attention to the signs of the approaching storm leads to blindness, panic, intense suffering, and death – or, as they are described in this poem, an experience of hell on earth (1.61–2). When "the leash of discipline was untied" in "The Great Feud" (1.199–200), the resulting disorder led to a hellish massacre. What the men on board the *Roosevelt* endured was perhaps even more frightening than any traditional concept of hell, as

> Behind the weather-cloth it seemed the world
> Was carried with the last gust to the void. (1.223)

The disorder pictured in *Behind the Log* is just as truly infernal:

> Upon the *Skeena*'s bridge the judgment fought
> With chaos. Blindness, deafness visited
> The brain. Through a wild paradox of sight
> And sound, the asdic echoes would not fall
> Within their ribbon-tidy categories
> ...
> Wake-echoes and reverbs, and *quenching* caused
> By pitch and roll of a heavy following sea,
> Had blended with the sharper pings from steel
> To give the effect of a babel and a brawl. (2.181)

The receiver in "The Radio in the Ivory Tower" proves to be an oracle of the coming holocaust. Through it

> With a new salute and macabre step,
> Chaos came in at the call of the horns. (2.44)

Frequently this chaos corresponds with the image of the primeval deep before the work of creation (Gen 1:2). At times, presided over by Vulcan[31] (*The Witches' Brew*, 1.131–2; *Dunkirk*, 2.123), it becomes the symbol for the instinctive level of the human psyche which lies beneath the conscious, and which, when directed towards aggression and death, is the source of all the humanly created versions of hell. Pratt refers to it, in this sense, in the poem "Silences" (2.3–4). Here there is no celebration of the rites of passage:

> No cries announcing birth,
> No sounds declaring death ...
> The drama is silent. (2.3)

Joy and sorrow, the basic emotions of life, give way here to a destructive instinct so primitive that it is "pre-reptilian."[32] Such "fury," however, is silent in that it is suppressed, or governed by "the ultimate economy of rage." Conscious hostilities that divide people may be purged or ended by the healthy expression of feeling:

> No one need fear oaths that are properly enunciated, for they
> belong to the inheritance of just men made perfect [Heb 2:23],
> and, for all we know, of such may be the Kingdom of Heaven.
> But let silent hate be put away for it feeds upon the heart of the hater. (2.3)

In the silent confrontation of the two persons which the poet observes he is aware that "A word would have dulled the exquisite edge of the feeling" (2.4). But such a word would also have ended the ultimate isolation that constitutes the suffering of hell. Cold hatred and fury driven back into the subconscious can find release only in aggression or self-destruction.

Although in this poem Pratt uses little specifically religious terminology, he is closer here to the images of eternal suffering that remain in the Gospels and in the Pauline epistles than are all the exaggerated horrors of apocalyptic literature – to the "great gulf" that isolates a Dives who did not recognize Lazarus as his brother (Lk 16:19–31), and to the exclusion of the contemptuous guest who chose to go unprepared to the wedding banquet (Mt 22:1–14).

While the submarine kingdom is frequently an image of hell in Pratt's poetry, its connotation varies according to the context in which Pratt uses it. He quotes his friends as having said that he wrote *The Witches' Brew* "to get hell out of [his] system" after he completed *Pauline Eschatology* (MS 9:69.4). To interpret this remark literally is to be led astray, as neither Paul nor Pratt has much to say about hell. It is true that this "Saturnalian feast" (1.131) seems to be set at the opposite pole from the transcendent "Apocalyptic dinner" (1.261) of "The Depression Ends," but the underwater region in which it takes place has greater affinity in its ambivalence with the depths of the psyche or the unconscious than it has with hell, as it is traditionally presented in biblical or apocryphal literature or in theological treatises. The devil and his legions must fly from hell to attend "the Bacchanals" (1.138), while the Shades, those incorporeal spirits good or bad which have undergone death, but which await the general resurrection, must come from Hades,[33] "that dry land."

With all due respect to Jay Macpherson's attempt to illustrate the parallels between *The Witches' Brew* and the Faust legend, I feel that her intuition about the influence of Celtic song and story,[34] from which no Newfoundlander could be totally immune, deserves further elaboration. On the mythological level, the setting of Pratt's party brings to mind *Tir fo Thuinn*, the land under the waves rich in food and natural delights, which was a place of retreat for Celtic gods and heroes.[35] At its centre stood a magic cauldron of plenty which needed a guard, since mortals often tried to steal it.

The water witches, too, are quite at home within this mythological framework. In addition, on the symbolic plane, this feminine triad, which stirs up and inverts the order of things,[36] represens instinctual drives in their natural development and growth.[37] To suggest that Pratt intended them as a parody of the Holy Trinity[38] is to attribute to him a lack of reverence of which he was entirely innocent. *The Witches' Brew* was rejected by the editorial board of Ryerson Press not because they considered it to be blasphemous, but because they found "the vintage too strong."[39] In their experiment the witches do stir up more than they have bargained for. They allow themselves to be directed by Satan into putting Tom to the test (1.144). The result is chaos and death, but the disorder gradually subsides, and the sea-cat leaves the scene of battle for the Irish Sea, where, according to legend, he belongs. If for a time in this poem, the underwater kingdom takes on the appearance of hell, there is every suggestion that it does not have to retain it.

Symbolically it may be said that both the creative and destructive powers of the imagination have been allowed free rein. Now, well tested, they may be held within bounds to be recalled as need requires.

After the scholarly demands which the writing of *Pauline Eschatology* had placed upon him, Pratt needed the freedom to indulge his imagination and to explore the limits to which he could allow it to run without creating a psychic if not a physical hell.

Satan and the Beast of the Apocalypse

Satan as he is most frequently recognized (DS 8–11; PE 71–2) appears rarely in Pratt's poetry, and when he does he is usually seen in a humorous or ironic light. In *The Witches' Brew* the "most sovereign and sulphurous lord" (1.144) arrives as a guest of the three sisters. His knowledge and experience are surprisingly limited, as his reaction to the experiment on the fish reveals:

> Not since the time the sense of evil
> Caught our first parents by surprise,
> While eating fruit in Paradise,
> One fateful morning, had the Devil,
> Used as he was to steam and smoke,
> Beheld such chaos as now broke
> Upon his horny, bloodshot eyes.
> Prince of the Power of the air,
> Lord of terrestrial things as well
> As subterranean life in Hell,
> He had till now not been aware
> How this great watery domain
> Might be enclosed within his reign;
> ...
> For all his wily strategy
> Since time began, the Devil saw
> No way to circumvent the sea. (1.139–40)

When the effect on the fish proves to be disastrous, and when he recognizes in Tom a higher level of creation, Satan is successful, as he is in the Book of Job (1:8–12; DS 9), in having the hero put to the test.

As Lord of Hell, "with a hoarse and bronchial laugh," Satan is seen again in "The Parable of Puffsky" (1.285–6), but his only duty is to appoint a commission to inquire into the nature of the "crack salesman" (1.286). In "Old Harry" (2.37–8), where he is associated by legend with a particularly dangerous rock off the sea-coast that appears to have been "built to incarnate a demon," he is, it seems, imprisoned and powerless. Pratt's ability to laugh at the devil does not detract from his vision of the evil present in the world. It does reflect something of an attitude which he admired in the poetry of Robert Burns, whose upbringing, he remarked, was that of a strict Calvinist. Burns, especially in his "Address to the De'il,"

... brought the Devil up from Pandemonium, examined him with a superb piece of descriptive and humorous analysis, and put the old fellow under a microscope as if he were a human bacillus. The last time that Satan was seen in the form of a star or planet was when Meredith trained a telescope upon him on a starry night in the celebrated poem "Lucifer in Starlight." Since then, Satan has forfeited not only those qualities of ambition and design which made him such a picturesque study in moral dynamics, but also his mass. He has become the classical example of the degradation of energy. (PPAA 268)

In Pratt's poetry, certain features formerly attributed to Satan are transferred to an image that appears more frequently, that of the apocalyptic beast or monster (Dan 7; Rev 12, 13; *PE* 13). This figure is usually the repository of power, whether it be the power of government exercised by human beings over the lives of others, the power inherent in nature, or that same power harnessed by humanity and channelled through the machine. It may even be that deteriorating power which in the "Address on Robert Burns" (PPAA 268) he associates with Satan.

The context within which Pratt places his beasts reveals, more often than not, an attitude of ambivalence on his part. He is clearly fascinated by power, whether manifested in the might of a steam engine or in a storm at sea – yet he is aware of the misuse to which it may be put in the rhetoric of "The Baritone" (2.5) or in the death-blows of "The Submarine" (2.30).

It might be said that the apocalyptic beast first makes an appearance in Pratt's poetry as Tom, the "uncouth primordial cat" from Zanzibar (1.137), whose "stock were traitors to the sea" (1.146). Associated by the observers at the party both with Lucifer, "that streamed / His fiery passage through the sea" (1.138), and with Satan, "who alone may trace / The dark enigma of this race" (1.137), Tom with his "electrifying fur," "galvanic tail," and "spontaneous conflagration" is a source of amusement to the Shades and to Satan himself, who demands that the beast be subjected to "The Supreme Test" (1.145). While he is sober, Tom exhibits little malice, but after he has fallen under Satan's power and has drained the liquor from the hundredth flagon,

The Shades then saw Hell's darkest fiend –
A sea-cat with an awful jag-on. (1.145)

As a source of energy Tom becomes blind, unable to discern the difference between his enemies and his allies:

> never was an errand run
> With means and end so much at one.
> For from his birth he was imbued
> With hatred of his racial kind;
> A more inveterate, blasting feud
> Within the world one could not find
> ...
> He had, upon his final flask,
> Resolved to carry out his task –
> To wit: – the full extermination,
> First, of his nearest order, male
> And female, then the breed cetacean. (1.146)

The real source of power in *The Witches' Brew* is not Satan but Tom, who, out of control, is able to bring about the undoing of creation, or the reduction of an orderly world to the state of primal chaos. Then, suffering from a hangover, and from loneliness when he discovers that he has disposed of all his kin, he

> Took one blood-curdling leap and left
> Magellan's for the vacant seas.
> Sullen and dangerous he ripped
> A gleaming furrow through the water,
> Magnificently still equipped
> For combat with rapine and slaughter. (1.149)

Once he has "stirred up the depths of hell,"[40] Tom is somewhat subdued, but unlike the apocalyptic beast in other poems by Pratt, he does not meet his destruction. The lonely voyage "pregnant of immortal raids / And epic plunder" (1.149) on which he sets out does not mark his end, but merely his relegation to the Irish Sea, where he is no foreigner but is at home as the sea-cat of popular Celtic folklore[41] whose periodic binges or rampages create violent storms and tempests.

Like the unleashed primal energy of the psyche, or the power of the imagination, which Tom may also symbolize, he requires direction towards constructive ends. While the sea-cat has wrought havoc, his spark is only temporarily diminished, and the reader is left with the sense that Tom may some day be recalled in other guises to be put to less destructive service.

Van Horne of *Towards the Last Spike* has something in common with Tom in his fabulous creative energy:

> Fast as a bobcat,
> He'd climb and run across the shakiest trestle
> Or, with a locomotive short of coal,
> He could supply the head of steam himself.
> ...
> Only the devil or Paul Bunyan shared
> With him the secret of perpetual motion,
> And when he moved among his men they looked
> For shoulder sprouts upon the Flying Dutchman. (2.231–2)

Like the sea-cat, the apocalyptic beast of "The Great Feud" is described in terms suggesting Milton's Satan (*Paradise Lost*, 9.505–30). Tyrannosaurus Rex is, however, even more destructive than Tom, and lacks the sea-cat's dynamism. Appearing on earth "three million years too late" (1.186), he is prepared by his adoptive parent, the moa, for his first appearance on the day of battle (1.186–7). Although the ape, with her slowly emerging power of reason, feared that the monster's coming "would cause a panic" (1.188), she found that Tyrannosaurus "filled the gap" in the ranks and seized the opportunity to harness his enormous energy and direct it towards her own destructive purposes (1.189).

Tyrannosaurus, who, like the drunken Tom, is the essence of blind power, is ranked at first on the side of the "tusk and claw." But when battle is far advanced, he,

> By some half-blinded route, began
> To scent the issue of the fight.
> Throughout the day he did not know
> Which was his ally or his foe;
> ...
> Fish and land animals alike
> Were objects for his fangs to strike. (1.196–7)

What causes the awakening of his "pulse of apprehension dim" is not clear:

> Perhaps some inland desert taste
> During the slaughter of the camels,
> Taught him his kinship with the lizard,
> His blood-removal from the mammals,
> And gave him nausea at the gizzard.

103 "Ghosts of the Apocalypse"

> ...
> Something in his racial birth,
> At variance with the things of Earth, –
> A tidal call that beat like pain
> From spinal ganglion to brain. (1.197–8)

Then, in response to the call of the sea-god, the "blind wanderer from the race marine" (1.198) plunges into the sea (Rev 19:20). Tyrannosaurus Rex, like a false prophet or an Antichrist (*PE* 133), can offer only spurious hope. Both in life and in death, he brings confusion and devastation in his wake.

The kraken of "The Cachalot" (1.153) is another monster of apocalyptic nature and proportion. Dwelling in "a dull reptilian silence" at the bottom of the sea, he never emerges from his "noisome pit / Of bones and shells":

> Moveless, he seemed, as a boulder set
> In pitch, and dead within his lair,
> Except for a transfixing stare
> From lidless eyes of burnished jet,
> And a hard spasm now and then
> Within his viscous centre. (1.153–4)

With his scabrous feelers "like a litter of pythons settling there / To shutter the Gorgonian stare," the kraken is an image of a purely destructive natural power which is overcome by the dynamic energy of the whale. Pratt does not allow his monster an eschatological destiny, as did Tennyson, whom he admired and sometimes imitated.[42] The narrative dictates of his poem do not allow for what would in this case be a digression. In another poem, it is to a lair like that of the kraken that the submarine (2.35) withdraws when, having disposed of her prey, she becomes in turn aware of the presence of a foe.

The topographical image which Pratt uses to convey the sense of the "passive corporal bulk" (2.230) of the Laurentian Shield in *Towards the Last Spike* is that of a beast which may share in the "ancient, dreamless, uninvaded sleep" of Tennyson's kraken:

> On the North Shore a reptile lay asleep –
> A hybrid that the myths might have conceived,
> But not delivered, as progenitor
> Of crawling, gliding things upon the earth
> ...

This folded reptile was asleep or dead:
So motionless, she seemed stone dead – just seemed:
She was too old for death, too old for life. (2.227–8)

But there are times (2.228) when the "Laurentian monster ... Top heavy with accumulated power" (2.228–9), and thus closely related to those other monsters, Jurania of "The Great Feud," and the iceberg of *The "Titanic"* (see 139, below), might convince us that nature had built it "to incarnate a demon" ("Old Harry," 2.37).

At first thought the Panjandrum of "The Truant" (2.125) seems to have little affinity with the beast of the apocalypse. A pure abstraction whose existence can be posited only by deduction, he is master of a universe run according to the principles of mechanics. Hence, he has no place for rebel humanity with its immaterial and immortal spark. He can only threaten to undo the orderly work of creation by reversing the evolutionary process, as does Death in *Dunkirk* (2.123). Once human beings recognize the Panjandrum's materialistic viewpoint as characteristic of the lord of hell ("The Parable of Puffsky," 1.206), or of Milton's fallen angels whose shout "frighted the reign of Chaos and Old Night" (*Paradise Lost,* 1.543), they have power to exorcise him. The degradation of power or energy according to the second law of thermodynamics – a degradation which, Pratt remarks, is an attribute of Satan (PPAA 268) – is characteristic of the Panjandrum, as it is in varying degrees of the other members of Pratt's apocalyptic bestiary.

Frequently, in Pratt's poetry, the machine takes on the appearance of the beast of the apocalypse. The mighty bird in "The Dying Eagle" (2.38–41) is broken in sprit at the sight of an ironically lifeless intruder which appears to have usurped his role. Although this creature is not necessarily evil, it is foreign to the environment, and the eagle sees it not only as one of the winged creatures of Ezekiel's vision (1:3–20) but also as a "supercilious bird" cutting through the air with "unconcern" and "extra-territorial insolence":

Was it a flying dragon? Head,
Body and wings, a tail fan-spread
And taut like his own before the strike;
And there in front two whirling eyes
That took unshuttered
The full blaze of the meridian
...
But something in this fellow's length
Of back, his plated glistening shoulders,
Had given him pause. And did that thunder

"Ghosts of the Apocalypse"

Somewhere in his throat not argue
Lightning in his claws? And then
The speed – was it not double his own? (2.40)

Pratt does little to conceal his admiration as he describes the *6000*, the engine "reared from the element of flame, / Designed to match a storm for speed" (1.257). The power and velocity of the machine are suggested by a series of comparisons with mythological creatures such as Mercury and Bucephalus, all of which suffer by contrast:

Those giants of Vulcan, leather-skinned,
Whose frightful stare monocular
Made mad the coursers of the wind,
And chased the light of the morning star
Away from the Sicilian shore,
Would have been terror-blind before
This forehead. (1.258)

Pratt finds a better parallel in the locusts of the ninth chapter of the Book of Revelation. The *6000*'s "armoured carapace" and his bottomless pit of a belly (1.250) with its heat, smoke, and noise "like chariots going to battle" (Ezek 1:24; Rev 9:9–10) are properties, too, of the giant apocalyptic insects, which, although they may sting, are nevertheless harmless (Rev 9:4–5).

But there are also monstrous machines that are instruments of Death "sweating at his lathe" (*Dunkirk*, 2.123). Submarines (2.31–2), although they possess great power and speed, are not the offspring of nature but expendable creatures whose only function is to carry death. They are not directed by human intelligence that is tempered by goodwill or charity, but are

Born of a mania of mind and will
And nurtured by a Messianic slogan. (2.151)

Other machines of war are as lethal as any beast of the apocalypse:

    those all but animate forms,
Mechanic myths of man's creative act
Transfigured into fact,
Endowed with perfect suicidal skill,
With power to fight unbleeding, yet to kill – ...
                        (*They Are Returning*, 2.140)

"Multipedes on the Roads" of *Dunkirk* appear to have no human origin. Having been "put together" by cranes, they are "unknowing and uncaring":

Born on the blueprints,
They are fed by fire.
They grow their skin from carburized steel
...
They breathe through carburetted lungs;
If pierced, they do not feel the cut,
And if they die, they do not suffer death. (2.120)

In the skies are creatures more ominous than that which confounded the dying eagle:

The great birds, carrying under their wings
The black distorted crosses,
Plunged, straightened out,
Laid their eggs in air,
Hatched them in fountains of water,
In craters of sand,
To the leap of flame,
To the roar of avalanche. (2.123)

"Myth and Fact" (2.193–4) is a strangely disturbing poem written around 1950 when the Korean War had become a reality, and when the widespread fear of the military power of the Communist forces had given new impetus to the rearmament race.[43] The apocalyptic monsters once safely confined to nightmares or fairy tales, and exorcised by daylight from the imagination, have become a reality. Pratt's image of humanity at this stage harks back to "The Demonology of the Synoptics" (6):

Was not the race just an incarnate child
That sat at wells and haunted ruins? (2.194)

But no feigned ignorance, no charm or spell, or even prayer, can provide the mind with an asylum from its fears:

For what the monsters of the long-ago
Had done were nursery peccadilloes
To what those solar hounds in tally-ho
Could do when once they sniffed the pillows. (2.195)

107   "Ghosts of the Apocalypse"

Yet any power unleashed through these "flying lizards" (2.194) is power that humanity directs against itself. Like most of the apocalyptic beasts that appear in Pratt's poetry, the monsters that contribute to the atmosphere of the "cold war" are instruments of death. Only if humankind is aware of its true nature and of theirs may it find consolation in knowing that the ultimate victory never falls to them.

THE APOCALYPSE AS AN EXPRESSION OF COSMOLOGICAL PERSPECTIVES

In addition to providing a literary expression for matters of eschatological concern, the apocalyptic form also makes available a context within which the writer is able to explore certain matters of cosmological interest, such as the mysteries of the origin and destiny of the world, of heaven and hell, and of the government of all creation by Divine Providence. The cosmological perspective, whether this is understood as astronomical or metaphysical – or both – is a significant element in Pratt's poetry, where it may be seen as a broadening of his eschatological orientation. In works from *The Iron Door* (1.204) to "Out of Step" (1.284), "From Stone to Steel" (1.260), "The Depression Ends" (1.261), and "Fire" (1.300) through "The Radio in the Ivory Tower" (2.41), "The Truant" (2.125), "The Unromantic Moon" (2.250), and "Summit Meetings" (2.186) to *The Witches' Brew* (1.131), *The "Titanic"* (1.302), and *Brébeuf and His Brethren* (2.46), it is viewed from many different but complementary angles.

One approach to Pratt's cosmology may be found in his narrative poems from "The Ice-Floes" (1.58) to *Towards the Last Spike* (2.201). Although the apocalypse is first and foremost literature of crisis, it presupposes an order beyond the natural and the temporal which throws the events set against it into proper perspective or enables them to be seen *sub specie aeternitatis*.[44] In "The Ice-Floes" (1.58), the apocalyptic battle between life and death both complements and sets off the Darwinian struggle for existence.

The historical events upon which this poem is based, the disaster that befell the sealing ship *Greenland* on 31 March 1898 and its starkly dramatic return to St John's weeks later,[45] occurred while Pratt was a youth in Newfoundland (MS 9:68.5). In recreating this incident, Pratt also explores the evolutionary implications of the circumstances surrounding it. Renaming the sealing ship the *Eagle*, he traces what Darwin calls the "web of relationships" among the species in their struggle for survival [46] which is complicated by the effect of climate in reducing the supply of food, and by the necessity of struggling with the elements.[47]

At the outset of the sealing expedition (1.58–9), the men are exhilarated not only by the beauty of the morning outrolling "on the fields its tissue of orange and gold" (cf. Is 40:22; Rev 6:14) but also by the prospect of the "harvest" of hundreds of thousands[48] of seals. But before the hunt has progressed far, the ice-floes have lost their pristine beauty and have assumed the appearance of a vast Armageddon (Rev 16:16) stained with enemy blood (1.60). Not content with their vast catch, the sealers are spurred on by the thought that "an added thousand or more" will beat the count of the previous day. Like the crew of the *Titanic*, they disregard not only the repeated signals from the *Eagle* (1.61) but also, and more significantly, the natural signs of danger in the changing weather, the colder wind, and the speed of the approaching storm. Isolated because communication is impossible, the men change quickly from "pursuing hounds" (1.60) into "helpless sheep" (1.62) as they struggle on, many of them to be subject to the "harvest" of death from exposure to the elements (1:62).

While the seals exhibit an instinctive care for their young and a marvellous adaptability to the natural environment (1.59)[49], the *Eagle* and her men become blind and lost (1.62). Nevertheless, the seals' search for food "to keep the brood alive" (1.59) is ironic in the light of their twenty thousand slain until we learn at the end of the poem that sixty men died "to help to lower the price of bread" (1.63).[50] Although the men appear, at first, to be pitted against the seals in a battle of apocalyptic colour and proportion, both species turn out to be closely related by nature in the struggle for survival. Both men and seals have basked in "that brisk hour before the sun," just as they have shared in the harvest of the sea, and have been subject to it. The superiority that humanity enjoys is suggested by rituals that embrace and lend a dignity to both life and death – "the story told," the flag at half mast, and the "muffled beat ... of a drum ... that filled / A nave ... at our count of sixty dead" (1.62–3).

The backdrop for the later narrative *Behind the Log* (1947) is, once again, the Greenland ice-cap. But Pratt's apocalyptic battlefield is no longer the primitive natural environment of the seal hunt where the combatants, though related, are not equally matched on the evolutionary scale. It is, instead, the zone of modern warfare, the setting for the story of the Convoy S.C. 42 and the battle of Cape Farewell (MS 9:70.3), where, behind all the technological masks and smoke-screens, Cain still slays Abel.

In *Behind the Log* (2.149), as dramatically as in "The Ice-Floes," Pratt recreates a situation that threatens the survival of a community. But the shortage of food in the later poem is not the simple result of natural causes or the outcome of the law of supply and demand in an unsophisticated economy. In describing the possible consequences of the human action that has precipitated the crisis in *Behind the Log*, Pratt uses physiological terms, thus emphasizing his vision of the heinousness of war:

> The crisis was the imminence of famine
> And the cutting of the ganglia and veins
> That vitalized the sinews, fed the cells
> Of lungs demanding oxygen in air.
> The wicks were guttering from the want of oil,
> And without oil, the bread went with the light,
> And without bread, the will could not sustain
> The fight, piping its courage to the heart. (2.151)

The enemy submarines, those "grey predatory fish ... pedigreed / With tiger sharks" (2.151), are all the more sinister in that they cannot share in the natural struggle for life, which, paradoxically, makes the men and the seals of "The Ice-Floes" both foes and allies:

> They did not kill for food: they killed that food
> Should not be used as food. They were the true
> Expendables – the flower of their type. (2.151)

The silent underwater kill of the submarines identifies them not as the offspring of creative human imagination but as monsters "born of a mania of mind and will" (2.151).

Ironically, the "harsh alliance of the ice / And fog" (2.152) that proves to be the undoing of the sealers in "The Ice-Floes" is, in this poem, like the fog at Dunkirk (2.124), the hope of salvation for the allied fleet. Light and communication, which could have saved the sealers from a natural disaster, can just as easily destroy human beings in a world dominated by technology. Here, light becomes a "pestilence" (2.166), and the human voice, usually welcome, betrays when it is picked up by the U-boat's direction-finder loop, waiting "like a human ear alerted" (2.155).[51] In this situation the greatest danger for the ships is not from the winds and the waves, for that is "their native element" (2.164). It is

> Not ice this time but moving steel submerged –
> Two hundred feet of longitudinal plate,
> Forged at the Krupp's and tested in the Baltic. (2.168)

In this drama of the hunter and the hunted, Pratt emphasizes the atavistic nature of the struggle by portraying the combatants in the animal imagery of the apocalypse (see 67, above), and dropping both sides to a lower rung on the evolutionary ladder. The supply ships are "herded like buffalo young inside the ring" (2.162), pursued by the enemy wolf pack in the moonlight "without the mercy of clouds" (2.169). The precariousness of the situation is further heightened by the image of the warships as huge mammals about to give birth (2.166). With thousands of sailors under the decks, sealed "As in vast envelopes," it is possible that

>   oil and fulminate of mercury,
> Nitrated cellulose and T.N.T.
> And the constituents of our daily bread,
> Fresh water and fresh air, could by a shift,
> Sudden and freakish in the molecules,
> Be transubstantiated into death. (2.167)

Death may come from a friend or from a foe, from within or from without, even from "excess of their protective zeal" (2.167). There is a moment of unnatural calm like that in "Come Away, Death" (2.112), accompanied by a revelation of the tenuous relationship between life and death – "to save to kill, to kill to save were means / And ends closely and bloodily allied" (2.170). But the explosion that follows the first direct hit, "like some neurotic and untimely sunrise" (2.170), makes insignificant the natural apocalyptic imagery of "The Ice-Floes." Falling prey to the submarines, the exploding tankers soak the sky "in orange fire" and kindle the sea (2.170). Nature reflects the terrible events with phosphorescence on the waters, and with signs and wonders in the heavens:

>   the Borealis
> Staged a rehearsal of the Merry Dancers
> Before the blood-red footlights till it paled
> The myth upon a tracery of starshell. (2.176)

In the wake of such vast destruction, ethical distinctions seem to be blotted out, "for fair [is] foul, and foul / [Is] fair, in that melee of strength and cunning" (2.171). The cataclysm that blurs moral distinctions also softens the distinctions between and within the crews, making their human antagonism less acceptable. Pratt sees them much as he sees the bodies of the dead in "Convict Holocaust" (1.216):

> The men with surnames blotted by their jobs
> Into a scrawl of anonymity.

A body-blow at the boilers would untype
All differentiations in the blood ... (2.179)

But even could they recognize their common humanity, the issue is, for the moment at least, too large and too complex for these men to remedy. Upon the *Skeena* judgment fights with chaos (2.181). With the approach of death, "blindness, deafness visited / The brain" (2.181). The self-destructive nature of war is emphasized by the value of the cargo. "Bread enough / To feed an army for a month" is consumed. The cost of the shipment of plasma preserved is "blood mixed with the sea-foam" (2.184). Nevertheless, in spite of the incalculable loss of life, some of the supply ships do manage to reach the northern outposts before making their way safely to Ireland.

Through his skilful juxtaposition of technical and apocalyptic language and imagery, Pratt is able in *Behind the Log* to reveal not only the barbaric wastefulness of war but also its universal reverberations. Throughout his lifetime he continued to exhibit an interest in science, and a fascination with technology, especially with those forms of it which could facilitate better communication among human beings.[52] But Pratt also saw that undue reliance upon the machine makes possible the abdication of humanity and regression to behaviour characteristic of the lowest stages on the evolutionary scale. If humankind is called upon to exercise responsibility in its relationship with nature, it is also called to do so in its use of the machine. Should it fail in either case, suggests Pratt, it may let loose another sea-cat or a Tyrannosaurus Rex.

Behind the Log, for all the carnage that it depicts, is not a pessimistic poem, for beneath the terse entries on the page, Pratt reveals what he finds also in *The "Roosevelt" and the "Antinoe"* – "mortality," finite human beings in command of the supply ships and their escort, at the radio and the radar, exercising judgment, making decisions, and performing actions that affect the lives of thousands unknown to them. In comparison with the loss of life that precedes it, the victory in *Behind the Log* may seem to be slight and temporary. However, an extract from a talk that Pratt gave close to the time of the poem's publication may indicate the perspective from which he viewed such an achievement:

If the giving of a life could be attended by the saving of another, the sacrifice could find its place in the Christian faith, but otherwise the process would stand for a symbol of the ironic in its ultimate rigour. Ever since life began, man has been calling for blood in all that polarity of mood from vengeance to redemption, from the curse to the prayer. (MS 10:46.4)

In the apocalyptic Greenland battle, Pratt explores "all that polarity of mood." He reveals the ironic, as he describes it here, and also what he sees beyond it. At the end of the poem, he shifts attention from the horror of death and destruction to the apocalyptic note of consolation that comes with the vision of a new order[53] "on a hoped tomorrow" (2.184).

"The Great Feud," first published with "The Cachalot" in *Titans* (1926), permits Pratt to extend the theme of the apocalyptic struggle between life and death from the personal and the historical to the universal and the mythological planes, conducting what Harold Horwood has described as "a romantic excursion into mythology."[54] While avoiding the pitfalls of the intentional fallacy, it is still possible to take advantage of the insights provided by Pratt's own comments on this work. In his introduction to a reading of "The Great Feud" he remarked:

The method of this poem is to invoke an evolutionary theme, and to work it out in terms of an imaginative symbolism. I want to show how colossal a catastrophe [could] occur, if certain natural instincts and passions such as self-preservation, a sense of family and racial pride, or even the feeling of honour or adventure, or the desire to possess and retain, were given absolutely free rein. (MS 1:5)

It appears that much of the difficulty in understanding and enjoying Pratt's *Titans*, as well as other of his extravaganzas, emerges not only from readers' inability to recognize his narrative point of view but also from their failure to appreciate the literary forms which he frequently chooses. Dorothy Livesay, in suggesting that the reader approach Pratt's narratives as documentaries, did the poet a favour by pointing out the amount of research and technical data that informs each poem.[55] Nevertheless, it is only if the reader is discriminating enough to distinguish between documentaries such as *The "Roosevelt" and the "Antinoe"* and *Behind the Log* and what are, in fact, parables or fables that he or she is likely to be satisfied. Pratt himself called "The Great Feud" a parable, and if he meant that, so too is "The Cachalot" (MS 1:5).

With all due respect to the helpful definitions provided by popular literary guides and handbooks, the observations of biblical scholars may shed more light on Pratt's work. C.H. Dodd, in what has now become a classic study, contrasts the use of the parable in a non-Jewish environment (a source of mystification, or a vehicle of esoteric doctrine), with its role in the rabbinical tradition to which he contends the parables of the New Testament belong. There they are the natural expression of a mind that sees truth in concrete pictures rather than in abstractions. He explains:

At its simplest the parable is a metaphor or a simile drawn from nature or from common life, and arresting the hearer by its vividness or strangeness, and leaving the mind in sufficient doubt about its precise application to tease it into active thought. Such a simple metaphor may be elaborated into a picture by the addition of detail or into a story instead of a picture ... The parable has one single point of comparison. The details are not intended to have independent significance as in an allegory ... The way to interpreting the parable lies through judgment on the imagined situation, not through the decoding of details.[56]

Pratt, whose imagination pictures truth in concrete rather than in abstract terms, frequently finds in the parable the most suitable form of expression.

Pratt subtitles "The Great Feud" "A Dream of a Pleiocene Armageddon" (1.168), although he remarks that he might more fittingly have described it as "a nightmare" (MS 1:6). By including in his parable elements of the dream form and certain features of the beast fable, two prominent types of apocalyptic literature (*PE* 113), Pratt is able to explore simultaneously, on a cosmological plane, both the psychological and the evolutionary[57] implications of his theme. While the dream form frees his imagination from the strict demands of logic, scientific accuracy, and history, the beast fable provides him with an excellent vehicle for satire. The juxtaposition within the poem of the gigantic and the minute, or of Tyrannosaurus and trilobite, constitutes a major form of irony. The total effect hoped for is the liberation of the reader's imagination, so that rather than be burdened by the problem of interpreting allegorical details she or he may be carried away by the movement and the humour of the fable, only to be "teased into active thought," at the end, by the serious implications of the parable. The poem describes an analogue to the apocalyptic war in heaven (Rev 12) – the great "Tellurian feud" (1.169) or life-and-death struggle between the inhabitants of the land and the primitive, instinctual creatures of the sea who are related through origin, yet are relegated to a lower step on the evolutionary ladder.[58] When the sea-creatures respond to the "unexplained disorder" invading their cold blood, and causing them to direct their sight "in far adventurous design / On footholds past the timber line,"

> It looked as if the destination
> Of all life of the stock marine,
> Was doomed to be, through paths unseen,
> The most profound obliteration. (1.169)

The question of what Darwin calls "racial life and death"[59] thrown like predestination "heavily upon the piscine soul" threatens the survival of the species and arouses the desire to strike back.

Justification for the fear of racial extinction is discovered and announced by the amphibious turtle who comes upon "the Great Consult" on earth (1.174). This gathering is convoked by a "female anthropoidal ape," who, through observing the penalty dealt by Fate on the murderer of her young, has "sniffed the raw material of the moral law" (1.175),[60] and seeks just and reasonable revenge, an "eye for an eye." Her message to "the prodigious Parliament" (1.174), which recalls the address of Milton's Satan to the fallen angels (*Paradise Lost*, 1.625–6) no less than the polemics of twentieth-century political leaders, draws upon all the traditional techniques of pulpit oratory.

But rather than urge her followers to reason and right conduct, the ape exhorts them to spend "in one grand consummating blow / Of death against the common foe, / Your strength to a triumphant end" (1.180). She binds them by a series of repressive or negative commandments, the "thou shalt not's" for which Pratt had little use (MS 1:3), to the ascetical practices of fasting, abstinence, and self-denial, or, in this natural context, to a system of wartime rationing so that they may be better prepared for the attack.

The muster of the land forces shows the full effect of "the persuasion of her tongue" (1.181). The ape's contagious "rage and hate" are echoed in the "gutturals blent with blasphemous umlauts," in the "earth-shattering roars," and in the screams of the birds (1.182). But it is upon the hungry carnivores that "the patriotic call / Falls with the greatest sacrifice," so that they are driven to prey on each other (1.183). Once on the "Isthmian battleground," their "mighty myrmidonian roar" and their "tocsin cry antiphonal" (1.184) are silenced. They are no less obedient than Satan's armies (*Paradise Lost*, 1.530 ff), or the crews in *Behind the Log* (2.170–1):

> The hordes were disciplined to order,
> Divided into army corps,
> Brigades, battalions and platoons;
> ...
> And regimented into shape
> By the anthropoidal ape
> Who, by her rousing martial speeches,
> Kept up to fever heat their zeal
> For the imperilled commonweal. (1.184)

115 "Ghosts of the Apocalypse"

Through the ape, the one creature in the poem endowed with speech and a measure of reason, Pratt examines the power of rhetoric to rouse to a destructive fury, or to subdue and bind to discipline and order.

The unforseen appearance of Tyrannosaurus Rex leads almost to a panic among the land forces. A throwback to an earlier geological age, a historically outdated despot or the beast or tyrant of the apocalypse (*PE* 12), he owes his advent to an unpredictable eruption of the volcano Jurania, and to the patriotic zeal of his foster-mother, who, inspired by the ape, has urged upon him "the chewing self-imposed, of cud" and "the fasting from all flesh and blood" (1.187). The evidence of his blind instinctive power convinces the ape, at first, that "the national cause" is lost, but regaining her composure she quickly gives the sign for battle,[61] thus directing Tyrannosaurus's energies towards the destruction of her enemy (1.189).

As the apocalyptic conflict (*PE* 133) between the land and sea forces begins (Rev 12; 1.189), the dawn is "blood-red" (Rev 12). The "wise" strategy of the ape and the repressive discipline she has imposed on her troops have stimulated their desire to kill "to the internal heat / Of a universal conflagration" (1.189; Rev 8, 9). In their blind fury they slaughter close relations[62] such as the walruses. The battle in its larger-than-life proportions (Dan 7; Jer 7:31; Rev 9–11) grows "wild as the tumult of Gehenna" (1.191). As the armies meet, "a thousand tigers of the land" fight "ten thousand tigers of the sea," oblivious of their common origin (1.191). Aggression, greed, racial pride, and the need for self-preservation, slipping free from any bonds of restraint, bring about widespread death and destruction.

Yet, like their human counterparts in Pratt's historical narratives, soldiers on both sides of the fray exhibit signs of the kind of nobility,

> As never, after or before,
> Was known within the files of War.
> Such acts of valour as were done
> Outshone the white flame of the sun;
> Such hopeless sacrificial deeds
> And feats of strength as might belong
> To men or gods, when weaker breeds
> Wrecked their bodies on the strong. (1.195)

Such heroism, rather than being redemptive, however, falls under Pratt's description of "the ironic in its ultimate rigour" (see 111, above).

But the outcome of the feud lies with "the alien Atavist" (1.197), Tyrannosaurus Rex, who allowed himself to be propelled into battle by the ape's manipulation of his "savage hunger" (1.189). It appears, by the terms in which Pratt depicts him, that he is not a "Christ-figure," as Sutherland suggested,[63] but rather the Adversary or the Antichrist (*PE* 133) who is the basis of a false hope for salvation (Dan 7:28, 11:36–45; Rev 12:7). At the height of the battle he fights blindly like the sealers of "The Ice-Floes" (1.60) and the seamen of *Behind the Log* (2.181), not knowing which is "his ally or his foe" (1.196). In the end it is the voice of the sea-god rather than that of the anthropoidal ape that prompts him to look back to his origins (1.198). His attempt to return to the sea is both a sign that he recognizes the common source of life and a death leap. Deprived of what little direction his leadership had provided (1.196–8), the remaining land-creatures turn upon each other:

> And now and then the storm would rise
> To unimaginable cries,
> As though a stubborn racial note,
> Goaded to the bitter-full,
> Had baulked within the cosmic throat. (1.200)

The reverberations of the battle are felt throughout nature (Rev 12:16). Jurania, which fifty years earlier had let loose Tyrannosaurus Rex (1.186), and which echoed the battle-cry of the ape (1.181), erupts once more (1.200–1) in true apocalyptic fashion (Zech 14). The earlier images of battlefield and slaughter are eclipsed by the vision of natural destruction common to the "little apocalypse"[64] of the synoptic Gospels (Mt 24; Mk 13; Lk 21), or to the Book of Revelation (6:12–17):

> And as the minutes passed, a flash, –
> An incandescent fork of blue,
> And now of green would struggle through
> The smothering pall of smoke and ash,
> Until with undulating sheet
> Of multi-coloured flame that beat
> The blank face of the sky apart –
> Just as the last convulsive stroke
> Unthrottled the volcano's heart –
> The storm flood of the lava broke.
> ...
> It poured its fury on the dead;
> Then the inexorable blast,

> Capping the horrors of the night,
> Pursued the living remnants, bled
> To the final pulses with the fight,
> And caught them as they tried to flee
> To the drowning mercies of the sea. (1.201–2)

It appears, at first, as if all the prophecies about the origins of the world and its end have, in Pratt's "dream," found their fulfilment. However, the lone survivor, the female anthropoidal ape, has, like Tyrannosaurus Rex, sniffed a warning scent. But rather than plunge into the ocean depths (1.199), she has chosen to flee to the safety of the mountaintops (Mk 13:14). While recognizing in an indistinct fashion "the incredulities of death" (1.202) for which she has been responsible, she nevertheless cuddles her brood "to withered paps" (Mk 13:17), and assumes the burden of life which Tyrannosaurus rejected (Rev 12:6;14:17):

> She gathered up her residue
> Of will to blot out from her view
> The awful fiction of the night,
> And take upon herself the strain
> Of the descent. (1.203)

Day returns and life, however fragile, persists. In terms of the dream, the ape's survival and "the strain / Of the descent" (1.203) which she takes up make possible the continuance of life, and, in terms of evolution, the appearance of the human race.

Among the questions that Pratt raises through his elevation of the evolutionary theme to a cosmological plane in "The Great Feud" are the Darwinian problems of adaptation and survival. On the literal level of interpretation, all the creatures in the fable, whether of land or sea, fear extinction, and are driven by the same emerging instincts and emotions to ensure the survival of their species.[65] Tyrannosaurus Rex, the tyrant resurrected from the past, who allows himself to be dominated by instinct, "that dark unreason of the mind" (1.199), cannot adapt to a new situation. Only the anthropoidal ape has reached the stage where she can order instinct by a measure of reason. While this ability distinguishes her from other creatures, it is not without its dangers, for it enables her to manipulate them for her own ends.

While few would agree with Sutherland that Pratt in "The Great Feud" is "personal," "introspective," and "relentless" in self-revelation,[66] it is true that, on the psychological level, the great evolutionary battle which Pratt presents in apocalyptic form and imagery finds a parallel in the Freudian struggle between Eros and Thanatos, between the instinct towards life and the instinct towards destruction, or between the ego and the id as it works itself out in the human species.[67] In "The Great Feud" Pratt allows us to see the results of the abuse of power that comes about through an undue reliance on either instinct or reason. The division or lack of psychological balance within the ape suggests that there is inherent in her descendants a flaw in the evolutionary scheme, somewhat analogous to original sin. The survival of the ape and the possibility of "the descent" comes about only when she is able to combine her "reasoning power" with her instinct to preserve life (1.203).

Pratt's studies in eschatology and his knowledge of apocalyptic literature were for him a great "commonplace book" from which he drew, often unconsciously. His application of apocalyptic language and imagery to times and situations apparently far removed from the biblical is significant. By 1926, when he published *Titans*, Pratt observed in national and international circles the fear of racial extinction, the will to dominate, the greed and the inhumanity that he felt could well bring about the equivalent of the apocalypse in his time. He was deeply convinced that the common origin of humankind, whether viewed from a scientific, a psychological, or a religious position, makes war an act of regressive self-destruction. Contemporary human beings, Pratt suggested, need not fear obliteration from on high when they can bring it about on a universal or a cosmic scale through their own misuse of the power of nature or technology. Not all the humour which gives life to "The Great Feud" can obscure that possibility.

Pratt was no mere alarmist. The signs and wonders associated with the apocalypse, as he well knew, do not necessarily announce the end. They can warn of the advent of false Messiahs such as Hitler ("The Baritone," 2.5) and of the Antichrist. But however terrifying it may appear to be, the apocalypse in Pratt's poetry, like the apocalypse in the Bible, is never a total eclipse. It may herald the cataclysmic end of one age, but it still allows for the possibility of a new creation.

Pratt is aware that the apocalypse as a literary form does more than announce the news that the present world, delivered over to the power of evil, is doomed to the wrath of God and to the final catastrophe (*PE* 21). In holding out as consolation the promise of a world to come – in Pauline terms, one that has already been initiated here – a transfigured universe in which the just will find their reward, the apocalypse builds upon the earlier prophetic tradition of the "remnant" which, purified by suffering and spared by God, is to become the cornerstone of a new creation, an instrument to carry on and bring to completion God's saving design *PE* 15). Although at times the prophets refer to "the remnant" in a negative sense to indicate the extent of divine punishment that the people deserve (Amos 3:12; Jer 6:9; 8:33; 24:8), or the fragility and the weakness of those who persevere (Is 16:34; Ezek 6:80), it is later revived by Paul (Rom 11:1–10) as the subject of eschatological hope. Without using the word, Pratt introduces one of the chief prophetic images for "the remnant" in "The Ice-Floes." Blinded by the raging blizzard, and cut off from the *Eagle* through their carelessness, the sealers are "like sheep in a storm" (1.62) without anyone to guide them (Ezek 5:10). The "count of sixty dead" (1.63) is a loss that the community can scarcely sustain. Nevertheless, there are those who survive the night, and who live to tell the story, and the community as a whole is brought together in mourning its lost (1.62–3).

In "The Great Feud" (1.168), that imaginative picture of a "Pleiocene Armageddon," Pratt uses the term "remnant" first in its negative sense to indicate the extent of the devastation wrought by Jurania:

Then the inexorable blast,
Capping the horrors of the night,
Pursued the living remnants, bled
To the final pulses with the fight,
And caught them as they tried to flee
To the drowning mercies of the sea. (1.201–2)

Even so, there is still a remnant left. The "female anthropoidal ape," small and feeble though she is, alone remains to take upon herself "the strain / Of the descent" (1.203), and in terms of the fable to ensure the future of humankind.

Pratt uses the same image in a different context in later poetry. The guests at the apocalyptic dinner in "The Depression Ends" (1.261) are "the remnant" gathered from the ends of the earth, "the blind and the lame," comforted and led into the feast "as a shepherd doth gather his flock" (Jer 31:7–12, 16). The reader can sense, too, that "the Truant" (2.125) who finds in spiritual rather than in material resources the strength to defy absolute power is the generic "remnant" of a humanity that can expect to be under siege until the end of time.

In Pratt's longer and carefully documented narratives, the image of the "remnant," while it does not imply the idea of an earthly Utopia, proves to be no less rich in its connotative value. After the third night of the dreadful storm in *The "Roosevelt" and the "Antinoe"* it seems that the "last remnant of the sky is blown / Out" (1.240), and that all hope of saving the crew of the *Antinoe* is gone. However, because Miller and his men take a risk that is outside the terms of the contract signed earlier by the crew of the *Roosevelt* (1.220),

> the remnant with their clothes
> Sodden and shrunk were, like drowsed children, gathered
> To the cargo hammocks. (1.246)

"Frost-bitten, thinned in blood, gnarled to the bone, / But everyone surviving" (1.247), they are "shepherded in the old way of the sea" (Is 63:11). Many of those who survive the sinking of the *Titanic* do so, too, as a result of the "uncontractual blood" (2.189) of others who freely step aside to make room for them. However, as the *Titanic* takes her "thousand fathoms journey to her grave," the survival of the remnant seems ironically like "the survival of the fittest":

> The swimmers whom the waters did not take
> With their instant death-chill struck out for the wake
> Of the nearer boats, gained on them, hailed
> The steersmen and were saved: the weaker failed ... (1.337)

In *Behind the Log* the allied convoy S.C. 42 off Cape Farewell suffers disastrous losses in its attempt to provide supplies and rescue lives in the Greenland battle, but it does not give up:

> The fourteen sunk and others just afloat,
> The remnant staggered on still north-by-east. (2.182)

Just as in *They Are Returning* (2.142, 144), or in *Dunkirk* (2.118), where the tattered remnant of earlier wars helps to rescue the men from the beaches, the remnant of the convoy, sorry though it appears, is still a source of hope and salvation:

> five
> British destroyers making thirty knots.
> This was the restoration for the hearts
> Of fifty ships – the maimed, the blind, the whole
> ...
> And so the S.C. 42,
> With mutilated but with fashioned columns,
> Covered the lap across the Denmark Strait
> With that same chivalry of knots which meant
> Rescue for hundreds in the Greenland battle. (2.185)

121   "Ghosts of the Apocalypse"

The fighting ships that "the remnant" has attempted to protect remain "miraculously unscathed" (2.185).

It is in these narratives of the 1940s, the war years when Pratt himself seemed tempted to lose hope, that the image of "the remnant" appears to have held most meaning for him. In *Brébeuf and His Brethren*, even more closely than in "The Ice-Floes," he associates the "remnant" with the flock. To save the Indian boys from the heritage of the brutality that Brébeuf sees their parents have learned, he hopes to send them east for education "shepherded by Daniel" (2.68). When the Iroquois menace is at its height the priests fortify their missions, including

> That of St Ignace where a double raid
> That slaughtered hundreds, lifted bodily
> Both town and mission, driving to their last
> Refuge the ragged remnants. (2.98)

As they care for the sick and provide rest for the travellers, asylum for fugitives, shelter for three thousand, and the Bread of Life for body and soul (2.98), the priests take on the likeness of the Good Shepherd (Is 40:11; Jer 23:3–5; Ezek 34:10–16, 23–31; Jn 10:11–18, 27–9). Even after the final attack and the martyrdom of Brébeuf and Lalemant, "Ragueneau, the Shepherd" looks on "a battered fold" (2.109). His is the task not only of recording the tale of the mission to the end, but also ironically of setting fire to Sainte Marie and leading the survivors to the island of St Joseph:

> But even from there was the old tale retold –
> Of hunger and the search for roots and acorns;
> Of cold and persecution unto death
> By the Iroquois; of Jesuit will and courage
> As the shepherd-priest with Chaumonot led back
> The remnant of a nation to Quebec. (2.109)

Had Pratt concluded his retelling of the saga here, the bloodshed and the destruction which mark the end of the Jesuit mission would have made it a tale of futile and sorry defeat. It is the living remnant of the faith, rekindled by the rediscovery of the past, that he believes to be the heritage of the twentieth century, and that alone can survive all the physical and material harm that human beings are able to do to each other.

No matter how total the eclipse or how precarious the state of civilization may seem, Pratt never leaves his readers without hope for recovery – but neither does he absolve them of responsibility for the human condition. Through the prophetic and apocalyptic image of the remnant, which he usually employs in its more positive sense, Pratt suggests that the salvation of many can be brought about through the perseverance, unselfishness, and fidelity of a few. The remnant can be one source of hope for besieged humankind, but Pratt suggests that unless the principles that direct or bind it together are more than the purely human will to survive, we will never again find the courage and the invincible hope to transcend our personal suffering and to cry,

> Faced with the sight of an entire
> Continent afire,
> We dare in this last phase of the eclipse
> To place the morning trumpets to our lips.
>
> (*They Are Returning*, 2.142)

4 "A Tendency to ... Fatalism Tempered with Humanity"

DETERMINISM AND FATE

To this point in our exploration, we have paid little attention to the part played by determinism and fate in Pratt's poetry. These forces cannot without distortion be separated from the totality of his eschatological vision, or from the apocalyptic language and imagery in which he expresses it most frequently. In the course of an interview with Ronald Hambleton which was broadcast over CBC Radio on 22 January 1955, Pratt remarked that, although he did not consider his work to be "of the same order as the *Apocalypse*," it was true that his earliest years had formed in him "a tendency to (perhaps you might call it) fatalism, tempered with humanity." He was, he continued, "tempted to believe at times very strongly in fate" (*PLP* 43). He held that this predisposition was reinforced by his university education, which had provided him with "a tremendous dose of Hardy in his prose and novels,"[1] in addition to "a cargo" of deterministic philosophy (*PLP* 44).

In this interview Pratt does not suggest that belief in either determinism or fate is inconsistent with belief in God,[2] or that it negates the fundamental freedom of the will, but he does indicate the source of a dramatic tension that is implicit throughout his poetry:

"God did not ordain tragedy, but permitted it." ... We were brought up in the belief of the goodness of God and yet we had to reconcile tragedy with it. We were always under that shadow. (*PLP* 44)

Pratt's preoccupation with determinism and with fate may be seen in his work as early as "The Demonology of the Synoptics." There, he traces in various ancient and primitive cultures the development of belief in evil spirits and in their power to take possession of human beings. He contrasts the elaborate rites of exorcism which were drawn up in the effort to liberate the victims from their fate with the simple yet authoritative word of Jesus, which, in response to an act of faith, sets the sufferer free (DS 12, 20).

In *Pauline Eschatology* Pratt comments on the rise of the mystery cults all the way from the East to Rome with their outstanding goal of "deliverance from the rule of the archons – an immortality freed from the trammels of Fate" (PE 169–70). He sees in the widespread practice of mysticism during the lifetime of Paul a quest for "the Salvation or the Redemption of the individual from the burdens of this life, whether these took the form of a belief in a ruthless Destiny, or in the hostile operations of demons within the body causing pain, disease and death" (PE 185–6).

In "Clay," which Pratt soon realized was "a deadly thing to read now," he claimed to have unburdened himself of "all the philosophic cargo" he had amassed at college (EL 1, 3). It seems, from the sheer weight that the drama is made to bear, that he did just that. In its lengthy speeches, which are more often monologues than integral parts of a dialogue, it soon becomes evident that once the role of God in the government of the world has been reduced to "the gambler's leaded throw" (2.320), and that of the man who claimed to be his son to the vain sacrifice of a deluded Galilean (2.335), there is no power to transcend the natural forces operating within the universe to which the human being is a helpless prey.

These forces find their expression, first of all, in the moral and psychological determinism from which humanity, without grace, seems unable to free itself. Julian sees the actions of his contemporaries in line with those of

> Cain's ruthless hand still clenched in bloody thrust
> Against a brother; Saul's dark javelin poised
> In silhouette against a curtain fold;
> The furtive bend of Borgia over a vial;
> Attila's sword and heel of Tamerlaine –
> All governed by this little vagus here [the heart]. (2.319)

Thus he is forced to demand,

> What wayward laws! Whose codes? Whose fond caprice?
> Where triumphs, gains, fulfilments follow sharp

Upon the heels of loss, and these again
Pursued by strivings unachieved. (2.320)

Although Julian does not deny, at this point, the freedom of the will, he does hold it up to question. In the light of the history of the human race, hope of moral progress seems to rest on no sure foundation. It seems that there is little to choose between this theory and Calvin's teaching of "double predestination" or, pushed to its furthest limits, "the horrible decree" of reprobation.[3] Stoicism seems to be the noblest response to the exigencies of life.

With no assurance of the existence of a personal God whose intelligent and loving providence both inheres in and transcends all of creation, humanity is left to strive alone against the determinism of a natural world from which it has become alienated:

The North wind calls the waters and they rise;
The East wind thunders and the deeps are stirred;
They know no other voice – no mastery
Save that of wind, and man's uplifted hands,
Clutching in frenzy at the spray, sink down
As helpless as his cries, and there is found
No eye to pity and no will to save. (2.324)

Even the obvious beauty in nature which Julian cannot honestly deny fails to provide a balance for its harshness and its cruelty. Julian, like Schopenhauer, sees nature in all its aspects caught up in an endless and meaningless struggle for existence in which all is tension, stress, and conflict. In a Darwinian universe in which only the strongest can survive,

Earth's wastes are full
Of miry swamps and quicksands. Compensates
The flower, rare and lovely though it be,
For the death-suctions of the stretching void?
It lessens not; it only swells the sum
Of terrors. (2.340)[4]

As if the burden of moral and natural determinism were not in itself more than enough to bear, the Julian of "Clay" envisions history repeating itself in endless cycles (see 82, above) to which the individual must submit passively or become another Sisyphus:

And must life's journey by some mocking fate
Just end where it began, where men, their eyes

> Blindfolded, every slip mistake for gain?
> Sterile progression! where each life repeats
> The racial circuit, and finds unrepealed
> The acrid law by which its parent died.
> Each loss, they say, is countered by its gain;
> The steep ascent repays the mountaineer
> In healthy pulse-beat, when the blue clear air
> Wipes from his brow the sweat, and the high peaks
> Summon his soul. Vain reason of the winds!
> The height is but the instrument of the fall;
> Each loss a gain, each gain a loss.[5] (2.334)

It is on a wheel that moves in just such cycles that Albert Schweitzer sees "the historical Jesus" crushed.[6]

Pratt never places Julian in a position where the reader feels that he is deprived of the use of his free will. If the hero could find some personal consolation in the memory of his child (2.348–9), or even commit himself to some meaningful course of action, he might entertain hope of redemption from the prison of "this baffling life" (2.349). But it is easier to find an excuse by professing belief in biological determinism:

> But no – the tides are set.
> Out there upon the shore today they move,
> With fixity of bounds as yesterday.
> And so within the veins the lines are drawn
> As hard, as fast, and hidden processes
> In cell and tissue play their destined part.
> This organism dies; its functions called
> By divers names as goodness, duty, right –
> These fail; the other lives because to it
> Was added marrow. Bring then sackcloth – ash. (2.349–50)

Not even the renewed life and beauty of the springtime can provide Julian with any surer grounds for hope (2.353). There is, in his case, no apocalypse or revelation (see 24, above), not even a momentary one of a higher order – merely a vague intuition, a "knocking in the clay" (2.355), like the rattling of the bones in the vision of Ezekiel (37:7), but without the certitude of promise that is the prophet's reward (37:12–14). While this natural "intimation of immortality" is preferable to utter hopelessness, it is, in terms of the poem, a feeble counterweight to the mass of deterministic theory, which, as it is presented, is simply too great to be convincing.

If by the time that he had reached the conclusion of "Clay" Pratt had purged himself intellectually from the overdose of determinism that he felt he had received, he does not seem to have succeeded as well emotionally or imaginatively. Its shadow, in one form or another, broods over most of the published poetry from *The Witches' Brew* to *Towards the Last Spike*. It appears in the burden of hereditary guilt borne by the suffering woman in *The Iron Door*, the Darwinian struggle for the survival of the fittest in "The Ice-Floes" or "The Great Feud," and in the inescapable reality of death which intrudes into the illusory world of *The "Titanic"*. The cyclical patterns and images of history in "From Stone to Steel" and "Cycles," though not wholly new to him (see 82, above), were probably reinforced by the poetic vision of Spengler (see MS 68:6.3). Whether it is present in the alien face of nature in *The "Roosevelt" and the "Antinoe"*, or in the holistic universe of *Towards the Last Spike*, determinism constitutes an important ingredient in the ironic tension inherent in Pratt's work, and remains a question with which both poet and reader must contend.

Fate is another matter, and Pratt is as careful to distinguish his understanding of it from determinism as he is to associate it with irony:

No, [fate] is different [from determinism]. I mean the convergence of the twain – after the fashion of Thomas Hardy – where two unrelated events or circumstances lead like converging lines to one end. Often there is the convergence of the manifold: things we lightly call coincidences ... Irony is connected with fate – and cannot be extricated from it. My father, you see, often could not go directly to break the news of a death at sea. Sometimes he had to combine this heavy task with his ordinary pastoral visit. This is the purest irony. (EL 1, 3)

The interplay of determinism and fate appears in Pratt's poetry as early as *Rachel*. First of all, nature plays a major role in the fortunes of a small fishing village. Then, determinism in its biological sense is reflected in the similarity, not only in appearance (1.34) but also in character and temperament, between the young Harry Lee and his father (1.21–2, 25–6) – a similarity which predisposes them to become victims of fate, and which leads to death for both.

In *Rachel*, as in many of Pratt's later poems, life assumes the proportions of a battle against the elements. The sea's "fateful summons" once heralded the untimely death of Rachel's father (1.29) just as it later marks the loss of her husband, a man

> Inured to rigorous blasts, scornful of fear
> And Death's white hazards in the sweeping waves.

> Where other men more ripe in age, more tamed
> By adverse shocks to parley with the winds,
> Tempered with caution and reluctant mood
> The seasoning of adventure, Lee would weigh
> His anchor, and with canvas proudly spread
> Before a threatening storm would gaily tempt
> The fortunes of a voyage. (1.21)

While Henry Lee is depicted as a good man, there is in his foolhardy tempting of fate a suggestion of hubris (see 73, above). The unpredictable sea remains master after all:

>   The tossing sea
> Strange bargains made. At times with lavish hand
> It opened up its treasures, then withheld,
> And then the ship, the master and the crew
> It gathered to itself. (1.22)

Lee's attitude is complemented by the romantic vision of his son, Harry. The boy's imagination has been fed by the "high recital of heroic deeds / Wrought out upon the Ocean's troubled face" (1.26):

>   everywhere the sea appeared to him
> The sanctuary of faith and sacrifice;
> The waters were its organ-notes that swelled
> With pomp of peal, and died with murmurous sound. (1.28)

Unlike her husband or her son, Rachel senses that the sea is neither a wild but playful animal nor a hallowed cathedral. Taught by experience, she alone

> Was fearful of its fury, of its peace
> Distrustful. Never did it speak, but sounds
> Of peril smote her ear, and in its smile
> There lurked a hidden gloom. (1.29)

She finds no other way to respond but by passive submission.

When her son's first voyage to the Grand Banks brings insufficient profit "to meet the needs / Of coming winter," he is tempted by the opportunity offered by the unseasonal and coincidental arrival of the *Swallow* "to swell / The summer earnings, and fulfil a dream / Till now unrealized of worlds unseen" (1.31).

129   "Fatalism Tempered with Humanity"

The chance that brings the *Swallow*, however, also brings the unusual calm at sea followed by the ground-swell, "the gusts of rain," the scurrying fog, and the dread north-easterly wind (1.32–3). Rachel is even more powerless than she was in the past while nursing her boy through nearly fatal childhood illnesses:

> Nor was left
> The mother's ancient right, inalienable,
> To challenge death within the last great hour,
> And from his hands to wrest the life she loved. (1.34–5)

She receives the news of the loss of the *Swallow* from the minister whose "high duty" it was, like John Pratt (see 127, above), "to comfort stricken ones," and "to break the news" (1.36).

Although the source of Rachel's grief is never concealed from the reader, her reaction to the death of her son, as Pratt depicts it, is even more melodramatic than the posturing of Julian in "Clay" (2.305–7). After her flight, Rachel is discovered wandering "in solitary places" (1.36) like one possessed (Mt 12:43; DS 14, 36). She is delivered from the effects of determinism and fate by death alone.

Pratt handles the relationship between determinism and fate with greater ease in the form of a parable in "The Great Feud." The weight of determinism which the sea-creatures must bear awakens in them not only the desire to retaliate against their enemies on land, but also the fear that the opportunity to do so will never come. The occasion is provided by Nature, that "quirky dame" who interferes also in "The Fable of the Goats" (2.18):

> But by some quirk that Nature flings
> Into the settled scheme of things –
> That old beldame, she gets so grumpy,
> No mortal vision may foretell
> Her antics, when her nerves are jumpy –
> It happened that she broke the spell
> By a freak shifting of the odds
> Within the sea-lap of the gods. (1.171)

Suddenly the atmosphere changes from gloom and depression to expectancy, almost hope:

> From igneous fissures in the ground
> Blue wisps of smoke with eerie sound
> Curled on the air to indicate

That some elaborate escapade
Was on the point of being played
By the royal clowns of Fate. (1.172)

It is over this "cone of sand" or Jurania (1.173), which becomes associated throughout the work with the unpredictability of nature, that the amphibious turtle climbs to lay her eggs, only to be distracted by the sight of the gathering in the amphitheatre below (1.173–4). Later, she becomes the messenger of fate, carrying back to the sea-creatures the news of "The Great Feud" (1.181). Once the strategy for the battle has been mapped out by the ape (1.176–80), and ratified by a "volleying symphonic roar" on the part of the "Great Consult" (1.181), the eventual "sultriness of peace" that follows is

Shaken only when a cloud
Of thick Juranian vapour, thrown
In a dark spiral, burst with loud
Echoes, like laughter from the cone. (1.181)

Nature's apparent mocking of the "human" instinct for order and ritual recalls the passage in *The "Roosevelt" and the "Antinoe"* that follows the reading of the funeral service. There, what is heard from nature is

a wild antiphonal
Of shriek and whistle from the shrouds ...
Blending with thuds as though some throat had laughed
In thunder down the ventilator shaft. (1.236)

The narrator of "The Great Feud" intrudes into his tale to emphasize the way in which the "settled scheme of things" (1.171) and the best-laid plans of the ape are disrupted by the unexpected interference of fate:

I claim
That by a wanton twist of Fate,
(To which I am by Hera sworn)
A creature of this sounding name,
Although three million years too late,
Stood on that peak this awful morn. (1.185–6)

Jurania, the instrument of fate, had preserved in her pitch the egg of a dinosaur laid long before mammals appeared on earth,

131   "Fatalism Tempered with Humanity"

> Until just fifty years ago,
> When the volcano underwent
> Her seismal periodic throe,
> The egg came bouncing through a rent. (1.186)

Even after the dinosaur's appearance, which merely confuses the issue of the battle in the "Juranian valley," fate continues to intervene:

> Reversals with the strangest luck,
> Unknown to contests in the sea,
> Took place where bulk and energy
> Matched themselves with skill and pluck. (1.195)

As Tyrannosaurus leaps to his death, "the leash of discipline" is untied (1.199):

> And now and then the storm would rise
> To unimaginable cries,
> As though a stubborn racial note,
> Goaded to the bitter-full,
> Had baulked within the cosmic throat.
> And yet the scale, for all this woe,
> Had still a higher note to go. (1.200)

"In 'The Great Feud' nature gives the finishing blow to the battle in the action of Jurania, the volcano," Pratt later remarked.[7] The ape's nascent ability to observe and interpret nature teaches her to flee what is beyond her control, and it prevents her from becoming a passive victim of fate (1.202).

The ambiguity that Pratt finds in nature is analogous to the ambiguity that he finds in humanity. The unpredictability of winds and waves and volcanoes, which Pratt does associate at times with fate, is not necessarily the manifestation of a malignant power. The "quirkiness" of nature that effects the outcome of poems such as "The Fable of the Goats" (2.18), "The Great Feud" (1.171–2), *Dunkirk* (2.124), and *Towards the Last Spike* (2.228–30) suggests that Pratt often sees in nature something of a lesser "truant," unreliable perhaps, but not totally determined by purely mechanical laws, or by Huxley's "cosmic process."[8] Like other aspects of nature, the tides that both kill and save operate

> Not with that dull, unsinewed tread of waters
> Held under bond to move

Around unpeopled shores –
Moon-driven through a timeless circuit
Of invasion and retreat;
But with a lusty stroke of life
Pounding at stubborn gates,
That they might run
Within the sluices of men's hearts. ("Newfoundland," 1.99)

The companion-piece to "The Great Feud" in Pratt's *Titans* is the satiric fable "The Cachalot." Well before the introduction of the human element in the final section of the narrative there is evidence of both determinism and fate at play in the world of nature. The cachalot can boast of as noble a lineage as can Brébeuf on the human level (1.150–1, 2.49), and his forbears are associated with the great explorers, navigators, and conquerors of human history (1.150). His "breed" is a determining factor in his ability "to win in all hostilities" and it leads him, still in his youth, to "the mastery of the herd" (1.151). In addition, nature has generously endowed him, and time has prepared him, for his entrance at the historically appropriate moment:

Another ninety moons and Time
Had cast a marvel from his hand,
Unmatched on either sea or land –
A sperm whale in the pitch of prime. (1.151)

If the full meaning of much of Pratt's poetry is to be grasped, and if the richness of its irony is to be appreciated, the reader must remember to take into account the narrative point of view. While Pratt frequently enjoys the liberty of the omniscient narrator, he is even more likely to combine this position with a shifting point of view, one in which he presents an incident or an object as observed by more than one person whose vision is limited by lack of full knowledge or by prejudice. Since he is able to circumnavigate his subject with the creative energy and the agility that he bestowed on his own Van Horne (2.231–2), he deserves more attention than he often receives.[9]

As omniscient narrator, Pratt first presents the cachalot in his historical or genealogical perspective. Then, moving in for a closer examination, he conducts the reader on a fanciful tour through the mammal's interior (1.152) that reveals the source of his natural power in workings every bit as wonderful as those of the *Titanic* (1.303–4). Next, he shifts the focus of attention to details of the exterior which foreshadow the outcome of the poem:

> Upon his coat of toughest rubber
> A dozen cicatrices showed
> The place as many barbs were stowed,
> Twisted and buried in his blubber,
> The brute reminder of the hours
> Of combat when the irate whale
> Unlimbered all his massive powers
> Of head-ram and of caudal flail,
> Littering the waters with the chips
> Of whale-boats and vainglorious ships. (1.153)

Any human being who would knowingly challenge such titanic powers must be foolhardy indeed.

The narrator's imagination then plumbs the depths of the sea where it finds in a "cave of murk and slime" (1.153) the kraken, a form of life far removed on the evolutionary scale from the mammalian. Sensing the approach of the cachalot, an enemy against which it is ill-equipped by nature to defend itself,

> The kraken felt that as the flow
> Beat on his lair with plangent power,
> It was the challenge of his foe,
> The prelude to a fatal hour.... (1.154)

Their battle takes on cosmic or mythological proportions. John Sutherland's comments upon the kraken and the cachalot as "differing aspects of the same principle of power – whether that principle be embodied in nature, or in the conscious or subconscious mind,"[10] are valid up to the point where he explores the "tentacles" of the theme in its relationship to Byron's "The Prisoner of Chillon" and applies them to specific details of Pratt's biography.[11]

In the grisly scene of slaughter in which the cachalot disposes of the kraken, little more effort is required of him than he had expended on "vainglorious ships" (1.153) in the past. Then the reader sees him with his task completed as "Maharajah of the seas / From Rio to the Celebes." At the height of his powers the cachalot, at home in his natural element, an amoral creature like the fish in *The Witches' Brew* (1.140; 111–12, above), is described in lyric terms which in their suggestion of an almost supernatural beauty can nearly hypnotize the reader into forgetting the previous violence:

> Over his back the running seas
> Cascaded, while the morning sun

> Rising in gold and beryl, spun
> Over the cachalot's streaming gloss,
> And from the foam, a fiery floss
> Of multitudinous fashionings,
> And dipping downward from the blue,
> The sea-gulls from Comoro flew,
> And brushed him with their silver wings. (1.156)

Having claimed his right to the supremacy of the deep by destroying the kraken, the cachalot falls asleep "upon the swell" (1.156), and thus resting in "the pride of his power" (Ezek 20:6) ironically makes himself vulnerable, at the dramatic moment, to the hubris of "the master whaler," Martin Taylor. If, as Sutherland suggested, the kraken and the cachalot may be seen as "differing aspects of the same principle of power" (see 133, above), so too may the cachalot and Martin Taylor, who mirror each other in pride.

Taylor does not pursue the whale as a symbol of evil with the monomaniacal fury of a Captain Ahab. He, too, is "flushed with triumph" (1.156) after a bountiful catch, and at first sees in the whale only a chance to "try his final luck" (1.157). Through his error in underestimating the power of the creature, the crew of the *Albatross* find themselves pitted against a Titan of nature. As the men look on, the beauty of the cachalot vanishes and he emerges from the cloud of mist "like a rock" (1.158), or like the iceberg of *The "Titanic"* (1.304–5, 338), with his "Terror of head and hump and brawn, / Silent and sinister and grey" (1.161).

For a while it seems that the cachalot with his tremendous energy has met in the *Albatross* and its crew his match, if not his nemesis. He cannot ignore them, nor can he shake them off,

> With that same large and sovereign scoff,
> That high redundancy of ease
> With which he smote his enemies. (1.162)

By nightfall he is clearly irked:

> 'Twas time to end this vanity –
> Hauling a puny bunch of men,
> With boat and cross-boards out to sea. (1.162)

As the cachalot summons his remaining strength and speed to reverse the previous luck of the crew (1.163), Taylor deals him a fatal blow to the heart:

> The odds had up to this been equal –
> Whale and wind and sea with whaler –
> But, for the sperm, the fighting sequel
> Grew darker with that thrust of Taylor.
> ... the flood
> That issued from this fiery rent,
> Broaching the arterial tide,
> Had left a ragged worm of pain
> Which crawled like treason to his brain –
> The worm of a Titan's broken pride! (1.163–4)

In the lines that follow there can be little doubt that Pratt intends to compare the death-throes of the whale and the passion of Christ in which divine power and glory appear to be eclipsed by human suffering (see Mk 15:1, 15–20, 24; Mt 27:2, 26–31, 35). It is necessary, however, for the reader to remain aware that the narrator can assume various points of view within the poem if he or she is not to misunderstand the implications of this passage as Sutherland did.[12] What Pratt gives us here is the Titan's projected image of himself:

> Was he – with a toothless Bowhead's fate[13]
> Slain by a thing called a second mate –
> To come in tow to the whaler's side?
> Be lashed like a Helot to the bitts
> While, from the cutting stage, the spade
> Of a harpooner cut deep slits
> Into his head and neck, and flayed
> Him to the bone; while jesters spat
> Upon his carcass, jeered and wrangled
> About his weight, the price his fat
> Would bring. (1.164)

Just as the earlier picture of the cachalot's beauty leads the reader to forget its violence, and to become lost in admiration, so this vision seduces the reader into a sense of wonder that a creature so magnificent should be brought so low. But this image of the greatest humiliation conceivable to human beings is one that the Titan rejects for himself. "The worm of a Titan's broken pride" (1.164) drives him to gather together the remaining threads of life for the final blow. The ironical "double stroke of death" dealt also to the troop ship in "The Submarine" (see 105, above) echoes "the hideous rupture of a stroke / From the forehead of the bull" that killed the kraken (1.155).

Throughout "The Cachalot" the basic iambic tetrameter line with the variation of couplets and of loosely interlocking rhyme scheme lends itself to a remarkable flexibility of timing, mood, and tone, and to the build-up and release of tension.[14] After passages of exuberant humour Pratt allows the narrative to rise to an exciting climax, then uses the same techniques of rhythm and rhyme to bring it to a remarkably effective conclusion, an exhibition of craftsmanship only slightly more polished than that with which he ended "The Ice-Floes" (1.62–3). The last lines in their masterful pacing and dramatic sequence of events might be compared for effect with the more detailed pattern of imagery at the close of Duncan Campbell Scott's "The Piper of Arll."[15]

> Then, like a royal retinue,
> The slow processional of crew,
> Of inundated hull, of mast,
> Halliard and shroud and trestle-cheek,
> Of yard and topsail to the last
> Dank flutter of the ensign as a wave
> Closed in upon the skysail peak,
> Followed the Monarch to his grave. (1.165)

Pratt had undoubtedly read Herman Melville's *Moby-Dick*,[16] Frank Bullen's *The Cruise of the "Cachalot"*, and Roy Campbell's *The Flaming Terrapin*,[17] before writing his poem. This fact makes as little difference to its interpretation as does the question of whether or not he had read Coleridge's *The Ancient Mariner*. "The Cachalot" is distinctly Pratt's own creation, and one in which the reader senses that he took delight. What is clear is that Pratt was well acquainted with both the prophecy of Isaiah (27:1) and the books of Jonah and Job, which present a vivid and, at times, playful picture of Leviathan. In the latter work the sea-monster is described through a series of rhetorical questions which, in the cumulative effect of their irony, remind Job that he is a creature, not the Creator, and that since he cannot understand the source of the power and the might of the physical inhabitants of the universe, he is ill equipped to penetrate the metaphysical dimensions of suffering and death. This description reduces both Job and the burden that he carries to proportionate size.

The cachalot, which from time to time throughout the poem bears an uncanny resemblance to the skipper of the *Albatross*, may well be, as E.K. Brown has suggested, a symbol of "the primitive overpowering the intellectual," or of "the natural crushing the artificial."[18] There is a sense, however, that before these inferences may be drawn the cachalot symbolizes and objectifies the hubris that leads Martin Taylor to abandon the caution that his long experience has shown to be necessary if he would not submit to the deterministic forces at work in the universe, or become a victim of chance or fate. Through hubris humanity becomes a victim rather than the master of the power that it longs to have at its command. The cachalot, no less than the kraken, is one of Pratt's apocalyptic beasts, a magnificent but dangerous repository of the power that so fascinated him. It is a "Monarch" (1.165) of nature, but none the less "a king over all the children of pride" (Job 41:34).

The most fully orchestrated expression of Pratt's vision of the ironic relationship between fate and hubris is to be found in *The "Titanic"*. Pratt remarked that if he had not been "predisposed towards fate already, the loss of the *Titanic* would have created a belief" (PLP 45). The impact of Marconi's reception of the first transatlantic wireless message on Signal Hill in St John's, on 12 December 1901, translated by newspaper headlines as "NO MORE LOSSES AT SEA," was juxtaposed in his memory and imagination with the sinking of the *Titanic* eleven years later just south of the spot where scientists received the telegraph message (EL 2, 3; 1.314–15). The whole tragedy, Pratt concluded, was pure irony – not merely in Hardy's sense of "The Convergence of the Twain,"[19] but also in his own sense of "the convergence of the manifold" (see 35, above).

The fascination that the theme held for Pratt is well expressed in a letter he wrote to W.A. Deacon while he was still in the early stages of composition:

I am simply swept away by the theme as I was in *The "Roosevelt"* only to a vaster extent. It is so much more complex, involves so many more philosophic, economic, and artistic issues that I don't want to hurry it too much ... *The "Roosevelt"* was a rescue of outright heroism, simple in its texture. The diapasons are all the time going in an event like that. But the alternations in *The "Titanic"*, the crescendos of cries and fears approaching panic, the terrible silences and innuendos, the tensions, the inward, voiceless struggles that issued in decisions, the stark outline of the iceberg remaining immovable while the ship takes her plunge, grim, alone, and triumphant – well, the subject is unique and will tax every resource for the treatment.[20]

As Pratt presents the *Titanic* on the day of her launching, she was a product of "mind and will / In open test with time and steel," but still "a shell of what was yet to be" (1.302). The "Primate of the Lines" from the day of her christening,[21]

> her proud claim
> On size – to be the first to reach the sea –
> Was vindicated, for whatever fears
> Stalked with her down the tallow of the slips
> Were smothered under by the harbour cheers,
> By flags strung to halyards of the ships. (1.303)

Completed, the *Titanic*, a gigantic machine, is described in terms proper to a huge mammal (see 89–90, above), with

> Levers and telegraphs and valves within
> Her intercostal spaces ready to start
> The power pulsing through her lungs and heart. (1.303)

Already the seeds of false faith, "faith in a material structure" (*PLP* 47), or faith in the accomplishments of science, are sown:

> An ocean lifeboat in herself – so ran
> The architectural comment on her plan.
> No wave could sweep those upper decks – unthinkable!
> No storm could hurt that hull – the papers said so.
> The perfect ship at last – the first unsinkable,
> Proved in advance – had not the folders read so? (1.303)

The "belief" that the *Titanic* can survive any collision with an iceberg, a rock, or a passing ship is pushed to the verge of credulity with the introduction of the wireless, the symbol of human pride in the "conquest over nature,"[22] a pride that is to betray humanity into the hands of fate (see 73–4, above). In the light of this belief, the risk at Lloyd's remains "a record low," and caution may be thrown to the winds (1.304).

While Hardy attributes the formation of his iceberg to "The Immanent Will that stirs and urges everything," and lays the responsibility for its collision with the *Titanic* on "the Spinner of the Years,"[23] Pratt's sense of causality is more complex. His iceberg, "calved from a glacier near Godhaven coast" (1.304), is clearly the offspring of nature. Moreover, it is in itself a symbol of "the convergence of the manifold," the centre of an archipelago, surrounded by "a host of white flotillas" and "fragments from a Behring floe." Its motion is "casual and indeterminate," and as blind as the progress of the *Titanic* is to become. Its passage through the "polar waste" is marked by "no smoke of steamships," and by "no sounds except the grind / Of ice, the cry of curlews and the lore / Of winds from mesas of eternal snow" (1.304).

In sharp contrast to chronological time, carefully accounted for in the poem by the marking off of the years, days, hours, and minutes which go into the building of the *Titanic* and her race for supremacy, is "glacial time," which combined with pressure in *Towards the Last Spike* to create the mesozoic rock (2.241–2). Here it has stratified the berg to "the consistency of flint," effecting at first the beauty and grace associated with the images of the cathedrals of Notre Dame and Rouen in *Brébeuf and His Brethren* (2.47–8; 54–5).[24] In this case such beauty is as illusory as that of "The Sea Cathedral" (1.167), "The Mirage" (1.282), or even that of the *Titanic* (1.325–28). Sun and weather soon reveal the features of another of Pratt's monsters of the apocalypse:

>   nothing but the brute
> And paleolithic outline of a face
> Fronted the transatlantic shipping route.
> A sloping spur that tapered to a claw
> And lying twenty feet below had made
> It lurch and shamble like a plantigrade. (1.305)[25]

Pratt sees the *Titanic* as the product of an age which considers itself too enlightened to accept the superstitions traditionally associated with ships and sailing (1.305–6, 312–13), yet which is not sceptical enough to question the "miracles" that science claims to perform. His description of the pleasures provided for the first-class passengers is almost Keatsian in its sensuous details, from the vivid itemization of food in quantities large enough "to feed the population of a town" to the listing of choices for recreation, leisure, and entertainment (1.307–9).

As "science responded to a button press," the smooth ascent of electric lifts, "the brilliancy of mirrors from tungsten chandeliers," the disguises of the Masqueraders' Ball in the glow of "mellow lights from Chinese lanterns," and "the andantino rhythms" of "The Blue Danube" combine to weave a magic spell that banishes all fear and creates

>   the feel
> Of peace from ramparts unassailable,
> Which, added to her seven decks of steel,
> Had constituted the *Titanic* less
> A ship than a Gibraltar under heel.
> And night had placed a lazy lusciousness
> Upon a surfeit of security. (1.308)

The *Titanic* resembles the sleeping cachalot which Pratt also associates with Gibraltar (1.161).[26] Even more ominously, it mirrors the iceberg in its silent and pristine beauty (1.305).

On board this "great machine," which of its very nature seems to call for "laconic speech," and on which it appears that even the judgment stands "in little need / Of reason" (1.309), human responsibility for directing the ship is waived in favour of blind reliance upon her instruments. The *Titanic* then is guided on her course by the refined technology of science which contrasts with, yet is not unrelated to, the impulse governed by "the raw mechanics of its birth" that governed the motion of the iceberg (1.305). When the contest for speed becomes the centre of attention, Pratt reminds the reader of the proportions of the game of chance in which the *Titanic* is a participant, and of "the human enterprise / That took a gamble on her navigation" (1.310).

As the *Titanic* gradually cuts herself off from communication with nature, she becomes more and more the victim of nature. Intrusions of reality in the form of periodic warnings from other ships about the presence of ice-floes in the vicinity are received by the crew with patient tolerance until they threaten to interfere with the concentration necessary in the race, and are cut off altogether.[27] The warning voices heard over the radio form an ironic counterpoint to the conversations and the actions of oblivious passengers which Pratt allows us to hear and see in more intimate scenes – in the comments of three men on deck (1.311–13); in the repartee in the dining saloon (1.313–16), in the love scene behind the deck house (1.317), and in the poker game (1.318–21).

These warm and human scenes on board the ship are set against a cosmic backdrop that reduces such affairs to apparent insignificance:

The sky was moonless but the sea flung back
With greater brilliance half the zodiac.
As clear below as clear above, the Lion
Far on the eastern quarter stalked the Bear:
Polaris off the starboard beam – and there
Upon the port the Dog-star trailed Orion.
Capella was so close, a hand might seize
The sapphire with the silver Pleiades.
And further to the south – a finger span,
Swam Betelguese and red Aldebaran.
Right through from east to west the ocean glassed
The billions of that snowy caravan
Ranging the highway which the Milkmaid passed. (1.316–17)

141   "Fatalism Tempered with Humanity"

The zodiac is traditionally associated with destiny, but Pratt does not refer here to its usual twelve astrological divisions, or to the seven planets, nor does he attribute to the stars any direct control over human life. While this passage is indisputably his own, it is possible that he had in mind Hardy's description of the starlit night in *Far from the Madding Crowd* (9–10), when the mere consciousness of the stars dwarfs the tiny human frame.[28]

Just as the clear sky is mirrored in the smooth sea, the image of the ship is reflected in the iceberg until it is difficult to tell which is the reality and which is the illusion. The irony becomes more complex as Pratt sets off the increasing speed of the ship, and the passage of minutes which leads to the doom of the passengers, against the almost incalculable age of the stars:

> The ocean sinuous, half-past eleven;
> A silence broken only by the seven
> Bells and the look-out calls, the log-book showing
> Knots forty-five within two hours
> ...
> Over the stern zenith and nadir met
> In the wash of the reciprocating set.
> The foam in bevelled mirrors multiplied
> And shattered constellations
> ...
> Under the counter, blending with the spill
> Of stars – the white and blue – the yellow light
> Of Jupiter hung like a daffodil. (1.318)[29]

Pratt then moves his point of view in from the infinite distance of the stars to that of the greatest narrative and dramatic advantage and views the fatal collision of ship and iceberg through the ironic lens of a poker game, a symbol of the contest with luck that the whole voyage represents. Though the sight of the iceberg startles the card players, the blow upon the ship's starboard and the answer of the helm that heels the ship to port appear to be so insignificant that they do not disturb "the sleep of hundreds" (1.323). Those who respond and go up on deck, ignorant of the fact that the electromagnets on the bulkhead doors have failed and that the call for help, postponed until further examination is carried out, cannot be answered by the nearest ship, the *Californian*, become

> satisfied
> That nothing in the shape of wind or tide

Or rock or ice could harm that huge bulk spread
On the Atlantic, and [go] back to bed. (1.323)

Pratt later wrote of *The "Titanic"*:

The ship itself may be taken as a protagonist of the story provided that other factors are taken into account. It is an illustration of beauty, grace, magnitude, and power, but it also possesses a "flaw" imposed upon it by its builders, the ambition of the White Star Line to make the "perfect ship," and to that end she ran at top speed though warned of the danger by other ships. The "flaw" was the belief in her invulnerability. Nature in the existence of an iceberg proved how overweening the hubris was. The iceberg struck at the "Achilles' heel."[30]

Pratt's description of the *Titanic* as a wounded mammal makes more evident its vulnerability and emphasizes the connection between its welfare and that of the human cargo that it carries:

As leaning on her side to ease a pain,
The tilted ship had stopped the captain's breath:
The inconceivable had stabbed his brain,
This thing unfelt – her visceral wound of death? (1.324)

Fearing panic, especially among the seven hundred passengers in steerage, the captain decides to maintain the illusion of safety through a deceptive silence:

No call from bridge, no whistle, no alarm
Was sounded. Have the stewards quietly
Inform the passengers: no vital harm,
Precautions merely for emergency;
Collision? Yes, but nature of the blow
Must not be told: not even the crew must know ... (1.324)

Like the captain, the passengers find the news of the collision and the prospect of mortal danger "inconceivable":

So suave the fool-proof sense of life that fear
Had like the unforeseen become a mere
Illusion – vanquished by the towering height
Of funnels pouring smoke through thirty feet
Of bore; the solid deck planks and the light
From a thousand lamps as on a city street;

> The feel of numbers; the security
> Of wealth; the placid surface of the sea,
> Reflecting on the ship the outwardness
> Of calm and leisure of the passengers. (1.325)

Even those who avail themselves of the lifeboats do so "convinced the order was not justified" (1.326). The flare of the rockets, looking "like a drill / A bit of exhibition play," seems

> more a parody
> Upon the tragic summons of the sea
> Than the real script of unacknowledged fears
> Known to the bridge and to the engineers. (1.326)

Maintaining the illusion of safety is the music of the band, which continues under the captain's orders "right through;/ No intermission" (1.326). Even as the tenth lifeboat goes over the side,

> How easy seemed the step and how secure
> Back to the comfort and the warmth – the lure
> Of sheltered promenade and sun decks starred
> By hanging bulbs, amber and rose and blue,
> The trellis and palms lining an avenue
> With all the vista of a boulevard:
> The mirror of the ceilings with festoon
> Of pennants, flags and streamers – and now through
> The leaded windows of the grand saloon,
> Through parted curtains and the open doors
> Of vestibules, glint of deserted floors
> And tables, and under the sorcery
> Of light excelling their facsimile,
> The periods returning to relume
> The panels of the lounge and smoking-room,
> Holding the mind in its abandonment
> During those sixty seconds of descent. (1.327–8)

Other boats leave less than half full (1.329).

Not all those aboard the *Titanic* succumb to the seductions of false faith, or to the instinct for self-preservation. Off-duty crew members decide freely to "join their mates below / In the grim fight for steam" (1.330). The captain of the Carpathia, "taking chances" to save the *Titanic* (1.324), attempts "to redeem / Errors of brain by hazards of the heart" (1.331). Some passengers, from the young boy to Jacob

Astor and Ida Strauss,[31] are characterized by a "pride" (1.331) which in contrast to the "sin" of hubris is the virtue of *parresia* (Lk 26:13; 1 Cor 1:31; 2 Cor 3:11, Gal 6:14). The Hebrew equivalent of this Greek word is related to freedom, so that it suggests the pride that enables one to stand erect, to have an elevated countenance, to express oneself openly, or "to exhibit self-respect shown by liberty of language and of bearing."[32]

Even as he releases the members of the crew from their duties, Smith stands at the door of the cabin, "with drawn, incredulous face" (1.335). As the last lifeboat vanishes there is no panic on board, no "besieging of the heavens,"

> But on all lips the strange narcotic quiet
> Of an unruffled ocean's innuendo. (1.335)

At this point something in the list of the *Titanic* recalls that of the iceberg after the sun has demolished "the last temple touch of grace" (1.305), but even then,

> In spite of her deformity of line,
> Emergent like a crag out of the sea,
> She had the semblance of stability,
> Moment by moment furnishing no sign,
> So far as visible, of that decline
> Made up of inches crawling into feet.
> Then, with the electric circuit still complete,
> The miracle of day displacing night
> Had worked its fascination to beguile
> Direction of the hours and cheat the sight.
> Inside the recreation rooms the gold
> From Arab lamps shone on the burnished tile.
> What hindered the return to shelter while
> The ship clothed in that irony of light[33]
> Offered her berths and cabins as a fold? (1.335–6)

As the minutes are counted off, and as the angle of the ship increases (1.335–7), Pratt allows the tension in the poem to mount. The "many thousand tons of shifting coal" in the bulkheads (1.329), the failure of the cargo ports to open (1.329), and the refusal of the passengers to respond to the rockets (1.336) are incidents numbered among the multitude that converge to bring about the destruction of the "indestructible." As the passengers remaining aboard crowd to the aft decks to avoid the "creep / Of the water" (1.336), "that last salt tonic which had kept / The valour of the heart alive," the bows of "the immortal seven," are stilled (1.338). Deck and port-hole lights are extinguished, and as the engines tear from their foundations, all cries are silenced, and the liner takes "Her thousand fathoms journey to her grave" (1.338). Meanwhile the Titan of nature remains untouched:

> And out there in the starlight, with no trace
> Upon it of its deed but the last wave
> From the Titanic fretting at its base,
> Silent, composed, ringed by its icy broods,
> The grey shape with the paleolithic face
> Was still the master of the longitudes. (1.338)

Augmenting the irony in *The "Titanic"* which is produced by "the convergence of the manifold," Pratt remarks, is the fact that "not a man on board was willing his own destruction or anyone else's destruction. Their volition was towards the living, but that volition was neutralized by ignorance" (EL, 46). On another occasion Pratt elaborates on the irony inherent in the sea-tragedy:

The loss of the ship was the greatest illustration of the irony of fate in marine history, the irony of circumstance where a human being makes a plan which he thinks is perfect, as in the so-called perfect crime organized by the so-called master-mind but where there is some little loop-hole or weak joint in the armour which he has overlooked or forgotten which causes the catastrophe. It is the irony of coincidence where a number of factors enter, each one taken by itself harmless, but taken in conjunction with all the others fatal, and it all comes down to man's belief in his power to control his own destiny ... The foundering of the Titanic, removed as it were from the bounds of belief, made the disaster the most distorted event in the history of the sea. It was the assumed omniscience of man in the perfection of his scientific plan, set over against Fate or Nature with its millions of factors beyond mortal calculation – it is that clash, ending in human tragedy, which is the essential thing in irony. (MS 9:70.8)

Pratt's sunken *Titanic*, like Hardy's, is an image of the "human vanity / And the Pride of Life that planned her."[34] *The "Titanic"* deserves to be called "apocalyptic" in the broadest sense of the word, but it is no coincidence that its language and imagery reflect Pratt's background in theology and biblical studies less than any of his other long poems. Pratt sees the *Titanic* as the product of a secular society that has become blinded and desensitized by purely materialistic values, one that worships the false gods of size, speed, security, wealth, and comfort. Such a society, as Pratt is convinced, and as history illustrates, contains within itself the seeds of decay, and places itself in the hands of determinism or of fate. Although Pratt's objectivity does not rule out compassion, it is evident that he looks upon the *Titanic* not as a Noah's Ark,[35] but as a Ship of Fools. "There is nothing very exalting about a tragedy like *The 'Titanic,'* a disaster due to stupidity," he remarks (*PLP*, 47).

"THE STOIC ANSWERS"

In his poetry Pratt frequently questions how the human being, a creature endowed with intelligence and free will, should respond to the demands of a universe that seems to be governed largely by the forces of determinism and fate. On several occasions he explores the validity of a stoical approach to the sufferings and the hardships that beset the human race. He first addresses himself to the question in "Clay" (2.322–3), where he has Penrose suggest stoicism to Julian as the least painful way of confronting the destruction of life and property wrought by nature in the form of the storm:

> It is a discipline that men have learned –
> To brace the soul against life's heavier blows. (2.322)

But to have "such eyes / That do not see, such ears that do not hear" (Mk 8:18) strikes Julian as inhuman:

> It is a lesson that before it's learned,
> A man must first unman himself to read.
> Teach him to think without his brain, to walk
> With shoulders paralyzed. It is an art
> Whose subtlety is such as human wit
> May not unravel ... Life moves not
> Upon such strange and jointless steppings. (2.323)

Describing the plight of a woman who is curiously like the Rachel of Pratt's earlier poem,[36] Julian illustrates the fact that stoicism, in such a case, can offer little comfort and no hope.

As one of the possible responses to the inexorability of death, stoicism was later to be exemplified by one of the dream characters in *The Iron Door*. The logical but closed nature of his position is suggested by the tightly controlled stanza in which it is expressed:

147 "Fatalism Tempered with Humanity"

> One who had sought for truth, but found the world
> Outside the soul betray the one within,
> Knew beacon signals but as casual fires,
> And systems dead but for their power to spin,
> Laid deeply to his heart his discipline,
> Looked at the door where all the roadways closed,
> And took it as the clench of evidence,
> That the whole cosmic lie was predisposed,
> Yet faced it with a fine indifference. (1.209)

Although the courage implicit in this attitude may be admirable, it is powerless to effect the opening of the door (1.211–12). There is, however, no indication that the dreamer sees its representative excluded from those who eventually pass through (1.213).

There are critics who claim that passages such as the foregoing are expressive of Pratt's personal philosophy. Paul West writes:

> For Pratt man is doomed but, in accepting doom bravely, can be commensurable with Nature and God (who have no pain nor joy nor love nor hate) ... Man has consciously to undergo what plants and minerals undergo without consciousness ... The only moral drama that attracts [Pratt] is that of enduring until demolition.[37]

This generalization is probably based upon a failure to recognize the irony springing from Pratt's facility in balancing off against each other within a single poem several apparently contradictory points of view.

The question of the stoic response emerges again and with greater frequency in poems written in the period from the beginning of the Second World War to the end of Pratt's poetic career. In *Brébeuf and His Brethren* the hero, after witnessing the Hurons torture a captive Iroquois (2.65–6), revolves in his mind the facets of the Native character (2.67). While he admires the braves for their code of endurance and their "impassivity," it is more than these natural virtues mirrored in Brébeuf that later (2.107) leads the Natives to seek,

>   the source
> Of his strength, the home of his courage that topped the best
> Of their braves and even out-fabled the lore of their legends.

Ragueneau, pondering the decision to abandon Sainte Marie and put it to the torch, weighs the motivation that has sustained the mission and can be confident that such an action will not be taken out of cowardice or lack of perseverance:

> all that torture
> And death could do to the body was done. The Will
> And the Cause in their triumph survived. (2.109)

Taken in their proper context, these lines indicate that it is not merely "stoicism" in Brébeuf that makes him a subject "ideally suited to the heroic vision," as Sandra Djwa contends.[38]

In "The Stoics" (2.131–2), which appeared for the first time in *Queen's Quarterly* in 1942, almost simultaneously with the first publication of "The Truant,"[39] Pratt expresses admiration for those sturdy species of an earlier age who discovered in their philosophy the strength to endure:

> Their tunics, stoles and togas were like watersheds,
> Splitting the storm, sloughing the rain.
> Under such cloaks the morrow could not enter –
> Their *gravitas* had seized a geologic centre
> And triumphed over subcutaneous pain. (2.131)

Nevertheless, Pratt is forced to question the adequacy of Aurelius's teachings in the light of the atrocious and hitherto unimaginable sufferings which members of the human race seem capable of inflicting upon each other, even upon the innocent, in this generation:

> Today we cannot discipline
> The ferments rattling underneath our skin.
> Where is the formula to win
> Composure from defeat?
> And what specific can unmesh
> The tangle of civilian flesh
> From the traction of the panzers?
> And when our children cry aloud
> At screaming comets in the skies, what serves
> The head that's bloody but unbowed?
> What are the Stoic answers
> To those who flag us at the danger curves
> Along the quivering labyrinth of nerves? (2.131–2)

Pratt's Truant, in replying to the Panjandrum, speaks for all those who, having already absorbed the lesson that stoicism has to teach, find that it falls short:

> "We who have met
> With stubborn calm the dawn's hot fusillades;
> Who have seen the forehead sweat
> Under the tug of pulleys on the joints,
> Under the liquidating tally
> Of the cat-and-truncheon bastinades ...
> We who have learned to clench
> Our fists and raise our lightless sockets
> To morning skies after the midnight raids ... " (2.130–1)

In the end it is not schooling in the philosophy of stoicism that gives the Truant the power to defy the Panjandrum and his materialistic universe (see 179–80, below).

In an address that he delivered early in the 1940s to the Women's Canadian Club of Montreal, Pratt elaborated upon what he considered to be the inadequacy of stoicism as a philosophy of life for the modern age:

> Neither is it enough to reduce the value of life to the will to endure, though that reduction may have an element of sublimity evoking our admiration, for the stoic reserve does throw a man back upon his own resources, which postulates a spiritual basis, a sense of inward dignity. Nevertheless, very few members of the human family possess enough stamina to keep their chins up in the fog of *Dover Beach*, however admirable that poem may be from the standpoint of expression. A melancholy roar, sustained indefinitely, can drown volition and initiative. (MS 9:68.6)

"THE STRAIGHTEDGE" OF REASON

If Pratt explored the stoic response to life and found it wanting, he seems to have discovered that the position of the rationalist has even less to offer. He firmly believed that survival calls for the use of all the human faculties, not the least of which is the intellect. Nevertheless, it must be admitted that Pratt's attitude towards pure reason or logic, expressed chiefly through his use of irony, is ambivalent.

The ambiguity attached to reason is evident as early as "Carlo" (1.49), where Pratt holds up to question the redemptive value of reason and the apparent injustice that makes the dog a victim of "predestination" while it leaves the human being, if free, subject to hubris:

> They tell me, Carlo, that your kind
> Has neither conscience, soul, nor mind;
> That reason is a thing unknown
> To such as dogs; to man alone
> The spark divine – he may aspire
> To climb to heaven or even higher;
> But God has tied around the dog
> The symbol of his fate, the clog. (1.49–50)

The fish in *The Witches' Brew* have "No Reason's holy light / To read the truth and no desire to search" (1.140). While, like Carlo, they may never aspire to heaven, they are impervious to the strategy of the Devil, they appear to enjoy themselves, and they remain "unfallen" creatures (see 69, above).

In describing the birth of reason in the female anthropoidal ape of "The Great Feud," Pratt does not depict it as an apocalyptic revelation of "the holy light" (*The Witches' Brew*, 1.140). Rather, he relates how "faintly" the ape

>   had sniffed the raw
> Material of the moral law;
> She had observed, one windy night,
> The skull of an alligator cut
> Open by a cocoanut
> Falling from a lofty height –
> An alligator that had torn
> And eaten up her youngest born.
> Then to a corner she had crept,
> And had not eaten, had not slept,
> But scratched her head and drummed her breast,
> And Reason entered as she wondered,
> Brooded in the trees and pondered
> On how the reptile was struck dead. (1.175–6)

As reason is associated with "the raw material of the moral law" in the mind of the ape brooding over the retaliatory, if accidental, death of her child's murderer, the origin of the *lex talionis* is suggested. There is also an implication that, in assuming the leadership of the land forces, the ape may not have been wholly disinterested in her application of reason.

The ape's rationality is exhibited in her qualities of leadership – in her ability to organize others and to unify them in a common cause. But the logic of her address to "The Great Consult," made even more persuasive by her ability to appeal to the emotions, fails to take into account "the wanton twist of Fate" (1.185), the irrationality of nature expressed through the eruption of Jurania, which, in turn, lets loose Tyrannosaurus Rex. For a moment she is almost confounded. "But instant as a thunderclap / The prescience of her soul [awakes]," and she is able, temporarily at least, to direct the monster's tremendous power to her own ends (1.188–9). Such power, however, is blind and unpredictable, and the ape is eventually to lose control. Only after the death of Tyrannosaurus, the reversal of the battle, and the final eruption of Jurania is she enabled "by subtle means that placed her head / Of land belligerents" to "sniff" the warning of nature, interpret it correctly, and flee with her offspring to safety (1.202–3). Having used her powers to bring about great destruction, she finally combines her reason with instinct and action to ensure the preservation of the species.

In the geometric world of the Panjandrum, humanity with "that strange precipitate" which is "not amenable to fire" falls "like a curse / On the mechanics of [the] Universe" (2.127). Even Puffsky's "watered soul," which is "non-inflammable," can find no place in the logic of hell (1.286). In like manner, it is the world of Father Time (2.132–3) with his "cool pre-Cambrian sense of sequence" that is upset by the appearance of

> this new adventurer –
> Which called itself a soul,
> With its mélange of pride,
> Courage, honour, suicide,
> Pursuing an eternal goal. (2.133)

The world of pure reason that cannot accommodate the human has offspring "born of a mania of mind and will" in the submarine (2.151), and in the *Titanic* (1.303–4). The *Titanic*, however, is less well equipped to confront the iceberg than is the ape to deal with the eruptions of Jurania. In contrast, the human crew of the *Roosevelt*, which uses reason as well as every scientific aid available, survives because the men are not surprised to have to reckon with "the slow / Unreasoned alternation of the sleet / With hurrying phantoms of hail and snow" (1.241).

What is even more frightening is that pure reason, or reason in alliance with baser motives, can lead human beings to torture one another, as in *Brébeuf and His Brethren*:

> A human art was torture,
> Where reason crept into the veins, mixed tar
> With blood and brewed its own intoxicant. (2.67)

It is without mercy or consideration for human frailty:

> Even the Great God of Islam
> Could find no escape for the faithful,
> When he knew the flight was regimented
> To the paces of a Mongol syllogism.
> ("The Old Organon," 2.28)

In *Towards the Last Spike* the logic of Blake's denunciation of the Pacific Scandal leaves "no loopholes in the facts" (2.211). It leads to the personal defeat of Macdonald, whether he is guilty or not, and to the delay in the building of the railway.

It is significant that reason plays a large part in the tragic loss of life at Dunkirk:

> Seven millions on the roads in France,
> Set to a pattern of chaos
> Fashioned through years for this hour.
> Inside the brain of the planner
> No tolerance befogged the reason –
> The *reason* with its clear-swept halls,
> Its brilliant corridors,
> Where no recesses with their healing dusk
> Offered asylum for a fugitive.
> The straightedge ruled out errors,
> The tremors in the sensory nerves,
> Pity and the wayward impulses,
> The liberal imbecilities.
> The reason reckoned that the allied guns
> Would not be turned upon the roads
> To clear the path for the retreat.
> It reasoned well. (2.114)

The reason can equip individuals or groups to "kill with ... geometry" ("Cycles," 2.195), or to attack with the inhuman logic of the guards in "Convict Holocaust" (1.216).

Pratt, however, does not suggest that men and women abdicate from rationality. "The Great Feud" illustrates what happens when reason loses control or is misused. Later, in *Behind the Log*, Pratt ponders on the factors that allowed the German people during the Second World War to become pawns in the hands of diabolical leaders. They were lost when they failed to guide by reason qualities which upon other occasions might be considered as virtues:

> Habits that would not heckle a command,
> Obedience that scaled the breach of fear,
> A frenzy that would spurn the slopes of Reason
> Under a rhetoric of Will which placed
> Before the *herrenvolk* historic choices –
> To scramble up a cliff and vandalize
> The sunlight or else perish on the ledges. (2.172)

In the same poem he indicated, as the *Empire Hudson* was torpedoed and as its hundreds of sailors, "unlifejacketed / Clawed at the jetsam in the oil and water," that there are times when

> High strategy
> Demanded of the brain an execution
> Protested by the tactics of the heart. (2.170)

The captains and the commodore of the allied convoy, aware of the danger that could well come from a stricken ship, have to set their priorities according to the greater good of the greatest number, although

> The triple task –
> To screen the convoy, counter-attack, and then
> The human third of rescuing the sailors –
> Seemed far beyond the escort's hope or effort. (2.169–70)

Even the tragedy of the *Titanic* is due, in part, to the sense of security that led people to live as if "Even the judgment stood in little need / Of reason" (1.309).

Pratt's distrust of pure reason is evident, too, in the poems which touch on religious experience. Within the context of *Brébeuf and His Brethren* his objectivity demands that he give it the dignity traditionally accorded to it by the Thomistic philosophy in which the Jesuits were schooled. The priests are fortified by visits to Rennes, where they once studied their theology, and

> Where, in the Summa of Aquinas, faith
> Laid hold on God's existence when the last
> Link of the Reason slipped. (2.54–5)[40]

While Pratt does not belittle the intelligence of the Jesuits, it is clear that his reason for admiring them is primarily that they are persons of faith (*PLP* 47).

In "The Mystic" (1.299), which first appeared in *Queen's Quarterly* under the title "Credo, quia non intellego,"[41] Pratt questions the source of "Such proud irenic faith as can refute / The upstart logic of this world of strife." He does not suggest that the mystic is ignorant of or even untouched by the chaos in the world about him, only that with his faith he is able to transcend it. The sestet of this sonnet ends with what are surely some of Pratt's most powerful lines as he observes,

> The proof that slays the reason, has no power
> To stem your will, corrode your soul – though lime
> Conspire with earth and water to devour
> The finest cultures from the lust of slime;
> Though crumbled Tartar hordes break through their sod
> To blow their grit into the eyes of God. (1.299)

In other works Pratt reveals more clearly the tension – even, at times, the dichotomy – between faith and reason that is part of his heritage (see 41–2, above). Each of the dream characters in *The Iron Door*, with the exception of the woman who represents the poet's mother, demands a reason for suffering and death. The little boy, for example,

> could not, by a rational way,
> Be fully made to understand
> That the mending of a lifeless body lay
> Beyond the surgery of his father's hand. (1.206)

No rational answer is forthcoming. When the door does open, the poet suggests that it may very well have been the wild argument of the frantic woman with "its strange unreason" that has proved "The case for life before the throne of death" (1.212). In "The Depression Ends" the persona declares that he needs no reason for his scheme "beyond the logic of a dream" (1.261). The mysterious behaviour of Cyrus in "The Fable of the Goats" can be explained neither by logic nor by science:

> But do not reason why the mind
> Should save the soul or seek to find
> Within the evolutionary dream
> An optimistic phagocyte.
> ...

Ye cannot know what Cyrus felt;
Ye only know that Cyrus knelt. (2.24)

Pratt suggests that pure reason in its attempt to explain away all mysteries becomes arrogant, failing to take into account not only the unpredictability of nature but also the element of freedom, a divine attribute shared with humankind. It would reduce the universe to a closed system like that of the Panjandrum, while leaving humanity with no possibility of exit. Further than that, Pratt's distrust of reason betrays a belief that the ultimate truth, and the access to it, lie beyond the reason's limited grasp.[42]

Had John Sutherland been granted more time to explore Pratt's work in depth, it is not likely that he would have concluded so readily that the poet was "deliberately hostile" to ideas, or that the apparent simplicity of his work depends initially upon "the abjuration of thought."[43] Such oversimplification would seem to contravene Sutherland's own interpretation of the poetry. Frank Davey's comments appear to be equally one-sided when he claims that Pratt "shows no ... interest in non-quantifiable or non-factual information," and that "the only reality which interests him is the knowable one – that of miles, tonnage, names, quotations, that which can be weighed, cited, documented, or otherwise rationalized." While Davey is speaking chiefly about the longer narratives, it is difficult to understand how he can insist seriously that "there is no mystery or ambiguity" in these poems, or that within their context "material reality is assumed to contain, if not be, the whole."[44]

There is more than a slight distinction to be made between rationalism and the awareness of the true capacity as well as the limitations of the reason; between materialism and love of the concrete – of rocks, and whales, and ships, and human beings. Pratt may have distrusted the use to which human beings often put their reason, but he did not despise it. He did abjure both rationalism and materialism. Pratt's use of irony provides evidence that though he may never have achieved it in its entirety, he sought, even unconsciously, the integration described by a contemporary philosopher, theologian, and literary critic who maintains:

It is necessary that there be a very close relationship and friendship between these two parts of us [reason and faith], so much so that it will be disastrous for either if it gets separated from the other. If we go about thinking only great thoughts in the name of faith, forgetting the human, we become mad dreamers, fanatical human beings, ruthless absolutizers, destroying and not redeeming the human. The human, in its weakness, needs the companionship and the redemption of faith. And faith seems more able to give this companionship and understanding than the pure intelligence. For the pure intelligence is more apt to wish to rise above the human condition and to despise the latter. But the most special concern of faith is redemption, the redemption of the parts of [us] that need to be redeemed.[45]

5 The Wheel Comes Full Circle: The Atoning Christ

It is not difficult to see how the image of God as an impersonal but powerful ruler of the universe, shaped in part by the influences of Pratt's childhood and reinforced by certain trends in the theology of his time, lent itself to an eschatological view of history, and encouraged him often to envision the world and the events of universal or local consequence that took place within it in apocalyptic proportion and colour. What is not quite as frequently acknowledged is the possibility that Pratt may have cultivated such a vision in much of his poetry for the rhetorical and dramatic effects that it helped him to achieve.

The abbreviated titles by which Pratt's theses are usually designated may be convenient, but they are nevertheless misleading in that they tend to obscure the Christological concerns of both works. The first thesis, "The Demonology of the Synoptics in Relation to Earlier Developments and to the Mind of Christ," is, properly speaking, not so much a study in historical development as it is an attempt to come to terms with a larger question of perennial interest in theology: the nature and the extent of Christ's knowledge (DS 19–21, 30). The particular focus of this thesis is upon the humanity of Jesus, and upon his comprehension of, and reaction to, traditions inherited from the past.

But Pratt reaches beyond the humanity of Christ in his doctoral dissertation, *Studies in Pauline Eschatology and Its Background.* Just as in his earlier thesis Pratt uses a survey of the demonology of the ancient civilizations to throw into relief the attitude of Jesus towards certain traditional beliefs, so in the second he employs a similar technique to illustrate Paul's gradual shift in emphasis from the accidental accompaniments of the Parousia (*PE* 196) to its one decisive event – the final return in glory of Jesus Christ, who, having suffered and died ignominiously, has risen and will come again as Lord (*PE* 124, 177, 189). It is, on the whole, the Christological element reflected in Pratt's poetry which brings its religious content into its proper focus. Since this element is rooted in a central mystery of faith, the Incarnation, it cannot solve in purely rational terms "the problem of God," but it does help, in religious terms, to give direction to Pratt's humanism, and it illuminates a more positive attitude towards religious matters than critics generally ascribe to him.

In "Clay" (2.305), Pratt attempts to work out, in terms of natural theology and philosophy alone, "the problem of God." Julian, unable to discover justice in the "divine plan," eventually rejects the divinity of Christ and the efficacy of the redemption although he does not question Christ's historicity or his motivation. If "the Galilean" failed to save humankind, as Julian tends to conclude, and if his suffering was in vain, then the fault lies with a God who, having accepted with favour the unbloody oblation of Melchizedek, and having prevented Abraham's sacrifice of Isaac, refused to speak again to save his own son (2.334). Calvary, "the final altar of the world" and the focus of its faith and hope, proves to be a delusion:

> The tender hands upraised in death had made
> High intercession, closing once for all
> The scourge that bled the heart, scouring the soul.
> ...
> O broken reed! O spirit! treble-crushed
> By the barbed insult where the iron failed,
> By dreams o'ershot, and courage spent for nought;
> ...
> And Calvary – is but a peak that flared
> An evanescent torch whose light was quenched
> In a red mist of sweat, and man's tired feet
> When once they scale the summit must, in shame,
> Re-walk the bloody gradient to the grave. (2.335)

Since Julian can find no evidence of divine justice on the natural plane, he is confounded by the scandal of the cross and is no longer able to believe in the possibility of the Resurrection:

> Whence did the Galilean win his right
> To ground earth's faith upon a soldier's rood?
> ...

> There, somewhere near the hill on which he died,
> Does not his dust blend with the earth he loved,
> But nobly failed to save? The charge, not his,
> Must elsewhere lie. If God's, then sovereignty
> Is as a sorry fable – shells of words,
> Without a kernel. (2.338)

Bereft of faith and hope, and overcome by the apocalyptic horrors of war described by his friend, Julian gropes in vain for another source of salvation:

> If the one,
> Who was the very rose-ray of all dreams
> The world's imagination fed upon,
> Yearned for through centuries before he came,
> And raised in retrospect to rank of God,
> ...
> – if he failed, as failed
> He has with the momentum of the years
> Of twenty centuries to make his name
> The lode-star of the race – pray, tell me then,
> Is there another yet to come, endowed
> With more resistless weapons of offence,
> With panoply more cunningly devised
> To stay the onslaught? (2.338–9)

Having found no Messiah more powerful than Christ, Julian concludes, "Then ruin waits / Upon his shrine, and dogs all pilgrim steps / That, flocking thither, search for peace and rest" (2.339).

The pilgrimage to the shrine in the ruins appears again at the conclusion of both *Brébeuf and His Brethren* and "The Truant," but in those later poems it is a symbol of hope rather than of disillusionment. If Pratt did, even for a moment, identify himself with the Julian of "Clay," he did not, like the character he created, cease trying to reconcile the exercise of divine power and justice (*PE* 153–4) with divine love and the mystery of "Christ's humility and weakness culminating in the Cross" (*PE* 191). The attempt at reconciliation remains a major theme in the poetry.

The general assumption that Pratt underwent a major crisis of faith probably owes much to a reading of "Clay" that is superficial, and that views it in a context apart from his earlier and later works. This tendency has helped to obscure the fact that, in addition to better-known and more widely discussed poems such as *The Iron Door*, "The Highway," and *Brébeuf and His Brethren*, Pratt wrote others on themes of a religious nature. Not necessarily because they are mediocre, but perhaps because, in keeping with their purpose, they are less reliant upon his characteristic irony and therefore less provocative, most have been, like the theses, consigned until recently to archives and dim shelves, obscuring an important facet of Pratt's religious sensibility.

After he had become established in the Department of English at Victoria University, and probably just after he had written *The Iron Door*, Pratt was asked to compose the lyrics of a series of hymns for "The Great Appeal and Final Triumph,"[1] a pageant to be presented in Massey Hall, Toronto, in 1928, by the United Church of Canada. These hymns were revived in 1954 for use in another pageant, "Triumphs of the Faith."[2] While the lyrics may not all be outstanding in originality or in inspiration, they nevertheless preserve, without excess of language or of sentiment, some of the best elements of the evangelical hymn tradition.

In these lyrics the distant and forgetful deity who appears in many of the familiar poems is seen in a different light in relation to the Son. Here God is the

> Father whose mighty heart would hold
> Mankind of every time and race,
> Who proved the richness of His grace
> In Christ, the Shepherd of His fold. (Hymn 3)

God, whose loving care extends to each individual (Hymn 1), is nevertheless "the God of all the peoples / That dwell upon the earth." God's "sacred covenant of grace" embraces "every time and place" in his plan of salvation (Hymn 1). He is the God of unity whose "spacious hand / Is spread with blessings manifold, upon this wide-receiving land" (Hymn 4). The love, worship, and service which human beings owe to God are seen as a response through grace of free will to the divine initiative:

> Divinest love that would reclaim
> The world from all its sin and loss[3]
> Whose theme eternal is the name
> Of Christ and a triumphant Cross,
> So charge our wills that they may draw
> Men's hearts unto Thy holy law. (Hymn 2)

However, such a full response to divine love is impossible without something of the motive later animating Pratt's "Truant." To persevere, one must pray for

> the starry faith serene
> That glows within a clouded night,
> The hold upon the things unseen,
> The promised core of morning light,
> That trust which in a burned desire
> Can take refinement from the fire. (Hymn 2)

With such faith and love, one may put on "the generous mind" of Christ (Phil 2:5–11), and see and respond to "the world's large need / Where blind men call out to be led, / And hungry souls cry out for bread" (Hymn 3).

These lyrics, at their best, certainly deserve to be ranked above some of the banalities included in many contemporary hymn collections. There is no suggestion here of any uncertainty about the relationship among the members of the Trinity. Nor is the question of divine justice ever raised.

During the 1930s, Pratt contributed other hymns and occasional religious poems to church periodicals, especially to *World Friends*, the children's magazine edited by his wife and published monthly by the United Church of Canada Women's Missionary Society. All of these pieces are marked by the universalism, at once Pauline and Wesleyan, present in the theses and in the earlier hymns. God is the "God of all the children of the earth" who pray that they may realize their close kinship to each other as offspring of a loving Father.[4] But this recognition, born of prayer, must be translated into deed:

> To human need I pledge my part
> This New Year's Day in loyal pact.
> Lord, may the motive in my heart
> Find no betrayal in the act.
>
> ("January the First," 2.294)

Christmas contributions to *World Friends*, notably "Mother and Child" (2.295) and "The Manger under the Star" (2.295), are marked by a tenderness devoid of sentimentality that could spring only from a genuine religious response to the subject. The posthumously published "But Mary Kept All These Things, and Pondered Them in Her Heart" (2.302) corresponds in form and approach to an Ignatian contemplation on a scriptural text (Lk 2:19).[5]

In another poem, "Thanksgiving," Pratt moves towards the longer and looser line with which he experimented in several poems included in *The Fable of the Goats and Other Poems* (1937). The lines in "Thanksgiving" are still held in check by the regular metre, rhyme, and verse form, but the stanzas are related to each other chiefly through anaphora, a common feature of biblical style that Pratt was to use more and more frequently. In this poem, Pratt also employs the harvest symbolism which he vested with greater complexity in *Brébeuf and His Brethren*. Here he presents God not as some remote overlord, but as a generous parent, source of life, to whom all creation must return:

> Lord of the autumn, when the soul's ripe grain
>   Is garnered in,
> And Christ's great heart rejoices as the world
>   Puts by its sin,
> Into thy love shall all thy people come
> With glad thanksgiving at the harvest home. (2.294)

At least two selections from *The Fable of the Goats and Other Poems*, for which he was granted the Governor-General's Literary Award in 1937, deserve consideration here with Pratt's lesser-known works. While they may not seem to be as specifically religious in their content as the other poems discussed in this chapter, they are no less important for what they reveal of the attitude of the Pratt of the 1930s. If "The Great Feud" is considered as a parable, "The Fable of the Goats," whose germ Pratt later claimed to have borrowed from Aesop (*PLP* 109–12), was his second attempt at a didactic narrative form. However, both the beast fable itself, which Pratt made, in part, the vehicle of Horatian satire, and the elements of language and the phraseology which he used in its narration betray its true source in the Old Testament. There he found the fable of the trees (Judg 9:8–15), a satire used against Abimelech, who was attempting to grasp the powers of kingship, and also the prophet Daniel's apocalyptic vision of the ram and the goat (Dan 8; *PE* 106), from which he derived the basic situation, with its reference to Cyrus, king of the Medes and Persians, who was to liberate the Jews exiled in Babylon.

However, while the beasts of Daniel's dream, the leading powers of Persia and Greece, meet in a headlong and bloody conflict that appears to herald the end of time (8:7–10), the goats in Pratt's fable representing the then-opposing powers of Europe and Asia are able to avert a cataclysm, not so much through the agency of any instinct for self-preservation, or even through an optimistic "moral phagocyte that had got the jump on the bacillus" (MS 3:21), but through the mysterious behaviour of the combatants. Cyrus, who up to this point has shown no trace of cowardice, suddenly kneels before his enemy, Abimelech, whose pride, arrogance, and scorn are replaced in turn by "a strangely warm / Infusion – a considerate care / That would not harm a single hair" (2.25). He steps reverently over his enemy, and takes the mountain pass without a blow. What Cyrus has lost in territory he has more than gained in honour, and nothing of importance is forfeited when both leaders with their herds pass on to more appetizing pastures.

On the moral plane, in this fable the *lex talionis* is replaced by the conduct advocated in the Sermon on the Mount (Mt 5:38–42), while Cyrus's action can only be described in Isaian terms as behaviour characteristic of the "suffering servant" (Is 42; 44:28; 45:1; see 177, below), in Pauline terms as one of "the foolish things of the world" that confound the wise (1 Cor 1:27), or in Wesleyan terms as the evangelical experience of conversion. The blending of the original fable with the dream vision and its infusion with Pratt's own blend of humour and irony, together with his choice of the iambic tetrameter line, carry the poem along at such a rapid pace that the crisis and conclusion appear, on the literal level, to be almost anti-climactic and to detract from what lies beneath the surface. The decision to omit this poem from the second edition of *Collected Poems* was probably based on the grounds that, like much satire, it became dated with the passage of time, and the solution to world problems that it offered, while it might still be held as an ideal, had not been realized, as Pratt was well aware. However, "The Fable of the Goats," and some of the poems that accompany it, illustrate the fact that Pratt, the steady contributor to the *Canadian Forum*, was not to be left behind by A.M. Klein or F.R. Scott as a capable satirist.

Included in the volume with "The Fable of the Goats" is "A Prayer-Medley,"[6] another little-known poem of the depression years. At first glance it appears to be a series of thanksgiving prayers, psalm-like in rhythm and structure and communal rather than individual in voice. While, apart from "The Fable of the Goats," the poems and hymns examined so far in this chapter have been fairly two-dimensional, "A Prayer-Medley" echoes with a reverberating irony. An extended choral ode in five sections, each of which expresses a contemporary attitude towards God and towards some aspect of life, it recalls the spectrum of opinion represented by the chorus and the speakers in "Clay," or by the dream figures in *The Iron Door*.

The first section of "A Prayer-Medley" (1.293–4) is a song of praise in which the distinctly masculine voices echo familiar but slightly emended biblical texts. The effect is that although man seems to address the Lord, he is actually heard to proclaim a paean to his own great wisdom and power over nature (Ps 8), which have led him to achievements greater than those traditionally attributed to God (Job 38). No longer reliant upon divine providence, he truly feels justified in proving the teaching of the Gospel (Lk 12:25) false: "By taking thought we have added cubits to our stature."

In the second stanza, the chorus continues to praise God for the progress of civilization, which, it is clear, it sees primarily as human achievement. In a secular world which prides itself on mass production, the Sabbath, the day when God rested and took delight in creation, has had to be replaced by statutory holidays. As the chorus is heard to list with pride the injustices of the past that men no longer perpetrate, and to rejoice that "the child, the woman and the slave have been made free," not in response to any divine decree but by "the Act of the Nation" (1.294), the choric tone sounds suspiciously like the voice of the Pharisee at prayer in the temple (Lk 18:10–12).

By the third movement, the human race has banished God altogether from its consciousness and is able to rejoice that "the curse of labour" (Gen 3:19) is past. Yet even as it does so, there intrudes the disturbing awareness that "we have multiplied the work that is not of our hands" (1.294), and that the natural and traditional rhythm of human work has been replaced by the inhuman thrust of the motors and dynamos, "stern and defiant and absolute." In this stanza, as in Dorothy Livesay's later poem "Day and Night" (1936),[7] the change from the free-verse line to the highly controlled rhythm and rhyme scheme of the three songs suggests not only the monotonous tyranny of the machine but also the uncreative pattern of human response that it evokes.

The world of the machine is not that of God the Creator (Ps 8, 19), but that of the Panjandrum (2.125–8), since it has no place for "wayward blood," "impredictable wills," and "clumsy fingers and thumbs" (1.295). However, "the pattern perfection of the weave," to which the "Truant" refuses to conform (2.128–9), is threatened here by the call of the saboteur, as the machines continue to overproduce and unemployment looms. As this section of the poem ends, the song of the machine and the angry and destructive cry of the saboteur are drowned by "the rugged antiphonal" of the individualists, who can only temporize, waiting out the cycle of supply and demand, and ironically urging a return to the law of the jungle:

Then brain and iron and brawn,
And every man for himself,
Will reinstate the Dawn
Of Freedom, Power and Pelf. (1.295)

The individual's will, ambition, and desire for power have replaced those of God as the centre of the universe.

In the fourth part of "A Prayer-Medley" the speaker proudly claims that man has become refined to the point where he no longer tortures for the faith, burns heretics, or crucifies his enemies. Through his speech, however, he makes it clear that while he now considers religion irrelevant, he may well be motivated by other concerns to commit similar atrocities. He looks upon the past, when men fought over the nature of the godhead, as "but nursery days when thy children scrambled up their picture blocks / in the vain attempt to puzzle out the features of thy face" (1.296). Now that he has "come of age," man attends secular councils rather than those of the Church, but, he boasts, "how orderly and admirable our conduct." The speaker notes that men meet "with the crossing of hands ... and wish one another well." They partake of secular communion services in the quest for peace and amity. Their committees form and adjourn, but do not dissolve. The only hope for man is to meet again "at Geneva, or London, or Washington," to confer once more, "to enter the halls full of wisdom and to depart void of understanding" (1.296). If man can still claim to live by faith, it is secular faith in his science, technology, and diplomacy.

The last section of the poem commences with man's reminder to the Lord that the human spirit is still kindled "by the flash of phrases ... by the cannonades of mottoes and ellipsis" (1.297). Those quoted, both secular and biblical, are the patriotic catchwords which attach glory or the Lord's blessing to the efforts of allies in the time of war. This stanza, however, moves from irony born of the speaker's lack of vision to a sense of awareness absent from other parts of this work. Man remembers that he may indeed honour those who fought for their country, "But our cenotaphs bear no testimony to those who moulder ingloriously upon the mattress" (1.297). The tendency to call upon the mythological spirits of destruction leads, at this point, to the realization that only evil can come of evil. As individuals turn in prayer to Buddha, to Confucius, or to "Christ, Lord of Love, Lord of Life," they are united in asking that "the dream may not entirely vanish" from their sleep. They conclude that there is no natural cure for the universal ills of humankind:

> Our physicians can prescribe for the ills of their own families.
> They can cure individual diseases, and heal the hurt of the body.
> But they have found no remedy for the deep *malaise* in the communal
>   heart of the world. (1.297)

But the closing lines suggest that even as human beings can say together "Our Father," they may be able to recognize each other as brothers and sisters and pray for forgiveness,[8] as well as for their common needs. On the whole, "A Prayer-Medley" is an interesting experiment. However, neither the approach to the theme nor the form of this poem was one with which Pratt could be entirely satisfied.

The poems and hymns discussed so far in this chapter reveal the more positive image of God reflected in some of Pratt's lesser-known or unpublished works of the 1920s and 1930s. Although some were commissioned for church use and are not always his finest achievements, there is no indication that in them Pratt was merely reformulating conventional pieties while he continued to believe otherwise. Since, in the context of these works, God's power is seen to be exercised in acts of love, and to be mediated through Christ, his son, the question of divine justice is never raised, and there is an absence of the conflict that we sense in some of the other poems.

In all of these works, Pratt, a pacifist in theory at least, with a deeply rooted belief in democracy, reveals his awareness of the poverty, the social ills, and the international discord of his time. Clear, too, is his conviction that prayer or worship that is not reflected in action, however limited that action may have to be, is in danger of becoming hypocritical. If the rest of his poetry does not, these pieces give the lie to F.R. Scott's charge that Pratt was unconcerned about social issues such as the fate of the Chinese coolies in the building of the Canadian Pacific Railway.[9] On the contrary, they reveal his deep sensitivity to them, as well as his conviction that the ills of the world could never be cured by political action alone. His Methodist background never led him, as it did others, into a purely secular socialism. Any healing process in society, he believed, had to begin with a change of heart in the individual. In the light of these early and often neglected works, the "religious poems" for which he is usually known, as well as those which he stated contained "undercurrents" of his convictions,[10] may be seen in a truer perspective, and what is generally considered Pratt's greatest achievement, his *Brébeuf and His Brethren*, may seem less surprising in its comprehensive embrace of the fullness of the Christian vision.

INTIMATIONS OF IMMORTALITY

Throughout the work of Pratt, the man who has been called "the rationalist technician,"[11] and the poet of science and of "the machine age,"[12] there runs unobtrusively but persistently a current of belief in the immortality of the soul, an awareness of a dimension of human existence that extends beyond the material and the temporal, beyond the here and now. While such a consciousness is by no means exclusive to Christianity, Pratt expresses it, explicitly at least, in the fundamental Christian paradox of life and death (see 82–3, above). Unfortunately, many critics, in overlooking the terms of the paradox, construct artificial limits to their interpretation of the poems and run the risk of misunderstanding their meaning.

Pratt is no more afraid to treat limited concepts of the afterlife, or of heaven, in a humorous or ironic context than he is to view in a less than serious light other traditional elements of eschatology (see 68, above). "Carlo" (1.49) and "The Parable of Puffsky" (1.285), though in different ways, refuse to take seriously the concepts of heaven as an exclusive club, or as a geographical location. In "The History of John Jones" (1.63), and in "To Angelina, an Old Nurse" (1.249), heaven is the future home of human beings (*PE* 103), and is depicted, of necessity, in material terms as a continuation of the earthly life led by the individual. While John Jones, whose all too human faults undercut the virtues for which he is eulogized, drifts "in his boat to the port of God" (1.63), the "sainted Angelina" is portrayed, with a mixture of the affection and fear that belonged to childhood, as

> Stalking at will, administrative, grim,
> With spoon or cup in hand full to the brim
> With oil designed for the felicity
> Of young and fever-spotted cherubim. (1.252)

In marked contrast to Pratt's hell with its characteristic silence (see 97, above), his heaven is distinguished not merely by the decorous "hum of multitudinous voices" (*The Iron Door*, 1.212), but even, perhaps, by "oaths that are properly enunciated" ("Silences," 2.3).

While "intimations" and even convictions of immortality recur throughout Pratt's poetry, *The Iron Door* is the most important of his early works for its religious overtones, and one to which he himself attached great significance (MS 1:5).[13] There is no reason to doubt his word that the nucleus of the poem was a dream which he experienced shortly after the death of his mother (see 62, above), although there is, perhaps, need for caution. It would be just as absurd to interpret Pratt's handling of the dream form solely in the light of Freudian or Jungian psychology as it would be to assess it from the purely literary point of view in terms of the Romantic "dream."

As early as "The Demonology of the Synoptics" where we find Pratt exploring the growth of belief in "extra-human agencies" he remarks:

Perhaps the most contributory cause is the significance attached to vivid dreams. It seems reasonable to think that the conviction of the reality of an unseen realm, and of the continuance of existence after physical death could be formed and strengthened by the visitations of the departed ones in the hours of sleep. (DS 10)

To support his point, Pratt then quotes from Professor Ernest Jones, then of the University of Toronto, with regard to the influence of vivid dreams, trances, visions, and similar intense emotional experiences in shaping the waking opinions of even the most cultured and educated of persons (DS 10).

This conviction of the importance of dreams and mystical experiences as a source of religious insight is one that is not at all foreign to biblical theology. While important examples may be found in the dream of Jacob's ladder (Gen 28:11–22), or in the conversion of St Paul (Acts 9:3–22), perhaps the fullest explication of their religious significance may be found in the Book of Job to which Pratt referred so often:

> For God speaketh once, yea twice, yet man perceiveth it not.
> In a dream, in a vision of the night, when deep sleep falleth upon man, in slumberings upon the bed,
> Then he openeth the ears of men, and sealeth their instruction
> That he may withdraw man from his purpose, and hide pride from man.
> (33:14–17)

This belief is reinforced by Pratt's development of the theme in *Pauline Eschatology*. After commenting that "the notion of eternal life in the sense of a new creation, which suffered a temporary eclipse in the apocalyptic writings, was continued by Jesus and by Paul as a fulfilment of the great prophets" (*PE* 77), Pratt adds that there is evidence within the epistles to indicate that Paul believed in the possibility of experiencing in this life some insight into the nature of the heavenly world. Drawing upon the Jewish apocalyptic writings, Pratt provides examples of some of the features of these epiphanies – suprasensory knowledge (Dan 10:1), privacy (Dan 10:7), and association with deep sleep and with physical weakness (*PE* 92). Pratt concludes that in the Pauline epistles, the dream, the vision, or the apocalypse in its literal sense becomes, as the apostle looks back upon it, a source of his insight into the gospel of Christ, into the knowledge of his character, or into his significance for the salvation of all (*PE* 92–3).

Pratt was well aware of the religious and psychological significance of the dream, just as he was aware of its place in the literary tradition of the West, from Virgil and Dante, and Langland and Bunyan, to Keats and Conrad. In *The Iron Door* he makes full use of its flexibility as a framework within which to recount a personal experience, to introduce the rationally inconceivable, and to free his imagination from the limitations imposed by time, space, and the necessity of fidelity to detail. While *The Iron Door* may be read as an allegory in that the main symbols and the dream characters have their parallels in actuality, it also functions, though in a less conventional sense than, for example,

Chaucer's *Book of the Duchess*, as a work of consolation, at the end of which the dreamer, together with those who have shared his experience vicariously, are strengthened in faith and hope.

It is interesting to compare Pratt's ode *The Iron Door*, with Francis Thompson's "The Hound of Heaven,"[14] a work that won Pratt's unreserved admiration (MS 10:72; see 188, below). Thompson's poem, the product of a baroque sensibility, with its theme of divine pursuit, personal flight, conquest, and surrender, is the more emotionally involving of the two. Pratt's work, which is about twice as long as Thompson's, looks more to an eschatological than to an immediate solution. By using both a first-person narrator and "dream characters" who represent various attitudes towards death and immortality, and in whose ultimate salvation the narrator is concerned, Pratt strives for a degree of objectivity that lends restraint to his expression.

Nevertheless, the similarities between the two poems in the combination of concrete and abstract language, in the imagery, in the casual introduction of the dream convention, and in the use of the irregular ode form are, without being imitative, too close to be coincidental. In both poems the variations in the basically iambic pentameter lines convey the vagueness, lack of precision, and hesitation born of the attempt to describe the experience. An element of order is introduced in both cases by the loosely interlocking rhyme schemes and by the occasional shift to trimeter or tetrameter lines – in Thompson's poem to suggest the inexorable pace of the pursuer in contrast to the frantic confusion of the pursued; in Pratt's to indicate, among other things, the ebb and flow of the tide, the transiency of the dream images, the emphasis on key phrases, the mood of the desperate woman (1.210–11), and the determination of the dreamer to see beyond the door (1.212).

The "traditional accompaniments of the apocalypse" (*PE* 14; see 68, above) are prominent in the settings of both poems. Thompson's psychological state of "Titanic gloom" (HH 52) corresponds with Pratt's symbolic "mass of gloom" (1.205–6). Wind (HH 53; 1.205, 208, 211), mist or fog (HH 56; 1.207), storm (HH 53; 1.207, 210), light and darkness (HH 52–4; 1.204–5, 206, 212), thunder (HH 53; 1.205), clouds (HH 54; 1.205), noise (HH 55, 57; 1.206), colour (HH 52–3; 1.211), the tension between time and eternity (HH 56; 1.208, 212–13), and chaos, fear, and flight (HH 52; 1.206) – all are present in larger than normal proportions.

Against this background is set, in Thompson's poem, not only the pattern of imagery suggestive of the love and beauty that his dreamer seeks in vain, but also the dramatic movement of the pursuit and flight. In Pratt's poem the dream characters and the cases that they plead in the face of an apparently deaf heaven constitute the dramatic tension. In both works the door functions as a major symbol. In Thompson's it holds out to the dreamer a possible source of escape into earthly delights until he finds that "the gust of His approach would clash it to" (HH 54). For Pratt the door represents the passageway between heaven and earth, although "It seemed the smith designed it to be swung / But once, then closed forevermore" (1.205). While this appearance is far from the reality, and the door does eventually open, the dreamer's attempts to penetrate the mysteries beyond, before his due time, prove futile when it closes "with a loud / Relentless swing" (1.213).

Thompson's dreamer attempts to escape

> From those strong Feet that followed, followed after.
> But with unhurrying chase,
> And unperturbèd pace,
> Deliberate speed, majestic instancy,
> They beat – and a Voice beat
> More instant than the Feet. ... (HH 52)

Pratt introduces a related image at the beginning of *The Iron Door*. As his dreamer first hears it,

> The noise as of stubborn waters
> Came in from a distant tide
> To the beat of Time with slow
> Immeasurable stride. (1.205)

Later, as the door opens, the longer line suggests release and freedom:

> A sound was heard, now like the beat
> Of tides under the drive of winds,
> Now like the swift deck-tread of feet,
> Steadying to a drum. ... (1.212)

Although the reader becomes aware early in both works of the convention in which the poet writes, neither Thompson nor Pratt mentions the word "dream" until the moment before the dramatic crisis, the point at which all sources of escape and all the arguments have proved to be in vain, and the hero in each case finds himself face to face with death. Thompson's hero, his dream having failed (HH 56), awakens to find himself "stripped of youth and strength" (HH 55). He is forced to cry out, "Whether man's heart or life it be which yields / Thee harvest, must Thy harvest fields / Be dunged with rotten death?" (HH 56–7).

Pratt's hero realizes that the cost of redemption was high and that the cost of being the human instrument of that redemption often seems excessive. The case of the young man who has died in a fruitless attempt to save another is not unique: "Life for a life! The grim equivalent / Was vouched for by a sacred precedent" (1.209). This awareness, however, does not prevent the youth from asking "why the one who should have been redeemed / Should also pay the price / In the mutual sacrifice." He suggests that he has somehow been short-changed. Similarly, the last person to appear before the door, the woman burdened by another's sin, questions the value of her sacrifice (1.210). At that moment the dreamer fears that her last cry went unheard, that "life was sinking in its cosmic trial / And time was running down before my eyes" (1.211). He feels "the world with its dead weight of burdens," and hears the calls of the seamen and their unanswered signals of distress:

And all the light remaining was bereft
Of colour and design in full eclipse;
No fragrance in the fields; no flowers left
But poppies with their charred autumnal lips. (1.211)

In the responses made to both heroes it becomes evident that in each case the dream has presented an illusion. Thompson's dreamer is answered by the voice of his pursuer, not in rational terms, but in terms of the experience that he has sought throughout a lifetime. In spite of his silent acknowledgment that he is "of all man's clotted clay the dingiest clot" (HH 57), he receives salvation as a free, unmerited gift. Pratt's dreamer receives a less personal answer, yet one that is no more logical. He sees the door open without knowing why. He watches as the dream figures pass through, and although his own immediate vision of what lies beyond is marred by "something heavy and as old as clay" (1.213), we sense that it may not always be so.

In *The Iron Door* the giant hand that appears to have formed the barricade (1.205) is related, at least by suggestion, to "the nescient hollow of God's hand" (1.211), which apparently has lost control over creation. While Pratt does not refer to the image again, it is not inconsistent with the meaning of the poem as a whole to relate it by association to the eventual opening of the door. In Thompson's poem the outstretched hand offered to the dreamer suggests the hand which the poet in "The Highway" (1.256) longs to grasp again. The apocalypse, or the moment of revelation, in *The Hound of Heaven* occurs when the dreamer "sees" that his own initial "gloom" is the shadow of his pursuer's hand "outstretched caressingly" (HH 57).

The central apocalypse in *The Iron Door*, like that in *The Hound of Heaven*, bears all the marks attributed by the authorities to a genuine religious experience. The "passivity"[15] that precedes the onset of the mystical state (cf. 1 Cor 15:8–10; 2 Cor 3:18) is not sought for, but comes about in the most natural fashion, frequently through sleep while the will is held in abeyance. Moreover, the impact of the experience is "ineffable," in that the narrator finds it difficult to describe (*PE* 94; 1 Cor 2:9). Such phrases as "it may have been," "perhaps," "I do not know," "I tried," "baffled," "I could not see," and "while it was not given me to know," recur to create both the vagueness proper to the dream convention, and the search for words to describe the vision.[16] In that the vision passes away (1.213) it is "transient," but the "authority that it carries with it for aftertime" and its "inner richness and importance"[17] are not forgotten: "But neither the gird of hinges, nor the feel of air / Returning with its drizzled weight of cloud,/ Could cancel half the meaning of that hour" (1.213).

It is, however, the "noetic" quality[18] of the experience described in the poem that is most significant. Like the "door in heaven" (Rev 4:1) that can be unlocked only by the "Key of David" (Rev 3:7–8), the iron door that at first seemed to be a barrier or a stumbling block (1 Cor 1:18, 23) is opened for an instant, and while the dreamer is not a visionary of the stature of John or Paul (2 Cor 12:1–4), he is granted a momentary insight into the nature of life beyond it, a level of knowledge that cannot be obtained by the discursive intellect.[19]

The narrator sees the characters who have peopled his dream, none of whom has received an explanation for his suffering, go through the cruciform passage with "keen impassioned faces / Transfigured" (1.213; 2 Cor 3:18; *PE* 107–8). Participation in the kingdom is the "recompense of patient suffering" (*PE* 142), and since in the Pauline sense they have shared, even unconsciously, "the fellowship of His sufferings," and have been "made conformable to Christ in His death," they have been found worthy to "attain unto the resurrection" (Phil 3:10–11; Rom 6:5; 8:17; *PE* 107). There is no hint that any has been excluded, not even the stoic or the aesthete whose honest search for truth or for beauty, like that of the dreamer in *The Hound of Heaven*, may have found its ultimate goal. What the narrator experiences vicariously through the dream figures is the conviction that those who have gone ahead of him have taken possession of an eternal kingdom in which he too may one day share. He is consoled by the knowledge that, like Rachel, they move on to "The stirring of new notes, tranquil and free / Pulsing their way into a deathless life" (1:37).

Existence beyond the iron door is characterized by "light" and "life" (*PE* 105, 108, 109), words which Pratt uses three times each in the last section of the poem, and words which, according to Evelyn Underhill, express two "cardinal aspects of reality to which the mystics return again and again in their effort to find words which will express the inexpressible truth."[20] It is not coincidental that Paul in one of the most exalted and hope-filled passages in his epistles should describe God in these terms (1 Tim 6:16; see 61, above), or that the culmination of the vision in the last chapters of the Book of Revelation should be replete with them. They are "manifestations of God," or "effects of [God's] power" (*PE* 109).

In spite of the light, the dreamer has to say, "I did not see, I only knew." In such an "intellectual vision," which usually carries more conviction than bodily sight, the consciousness is at its highest, and hallucination, according to Underhill, is least likely.[21] The dreamer becomes one of those who is blessed because he has not seen and yet has believed (Jn 20:29). The vision must eventually "fade" into the light of common day, but the experience has been so intense that the regaining of ordinary sight can only be compared to blindness (cf. Acts 9:8). The luminosity of the dream, so different in its quality from daylight, is "enfeebled" by the harsh "solar glare."[22]

Harold Horwood's claim that *The Iron Door* closes upon an unanswered question[23] can be accepted as valid only in that neither the dreamer nor any of the dream figures receives an answer in terms of human wisdom or justice. Horwood seems to miss the point that all of the questions are thrown into insignificance by the opening of the door. Neither can the poem be said to express what another critic calls "Pratt's rejection of his belief in the Afterlife ... related to his rejection of the moral universe."[24] The triumphant tone of the apocalyptic moment, followed by the gentle return to the everyday world, which might be compared for effect with the ending of *Brébeuf and His Brethren*, indicates, too, that the poem is more than a "lyrical lament for lost friends, and song of hope that they have all met a just and spiritual reward."[25] Only too frequently the reader who is deaf to Pauline paradox cannot hear the Prattian irony. *The Iron Door*, which was born of personal experience rather than theory, provides the alternative to the wistful conclusion of "Clay," and suggests that there was in Pratt a relationship between the poet and the mystic.

Among other poems which Pratt mentioned as containing "undercurrents" of his religious convictions[26] are four short lyrics related to *The Iron Door* in that three centre around the declining years and the death of his mother, and all are reflections on the theme of eternal life.

In the four quatrains of "Old Age" (1.214), Pratt meditates on the physical limitations brought on by advancing years which restrict existence to "the round of a wheel chair and four dull walls." The opening exclamation, "So poor again!," suggests a return to the state of poverty and dependence which is humanity's at birth (Job 1:21). Interior and exterior rhyme combine to emphasize the loss of the qualities that once characterized the human being – "again," "taken," "gone," "forsaken." The "mountain stride," the "eagle vision," the "*All Hail*" of the voice are replaced by the shaking hand, the falling step, and the faded will. But even as the observer looks on, he participates in a momentary apocalypse of a life that transcends the present one:

> And yet to-day as I watched your pale face yearning,
> When the sun's warmth poured through the open door,
> And something molten in your soul was burning
> Memorial raptures life could not restore,
> I knew, by some high trick of sight and hearing,
> Your heart was lured beyond the window sills,
> Adventuring where the valley mists were clearing,
> And silver horns were blowing on the hills.

In this poem, as in "The Lost Cause" (1.217), "Doors" (1.252), "Horizons" (1.289), and "Blind" (1.217), sensible blindness, usually considered a source of limitation and suffering, seems to sharpen the perception of an infinite horizon which extends beyond the boundaries of the material world.

The short poem "A Legacy" (1.286) plays again upon the paradox of poverty and riches (1 Tim 6:7–19), and as in *The Iron Door* and "Old Age," death is pictured as a casual passage through an open door. There can be no strife over the legacy left by the poet's mother, whose life has been an illustration of the teaching of the Gospel on the primacy of charity over concern for material possessions (Mt 6:19–21). Where her heart has been, there is her treasure, an incorruptible one that can never be exhausted. Pratt still sees in Pauline perspective the present life as a preparation for the future, and "eschatological resurrection as the mature fruit of the ethical resurrection which is wrought in Christ in the earthly life of the Christian" (*PE* 97).

In "The Empty Room" (1.291), published in *The Fable of the Goats and Other Poems*, Pratt again expresses his belief that those who have died have merely passed from one form of life to another. As he tries to recall the spiritual presence of his daughter[27] not in terms of "make-belief" but of "faith" and "miracle," he suggests that he may be willing to entertain the possibility of some form of communication with the souls of the departed (see DS 10; 167, above).

"The Decision" (1.67) is a lyric which Pratt dedicated to the memory of a former student. He first presents the immediate human reaction to the news of the untimely death of a young athlete: "We / With burning look and stubborn word / Challenged the Referee." The question is why the referee would call the contestant back before he was, to use the Pauline metaphor of the race (1 Cor 9: 24–6; 2 Tim 4:6–8; *PE* 95), "half-way round the track." The possible answer is presented in the last stanza in lines that, combining casual simplicity of style with serious content, evoke Emily Dickinson:

Unless he had contrived, instead,
To start you on a race,
With an immortal course ahead,
And daybreak on your face. (1.67)

It is the image of daybreak that marks the consummation of the apocalyptic feast in "The Depression Ends" (1.267). But Pratt's vision of "a deathless life" (*Rachel* 1.37), which is grounded in the Pauline epistles, becomes possible only through the Atonement – bringing back to God, through the Son, not only an alienated human race but also the whole of creation (*PE* 112).

The question of atonement or redemption persists throughout Pratt's poetry, whether it is treated lightly, as in "Carlo," or seriously and more subjectively, as in *The Iron Door*. But in both of these works an answer in Christian terms is merely implied. In other poems, Christ's role in the reconciliation of divine power with human weakness is more explicitly stated.

The Christ who emerges at the end of Pratt's lyric "The Highway" (1.256) is not the suffering and deluded human being of "Clay" whose heroic actions, according to Julian, ended only in failure and death (2.338). Yet Pratt constructed the shorter poem around a series of images which he drew from "Clay" and employed in a different manner, to evoke richer levels of connotative meaning. In "Clay" these images function as indices of Julian's disillusionment and cynicism. Once Julian has lost his faith, what he once regarded as "the highway" of life (347, 355) and of the world's progress (319–20) seems to lead only to the grave (335). Man, he concludes, must beware of the "errant step" that turns from the road and "moves into night and vacancy" (320). Christ, whom Julian earlier believed to be the "rose-ray of all dreams" and "the lode-star of the race," he sees as a man whose power to act "fell most tragically in far arrear of claims" (338), since he was unsupported by a father's hand (324–5). Julian rejects both the God of power and the purely human Jesus. Nor does he ever recover his faith in them.

In "The Highway" these images are transformed into symbols which lend to this short poem an ambiguity and a richness of texture lacking in "Clay." On one level only, "the highway," as Sandra Djwa has suggested,[28] may be interpreted as the path of evolutionary development, or, as Thomas Huxley called it in *Evolution and Ethics*, the "upward road of living energy"[29] moving through successive stages in the unfolding of the universe, from the "endless growth of the cosmic" to the "short span" (*EE* 4) of the human. In this context, the star, the rose, and the Son of Man emerge as the finest products of natural selection, or of each stage of "the cosmic process," which, according to Huxley, is "full of wonder, beauty and pain" (*EE* 5, 7). It is possible to see Pratt's "Son of Man" as a fitting representative of Huxley's "ethical process" (*EE* 33) at its height, repudiating at the cost of self-sacrifice "the gladiatorial theory of existence" (*EE* 33). Humankind in general, by following its "ape and tiger promptings" (*EE* 6), or by ignoring the demands placed on it by the nature of the universe in which it lives (*EE* 6), has, in terms of the poem, "missed the path," or become aberrant and retrogressive. Only by heroic actions, such as those exemplified by the Son of Man, can it bring about conditions essential to the development of its noblest powers (*EE* 5).

While "The Highway" clearly illustrates Pratt's interest in evolutionary themes, it must be admitted that a rigidly Darwinian or Huxleyan interpretation of this poem is not entirely satisfactory. For example, such a reading fails to provide an adequate explanation of the last three lines. Huxley could hope to oppose the relentless and impersonal universe only with ethical humanity. He looked to no power beyond the "cosmic process," and expected no real salvation from it. In "The Highway," however, the poet looks to the "Son of Man" to discover how he may "grasp again" the creative hand, which he sees here as a source of good and beauty. But this same hand is that of "the cosmic seneschal," and "the marshal," responsible for power and order in the universe. The problem of reconciling the "Lord of Hosts" with the "Lord of Love" is evident here, as it is in the later poem "Cycles" (2.195).

A contrapuntal movement is established within "The Highway" by another frame of reference which contributes to the poem's complexity, even as it elucidates some of its obscurity. The series of images in this poem which Pratt used earlier in "Clay" is employed in a Messianic context in the Old Testament, especially in Isaiah, the prophetic book to which Pratt refers most frequently (*PE* 11, 125; MSS 1.3; 9.69,1). The highway, a recurring image in Isaiah, is the way of salvation (35:8; 43:19), the road through the desolate and waste spaces, by which all people may walk until the end of time (35:8), the path for the Messiah (40:3), and to him (42:16; 19:9, 11). The Messiah is symbolized, in an eschatological frame of reference, by the "star out of Jacob" (Num 24:17), the "bright morning star" (Rev 22:16). The desert garden which blossoms with its rose (Is 35:1–2; *PE* 15), and which Pratt has already used to good effect in the earlier poem "Magic" (1.288), is a sign of the Messianic age (*PE* 15) prepared by "the hand of the Lord," an image which Isaiah associates with the work of creation (40:12), as well as with the acts of redemption and salvation (40:10; 50:2; 51:9; 59:1). The misstep occurs when human beings, like sheep, go astray, and turn "every one to his own way" (53:6). It is the mysterious "suffering servant" (42; 53) who, by bearing the burden of their iniquities, and by making intercession for them, "justifies" many and reconciles them with God (53:5, 10). Pratt treats this role of the Messiah, attributed to Christ by Paul (Rom 8:9), in *Pauline Eschatology* (175–8).

"Son of Man" is not an Isaian term, although it has been applied traditionally to the "suffering servant" by association. Aramaic in origin, this title brings together seemingly opposed qualities. In Ezekiel (2) it implies the lowliness of the prophet. In Daniel (7:13) it signifies a person who is mysteriously more than human, and it becomes a Messianic title. The author of the Apocryphal Book of Enoch applies it to a transcendent figure, heavenly in origin, who is to receive from God's hand the eschatological kingdom at the end of time (1 En 37:71). In the Gospels it is the title which the evangelists allow Jesus to use of himself. At times it refers to his lowly state (Mt 8:20; Mk 8:31; Lk 9:58). Again it refers to the triumph of the Resurrection (Mt 17:9), or to Christ's return in glory (Mt 24:30; Mk 8:38). Since Paul does not apply this title to Christ, Pratt does not discuss it in the text of *Pauline Eschatology*, although he includes it in his chart of the features of apocalyptic literature at the beginning of his thesis (*PE* 18+, table 1, Ezra).

To assume that in "The Highway" the poet is specifically invoking "the historical Christ of Strauss"[30] is to ignore the fact that Pratt was aware of the long history and connotative richness of this title, which, in its apocalyptic and eschatological association,[31] embraces both immanence and transcendence, and which harmonizes the two frames of reference operating within the poem. The Son of Man in Pratt's poem can be seen as an ironic figure representing, as he did for George Blewett, both the finest product of the natural evolutionary process and the fulfilment of humanity's highest religious hopes over the centuries. In him, the Lord of History, the human race hopes to rediscover "the highway," to grasp again the creative hand, and to see the close but ironic relationship between the God of Power and the God of Love.

While Pratt must have been well aware of Blewett's Christian view of the world, there is no evidence that he was acquainted with the thought of his contemporary, the French paleontologist and philosopher Teilhard de Chardin (1881-1955), most of whose works were published and translated posthumously, but whose longer life allowed him to spell out more explicitly what Blewett could only suggest. Pratt might not have agreed with some of Teilhard's ideas, but there is little doubt that Blewett and he would have appreciated Teilhard's attempts, in terms of Pauline theology, to achieve a synthesis of the scientific and the religious views of creation and evolution. Eschatology is the most fundamental element in Teilhard's thought, for he believed that in this area faith and profane activity reach their climax and consummation.[32] Pratt's "The Highway" might easily be read as a poetic synopsis of Teilhard's evolutionary thought.

The road of evolution is also a central image in "From Stone to Steel" (1.260), but in this lyric, which seems less hopeful than "The Highway," its cyclical path expresses Pratt's scepticism about the progress of civilization. It is closer to Huxley's "upward and downward road" (*EE* 3) than to an Isaian path of salvation. By establishing Geneva, in its association with such cultural institutions as Calvinism, the League of Nations, and the Red Cross Association, as one pole of human evolution, and Java with its earliest known human being as the other, Pratt is able to draw out the ironic tension between the "civilized" and the "primitive," between the "temple and the cave." He describes the convergence of these strains in contemporary behaviour where "the snarl Neanderthal is worn / Close to the smiling Aryan lips."[33] He suggests that all the centuries that separate humanity from the cave have not quenched its thirst for blood. Set off against each other by implication throughout the poem are the opposing yet closely related concepts of the legal and rational terms of international agreement and the instinctive ones of the cave; of just reparation and primitive retribution; of victimhood and martyrdom; of the praying fingertips of religion and the preying ones of barbarism, all the polarities in human beings that are kept apart by a boundary that is "tissue thin."

Pratt indicates that the key to distinguishing between appearance and reality in this context, and the only way out of the endless Spenglerian cycles,[34] may lie somewhere outside the situation itself – in the purifying experience of Gethsemane, where, like Christ, humanity may reorder its motivation, exercise its will, and find the strength to accept what it may be powerless to change. It is this moment that lends meaning to the cross of suffering, or to the crown of victory. The Julian of "Clay" did not see the connection between Gethsemane and the Cross. The Pratt of "From Stone to Steel" did, and never thereafter separated them.[35] Pratt frequently associates the Cross and the garden of Gethsemane with the archetypal Tree of Paradise from whose roots springs the Fountain of Life (Rev 22:1–2).[36] The Julian of "Clay" still conceives of the sacrifice of Calvary in these terms, although, as far as he is concerned, the fountain has run dry:

> A cross was raised,
> And at its foot a river ran whose fount
> Welled from the noblest veins that ever bore
> Imperial tides. This was the last great stream;
> The hill – the final altar of the world. (2.335)

But the dreamer of *The Iron Door* is less disillusioned after he attempts, though as yet in vain, "With an insatiate hunger, to discover / The fountain of that light and life inside" (1.212).

Pratt's later poetry depicts the Cross as a well-spring of new life and courage for besieged humankind. In "To an Enemy" (1.130), in effect a meditation on the implications of a Pauline text that is of great significance with regard to the doctrine of the atonement (Eph 2:13–17), the speaker's raw wounds help him to realize the suffering he has inflicted upon his foe. While their previous encounter has been in terms of the "burn for a burn, wound for a wound, stripe for a stripe" of the *lex talionis* (Ex 21:23–5), he now "thirsts for" forgiveness, hoping that when the audit is made the accounts will be balanced, not according to the retributive justice of the Old Law, but according to "the heart's own codeless bargaining," or the charity of the New (Mt 5:38–43). As he sees in his enemy the image of the suffering Christ (1.130), he conceives of their reconciliation as sacramental rather than purely human, and suggests that it can come about only through him "by whose stripes we are healed" (Is 53:2–5):

> And he, with wound adjuring wound, shall draw
> His equal measure to the sacrament
> From an old well to which some mortals went
> When, with their thirsts ablaze, they looked and saw
> An Orient form uplifted in the skies,
> And quenched their hate in his forgiving eyes. (1.131)

The reconciliation of the enemies is possible, however, only when, in imitation of Christ, they have laid aside all purely human power. In this poem, as in others, "the blood that is shed is the blood that unites."[37] The mystical insight into the nature of the Atonement throws into insignificance any questions about its judicial implications.

The language and imagery of the last four lines of "To an Enemy" may shed some light on the last lines of the later and more important poem "The Truant," in which Pratt still tries to reconcile the exercise of divine power and justice with the humiliation and abandonment of the Passion. In "The Truant," suffering genus *homo*, who has already learned the lesson of stoicism (2.130–1) and has countered with superior humour the threats of the Panjandrum, finds a well of living water flowing from the temple (Ezek 47; Jn 4:14; Rev 22:1) from which to quench "a dying thirst" (2.131). In the "Galilean valley" – the experience of Gethsemane, symbolized by the cathedral ruins – when all the visible supports of civilization have been torn away, he or she, like Jesus, consciously faces the prospect of passion and death, accepts the cup if necessary, and opposes the mechanics of the universe with the ironic power of the Rood.[38] The "Truant" exhibits that Pauline "steadfastness in persecution and suffering which is a condition of being counted worthy of the kingdom of God" (*PE* 95).

"The Truant," Pratt remarked on one occasion, "is a Christian who defies the giant of might and is willing to suffer pain and death to submission. The poem ends on the Rood, the sublimest symbol of Sacrificial love."[39] Like William Faulkner, Pratt is conscious that there is much more to humanity in the end than the sound of the "puny, inexhaustible voice still talking."[40]

It is possible that Pratt, writing this poem in the summer of 1942 (see 181, below), had fixed in his imagination the widely circulated photographs of the ruins of Coventry Cathedral in whose rubble the Cross was the only recognizable object. In a toast which he proclaimed at a St George's Day dinner, Pratt contrasts with the destruction of Coventry Cathedral the irrepressible English sense of humour as a sign of the spirit which enables one to carry on and to endure. In the same talk, Pratt discusses the Churchillian pause, such as that preceding the last line of "The Truant," which he uses for special effect when, like its originator, he wishes to express "a jauntiness in the heart, though the sweat may be pouring over the face, ... like calling out *en garde* in an encounter with death who has 99 chances out of 100 in his favour" (MS 9:67.1). In the end, the strength and courage demanded of Pratt's "Truant" are expressions not of mere bravado or of absolute power, but of the power which, according to Paul, "is made perfect in weakness" (2 Cor 12:9). This ironic power is described by another writer in prose:

The irony of Christ is unique. It involves the mastery of the world, spiritual freedom, freedom from the past and from every form of that which imprisons; it works through death and weakness; it therefore dethrones every other pretentious idea and establishes the movement through the human condition and total human condition (not the human condition of the beautiful people) as the way. Weakness becomes one of the great forms of power. Age, sickness and death lose their power ... and take on another form of power. Precisely what we are becomes the ironic mode of transcendence of what we are.[43]

It is in "cathedral rubble" (2.131) as in "Ragueneau's ruins" (2.110) that twentieth-century man or woman quenches thirst when he or she rediscovers the original source of the life of the spirit.

In *They Are Returning*, Pratt again uses the metaphor of sacrificial blood as a fountain of life, but in this poem it conveys the sense of disillusionment in the wake of the Second World War. Such horrors lead humanity to question not only the ultimate value of the sacrifice of the Cross but also of the faith born of it:

> We have known blood to run
> Like this before – blood of father, blood of son,
> And we had read
> That out of blood from hands and feet and side
> A faith once came to birth
> And found its test of worth,
> Or were we so misled
> And so unprofited,
> That in the self-same stream the faith has died,
> Lost in the periodic ebb and flow
> That left an aftermath upon the earth
> Of terror, greed and woe? (2.141–2)

Pratt employs the related image of a blood transfusion in "Cycles" (1951). Here his attitude towards power appears to be more ambivalent. The weariness and frustration in the face of the mounting tensions of the "cold war" are evident, as Pratt attempts, once more, to reconcile the polarities of power and love. Tactics have evolved to the stage where an individual, now unable to see the enemy's face or to meet him in hand-to-hand combat, and consequently denied the human contact that might lead to compassion and forgiveness as in "To an Enemy," kills coldly and impersonally with silent "geometry" (2.195).

Since the "Lord of Love" seems to have been slow to contain "the range of hate," human beings feel justified in calling on the "Lord of Hosts," the origin of whose power is dubious. He may well be the God who "giveth power to the faint" (Is 40:29). But, in the context of this poem, he could just as easily be related to the deity of Kipling's "Recessional" or to the Panjandrum of "The Truant" as a source of power and justice that is limited in its nature. He is called upon to act as the "judge of Nations," or as the referee in the international boxing match. There, he may not only split the "foul from fair," but also reverse the cycles by reducing warring humanity to its primitive state, a function which Pratt usually assigns to Death (see "The Truant," 2.127; *Dunkirk*, 2.123). Perhaps then, when extinction is imminent as at the end of "The Truant," we may be ready for the "Lord of Love and Life / To lead our ebbing veins to find / Enough for their recovery / Of plasma from Gethsemane" (2.196). The transfusion may only strengthen humanity before its passion, but it may also, by extension, imply the possibility of resurrection or renewal. Overriding this conclusion, however, Pratt implies, is the uneasy sense that in the struggle for survival human beings may, at times, be forced to align themselves with power and death before they can embrace love and life.

The poem "Displaced" (2.190)[44] was one of Pratt's last poems of a specifically religious nature. Published in 1949, after "The Truant" but before "Cycles," it does not employ the image of the blood transfusion but it does reflect the sense of weariness and discouragement implicit in the latter poem.

The late 1940s were the years of the "displaced persons" or "DPs" as they were commonly called. Driven out of home and country by postwar political settlements, or by the growing wave of Soviet-bloc invasion, they were not always welcome in the lands to which they fled for refuge. One "displaced person" of Pratt's poem appears to be the suffering Christ whom men and women now "come of age" have rejected as a "Romantic figure for a creed fixation," an outdated and, in Freudian terms, unhealthy[45] focus of attention.

Pratt suggests that Christ leaves with a feeling stronger than sadness – perhaps anguish (Mt 23:37; Lk 19:41–4), or justified anger (Mt 23:33; Lk 19:46). His embarkation is accompanied by "the sough of surf on limestone," a sound which recalls, yet is weaker than, the "grating roar of pebbles" in Arnold's "Dover Beach," or its analogue in "the melancholy, long withdrawing roar" of the world's ebbing faith.[46] The compass needle pointing vaguely "outward bound" suggests that Christ's destination is unknown or insignificant, but Pratt warns that what he leaves behind will be a wasteland (Is 21:1) of roots, rubble, and ash, even more barren and desolate than that at the end of "The Truant" (2.131).

The poet then addresses in turn three human substitutes, seeking the direction once expected from the displaced "figure" of the first stanza. But the distant reassuring voice of the prophetic watchman (Is 21:6–12; Ezek 3:14) is inaudible to human beings of this century. The stanza ends with the anguished question, "How can we sift your midnight's 'All is well' / From faiths confronting faiths with slit-throat edges?"[47] The navigator may be able with the aid of his charts to forecast the weather or chart the course, but he cannot read the apocalyptic signs of the times, or "Decipher black-and-scarlet palimpsest." Even the "wisdom" of the economist who "curved the cycles, carved their epitaphs" is limited in that there is no place on his charts to record the real "tidal booms" and "depressions" of humankind and its history.

Since no sense of direction can be provided by human beings, the world seems to be adrift. Pratt's last resort is to the image of the woman. When he orders her to "eat of the children's crumbs" (Mt 7:28), and to free her fingers for prayer, he refers to the foreign woman of the synoptic Gospels who begged Jesus in spite of his apparent indifference and even rudeness, to heal her sick child (Mk 7; Mt 15; DS 20). Her dogged perseverance in faith and humble prayer won her the praise of Jesus and a cure for her daughter. For one of such faith, suggests Pratt, "the limits of her husbandry" or the extent of her effectiveness will be measured by the number of faithful followers that she finds.

In the final stanza Pratt suggests that in response to the kind of faith and intercession expressed by the woman on behalf of her child there yet may be an answer:

Perhaps an ancient God who dealt in wonders –
Trading a heart of flesh for one of stone – [Ezek 11:19]
Will offer benedictions, not his thunders,
Bending his ear to catch a cradle moan. (2.190)

In the Gospel narratives, Jesus did hear the woman's prayer, praise her faith, and heal her child. Indeed, as Pratt suggested in "The Demonology of the Synoptics" (20–1, 32), Christ performed miracles or wonders only in response to faith, not to elicit it. Even in his own country "he did not many mighty works there because of their unbelief" (Mt 13:58; Lk 4:23), and at the request of the Pharisees he "refused to perform a sign for an evil and adulterous generation" (Mt 12:39; Mk 8:12; Lk 11:29). Since humankind has rejected the incarnate God whom it needs, the only alternative for the present generation seems to be a return to the God of the Old Testament, who may still be moved by mercy.

The image of a displaced Christ does not derive merely from Pratt's familiarity with the nineteenth-century poets such as Arnold, Clough, and Hardy, from the German philosophers of his past, or even from the "death of God" theologians who were his contemporaries. It is an old theme implicit, as Pratt knew, in the beginning of the story: "He came unto his own, and his own received him not" (Jn 1:10–19).

What Pratt mourns for here is not "the death of God," or his own loss of faith, but the apparently universal rejection of Christianity. The turning back to the God of Ezekiel could suggest a new beginning and it does imply a certain degree of hope. But the Incarnation has taken place. Humanity has been redeemed, and if it does not recognize Christ in its midst, it can only fear the apocalypse. Juxtaposing the image of the Syro-Phoenician woman with that of the God of the Old Testament, as Pratt pictures him, is, ironically, to displace both again.

While there is irony in "Displaced," it is obscured, not only by the obvious weaknesses of a mediocre poem, but also by the dichotomy that the reader may still sense in Pratt's subconscious between a thundering "ancient God who dealt in wonders" and the Christ who has been rejected by humankind, between the Ruler of the Old Testament and the Saviour of the New. While the split in the poem is intended, in part, to reflect the situation of the modern world, there is here, as there is in "Cycles," a suggestion that the relationship among the "Four Daughters of God" (see 40, above) has become for Pratt temporarily strained.

In *The "Roosevelt" and the "Antinoe"* (1.219), *The "Titanic"* (1.302), and *Behind the Log* (2.149), the question of a just exchange of life for life is raised again, as it is in *The Iron Door* (1.209), though not, perhaps in keeping with the nature of the poem, as insistently. In the crisis around which each poem is built, most human beings respond spontaneously in order to save others. But the pragmatic value of their self-oblation is often held up to question by the irony of their situation. The crew members of the *Roosevelt* (1.234–5), like those of the allied convoy in *Behind the Log* (2.184), become other Christs, not only in that they give their lives to save others but also in the ironic sense that their anointing with oil is the cause of their death. Against the background of the blindly misplaced faith which the *Titanic* represents, many of the passengers behave with generosity spelled out in terms beyond question:

> The boat was drawn up and the men stepped out
> Back to the crowded stations with that free
> Barter of life for life done with the grace
> And air of a Castilian courtesy. (1.333)

As he allows the reader to become aware that other lifeboats set out half-empty (1.332), Pratt queries the need of the sacrifice, but not the motive for it. In later poems, with the exception of the execution of Riel in *Towards the Last Spike* (2.244), the exchange of a life for a life is even less a matter of justice than one of love. "The Deed" (2.196), *Dunkirk* (2.113), *They Are Returning*, "Newfoundland Seamen," and *Magic in Everything* are celebrations of purely gratuitous human acts, executed "without terms and without drill commands" (2.189). The cost is simply not counted.

There are times in this life-for-life relationship when Pratt perceives self-sacrifice, or service of others, as a blood transfusion for the community, for the human race, or even for the whole Mystical Body of Christ, as it is in Brébeuf's France (2.48). In contrast to the widespread destruction around them, the work of the nurses in *They Are Returning* is described as

> finding
> The death-range near the Lines in Italy
> Where, standing by a soldier's bed,
> They could direct the pale-gold
> Drip of the plasma or the *mould*
> Into a median vein and see
> It re-enact
> The Resurrection from the Dead. (2.143)

The sacrifice of the members of the crew of the *Roosevelt* appears, at first, to be in vain as the sea contests, "with its iron-alien mood, / Its pagan face, its own primordial way, / The pale heroic suasion of a rood" (1.238). The priest's absolution and the burial service with its prayers of petition and the reading of 1 Corinthians 15 seem to be mocked by the diabolical spirits of the storm. But just as the ocean is no Gennesareth of Galilee, the clergymen are not Christ. Their rituals are not magic formulae (DS 6–7), and no automatic or simple solution is immediately forthcoming. This incident, like others in Pratt's poems, can be seen in its true perspective only in the light of his focal scene of Gethsemane, where Christ, or his human image, prays to avoid extinction. His prayer appears not to be heard and he must undergo death, but as a result "we are all of us saved" (Heb 5:1–9). As far as Pratt was concerned, no religious ritual or practice could excuse human beings from responsibility. It might change them by making them less selfish and by bolstering their courage, but it could be meaningful only in so far as it was backed by their willingness to lay down their lives for others (1 Jn 3:16).

Pratt regarded what he called "sea-shepherding" as a human participation in the work of redemption, "the going out to seek and to save a life which was otherwise lost" (*PE* 17; MS 2:11), or "God's art of salvage" ("Clay," 2.341). In the end, not one of the *Antinoe*'s crew perishes:

> All were brought
> Below where ocean miracles are wrought,
> Where the heart's furnaces are stoked and blown,
> Where men are shepherded in the old way
> Of the sea, where drowned men come to life, they say,
> Under such calls to breathe as never come
> To those that roam the uplands of this earth. (1.247)

Although the *Roosevelt* has witnessed the loss of several of her men, the notes of her whistle come from a "silver throat aglow / With life and triumph" (2.247), like the trumpet of the Resurrection (1 Cor 15:55). Of the work of "that fine mixture of nationalities, all engaged in a death struggle for the preservation of life," Pratt later wrote:

> The job was done just in time. It was a call well answered. The call of the instruments, joined with the hail of the human voice and the sacrificial blood beating at the pulses. Science in league with good will, individual courage and humanity behind the machine. It is that sort of thing, and only that sort of thing, which is the hope of the world. (MS 2:11)

Pratt's moral vision informs all of his narratives, but it seems especially evident in those over which he took the greatest pains to be "objective," or faithful to historical detail.

After the terrible expenditure of life in *Behind the Log*, Pratt questions, as he did in "The Toll of the Bells" (1.68), the meaning of 1 Corinthians 15:

> Where was the cause which once had made a man
> Disclaim the sting of death? What ecstasy
> Could neutralize this salt and quench this heat
> Or open up in victory this grave? (2.184)

In the midst of such chaos any immediate answer would be absurd. Time alone can unfold the truth:

> But oil and blood were prices paid for blood
> And oil ...
> ...
> And blood mixed with the sea-foam was the cost
> Of plasma safely carried in the holds
> Across an ocean to a continent,
> There to unblanch the faces on the fields,
> There to revein the vines for fresher fruits

187   The Atoning Christ

> In a new harvest on a hoped tomorrow;
> And over all, the purchase of the blood
> Was that an old dishonoured postulate,
> Scrubbed of its rust, might shine again –
> *Granted that what the mind may think, the tongue may utter.* (2.184)

This extension of the idea of the Mystical Body of Christ, which embraces within itself the mystery of the Atonement, receives a fuller and more explicit treatment in what is generally agreed to be the finest of Pratt's narratives.

THE FULLNESS OF THE VISION

In *The Jesuit Relations and Allied Documents*, as well as in secondary sources, Pratt found the wealth of historical detail that he drew upon for *Brébeuf and His Brethren*. He also discovered what might have been to him the less familiar aspects of Catholic Christianity spelled out, not in the abstract terms of theology, but in the existential terms of the daily lives of a group of men committed to living it under the most difficult circumstances imaginable. Apart from any specifically Catholic teaching, however, such as the manner in which Christ is believed to be present in the Eucharistic species, Pratt would not have found himself on totally strange ground. His previous training in philosophy and theology and the influence of George Blewett stood him in good stead. He sought competent advice from Jesuit and Basilian priests and from Catholic contemporaries, and through his practice of "objectivity" he was able to put aside any prejudice that might have proved an obstacle.

There is evidence, too, that Pratt, the Wesleyan Methodist by upbringing, discovered himself to be surprisingly at home in the atmosphere of Ignatian spirituality. Accidents of nationality and temperament or of practice and expression apart, Wesley and Ignatius Loyola, both mystics, are as one when they touch upon the centre of the Christian message.[48] Both were masters of an incarnational spirituality which owed much to Paul and to the *Devotio Moderna*. They preached docility to the work of the Holy Spirit, and an ardent attachment to the person of Christ, especially through a life of imitation of him in prayer, the discernment of spirits, the practice of the Christian virtues, penance such as fasting, abstinence, and almsgiving, and the service of others through the spiritual and corporal works of mercy.

It is of no little significance that, apart from Milton, whose work he considered "sublime" (MS 10:75.1), and Burns, whom he admired for his ability to turn abstract theological disputations upside-down in order to demonstrate their irrelevance (MS 9:66), Pratt preferred the religious poetry not of seventeenth-century metaphysical poets such as Herbert, Vaughan, and Traherne, who are barely mentioned in his lecture notes or in other manuscripts, or of later Protestant or Nonconformist poets, but rather the achievements of certain Roman Catholic poets whose work is strongly influenced by the baroque. Pratt's studies in theology, his knowledge of comparative religion and mythology, and his grasp of the history and psychology of religion might well have gained him entrance into the twentieth-century school of T.S. Eliot or W.H. Auden, but his concept of faith and its consequent effect on his imagination prevented him from sharing in their type of religious experience and desiring to reflect their style.

It seems strange that Pratt was convinced that in the religious poetry of the twentieth century there was nothing to equal Francis Thompson's *The Hound of Heaven*, until he reveals the fact that what he most admires is the sense of the poet's "surrender to God in the ecstasy of faith" (MS 10:72). In contrast, he remarks that Eliot's "dislike of passion or intense lyrical sentiment, his intellectualism," prevented him from making "that complete emotional surrender" seen in Thompson. In the light of this comment, Milton Wilson's observation in his monograph *E.J. Pratt* of "traces of Crashaw-like sensibility" in *Brébeuf and His Brethren* is perceptive, even if it is not developed in full enough detail to be satisfying.[49]

In another of his lectures at Victoria College, Pratt commented on the fact that while Auden was influenced by Hopkins' sprung rhythm, "nowhere did Auden come close to comprehending the depths of Hopkins, because the religious fervour simply wasn't there" (MS 63). It would appear that in Ragueneau's account of the Jesuit mission in North America and in the letters and journals of the missionaries themselves, Pratt rediscovered the "ecstasy of faith," the "fervour," and the mysticism that were marks, too, of the evangelical experience.

The complex image of Christ which is central to *Brébeuf and His Brethren* indicates that Pratt's comprehension of certain religious concepts continued to develop after he had finished his formal theological studies. One of these concepts is the Pauline notion of "the Body of Christ" (1 Cor 12:12-27; Rom 12:4-5; Eph 4:4-16, 5:22-33), which constitutes the organic unity of Pratt's poem. While this image is not at all foreign to Methodist spirituality,[50] and while he had explored its significance to a considerable extent in *Pauline Eschatology* (43-53, 183, 186), there are indications that Pratt did not begin to grasp its fuller implications until he had begun to write *Brébeuf and His Brethren*.

189 The Atoning Christ

Pratt locates the historical account of the Jesuit martyrs within the symbolic context of the Church as the Mystical Body of Christ. The France of the seventeenth century, of which Brébeuf and his fellow Jesuits are representatives, is depicted in the introduction to the poem (2.46–8) at the height of the religious revitalization that swept through it after the Council of Trent.[51] The "winds of God" blowing over France and bringing back the saints "in their incarnate forms" (2.47) are the poetic equivalent of the "Spirit of the Lord" in the prophecy of Joel (2:28), to which Pratt in *Pauline Eschatology* had attributed the great religious awakenings of the Jewish nation (*PE* 53), marked by spectacular manifestations and by the developing apocalyptic imagery of the age.[52] It was the activity of the same Spirit (Acts 2), he remarked, which established the primitive Christian Church (*PE* 56). In *Brébeuf and His Brethren*, the vitality of the Mystical Body has all the marks of a new Pentecost – prophecy, speaking in tongues, dreams and visions, healing, the working of miracles, and the discernment of spirits (*PE* 56). The Pentecostal theme is reinforced by the imagery associated with the Old Testament harvest festival (Lev 23:10–22), the elements of fire, earth, and water, together with oil, wine, wheat, and bread, and the blood of the sacrifice, all of which lend another dimension to the natural imagery of Pratt's poem.

In *Brébeuf and His Brethren*, Pratt also associates the prompting of the Spirit, which impelled the expansion of the early Church from Jerusalem to Rome (*PE* 56), with the call of the frontier which provided similar scope for apostolic activity in the seventeenth century. Like the sound of the clarion that echoes throughout the poem (2.46, 49, 55, 56, 64, 89, 108)[53] it awakened the Mystical Body to new life:

> It caught the ear of Christ, reveined his hands
> And feet, bidding his marble saints to leave
> Their pedestals for chartless seas and coasts
> And the vast blunders of the forest glooms. (2.48)

The dynamic imagery of the Incarnation and of the revitalized body introduced in the first lines of *Brébeuf and His Brethren* enables Pratt to bring together throughout the poem, sometimes in harmony and sometimes in tension, the immanent and the transcendent, the temporal and the eternal, the "already" and the "not yet." The poem links the past of the primitive Church, the historical present of the seventeenth century, and the future hidden in the dreams of the new apostles. If, at the end of the poem, "the wheel [has] come full circle" (2.108), it does not stop with the death of Brébeuf or Chabanel, or even with the destruction of Sainte Marie. Three hundred years later, the winds of God are still blowing through "the pines / That bulwark the shores of the great Fresh Water Sea" (2.109). Past centuries come back with the turn of the spade and the relighting of the candles. The Mystical Body is renewed once more, even as the Eucharistic Body is broken (1 Cor 11:26), and Pratt inserts his own age into the context of the cosmic Body of Christ which embraces all time and all creation (Rom 8:21), and which still looks forward in eschatological hope to the fullness of redemption (*PE* 97, 183, 186).[54]

Pratt had observed that, according to Paul, the Mystical Body is built up by the growing conformity of its members, in faith and in love, to the likeness of Christ, their head (*PE* 43). In Pratt's poem, Brébeuf and his brethren are Joel's young men who see visions (*PE* 53, 89). They are other Pauls for whom the vision or apocalypse is not only a source of insight into the Gospel of Christ and into his eschatological character (*PE* 92), but also the personal experience that motivates them to imitate him. That Pratt wished these experiences to be construed as authentic rather than as hallucinatory or illusory is suggested by tone and context.[55] They usually take place during prayer (2.48), are subject to the discernment of spirits (2.49, 87),[56] are grounded in a solid foundation in the spiritual life (2.49), and are most often related to a strong natural constitution (2.49, 56). When they come as a consolation after moments of great suffering or sacrifice, they are in keeping with the mystical tradition,[57] and are not necessarily a bow, on the part of Pratt, to the theory of compensation.

While Pratt's sources ascribe mystical experiences to all the martyrs, nowhere in the Jesuit *Relations*, in the allied documents or letters, or in the secondary materials which Pratt consulted is there any record of Brébeuf's first vision, or of the vow which follows it (2.48–9). It is evidently Pratt's own invention and one that is of prime importance to him, since it reveals Brébeuf's personal motive for his sacrificial life and death. As far as Pratt was concerned, neither the general religious enthusiasm of the day nor the "iron code" of Ignatius (2.64) could justify or account for his hero's acceptance of martyrdom.[58] It seems that Pratt wishes us to understand Brébeuf's vision of the suffering Christ not as a simple exercise of the imagination proper to Ignatian contemplation, but as a special grace of consolation without previous cause or of "infused contemplation":[59] "No play upon the fancy was this scene / But the Real Presence to the naked sense" (2.48).

In an apocalyptic moment which corresponds to the experience of Gethsemane in other of Pratt's poems, Brébeuf sees what may lie ahead of him, chooses freely, and commits himself to follow Christ, "*per ignem et per aquam*" (2.48). The prophetic words of his vow, "*I shall be broken first before I break them,*" resound throughout the poem, gathering greater significance as the climax approaches. They take precedence, from Pratt's point of view, over Brébeuf's canonical vows, his ordination, and his first Mass (2.49, 55).[60]

Through the vision and the vow, it appears that Pratt wished to indicate that his hero was not a neurotic seeking martyrdom as the fulfilment of a subconscious death wish. Indeed, at this point, Pratt is more likely to have seen in Brébeuf's vision the type of religious experience that Wesley would have considered fundamental to a true conversion.[61] It is possible that he may also have found a parallel in the Wundtian theory of "apperception," which for all its outdated clumsiness underlines freedom of choice and relates it to the function of the will. Brébeuf's vision during prayer provides the opportunity for "apperception." He first "sees" Christ on the Via Dolorosa (2.48). During the period of waiting and reacting to the image, there is a noticeable increase in muscular tension as his fingers are "closing and tightening on a crucifix" (2.48).[62] Voices speak to his ear and to his heart informing him of the consequences of his choice. Thus, when Brébeuf binds himself by his vow, Pratt suggests in Wundtian terms that he "acts freely from within, with a consciousness of the significance which the motives and purpose involved" have for him.[63] Having freely exercised his will, Brébeuf becomes, like Christ in Gethsemane or Shaw's Saint Joan (MS 4:28), another "Truant" rather than a passive victim, and from that moment nothing that Fate or the Indians have in store can touch him.

Brébeuf's companions are motivated by visions or by experiences similar to but less extraordinary than his (2.55–7), and they also bind themselves by vow to remain faithful. Later, amidst the terrible deprivations of the mission fields, they are provided with opportunities to renege or reaffirm their initial promises.[64] Mystical experiences in prayer (2.71, 80, 86), visions (2.80), dreams (2.80), memories (2.65), and visits to France (2.89), Quebec (2.90), and Sainte Marie (2.93) allow them to choose freely again. Champlain (2.75, 95), Richelieu (2.75, 95), the Indians (2.51, 70, 99), even the soldiers (2.92) and the traders (2.95) are dreamers too, but their secular visions, whether of power or glory, of death and destruction, or of financial gain and adventure, are all subject to time and change. These visions pale in comparison with an almost Dantesque perspective (*Paradiso*, 33.130–4):

> The priests were breathless with another space
> Beyond the measure of the astrolabe –
> A different empire built upon the pulses,
> Where even the sun and moon and stars revolved
> Around a Life and a redemptive Death. (2.95–6).

Apart from their visions, the lives of Brébeuf and his companions seem to abound in other manifestations of the Spirit (*PE* 56), which Pratt often handles with characteristic irony. The "putting on of Christ" (Phil 2:5) does not deify (*PE* 184) the Jesuits, who retain their human frailty. They are sorely tempted to give up: "How often did the hand go up to lower / The flag? How often by some ringing order / Was it arrested at the halliard touch?" (2.64). It requires effort to sublimate hoary "Gallic oaths" into the *Benedicite* (2.64). Brébeuf's methods of instruction are too sophisticated for the Indian mind, which cannot grasp abstractions (2.72). Yet he does not see that the Indians grasp better than do the Jesuits "the visual affirmatives of hell" (2.73). Brébeuf's desire to educate the Indian children in Quebec is rational and well intentioned, but clearly short-sighted (2.67–8). At times the Jesuits are intolerant and they take advantage of Indian credulity by employing as a basis of persuasion their marvels – the clock, the magnet, their use of writing, and French strategy in war (2.60–3).

On the other hand, Pratt frequently in Brébeuf's words attributes to the Indians "faith," "deeds," "the grace of martyrdom," "Pentecostal meetings" (2.94), "courage," "endurance," and "charity and gentleness to strangers" (2.67). These qualities, Brébeuf observes, give "a balance to the picture" (2.67–8). It is quite obvious from the poem itself and from the sources from which it was derived that neither Pratt nor the Jesuits saw the Hurons as "part of the unfocused evil of the narrative."[65] Moreover, to accuse Pratt and his Jesuits of prejudice because they call the Indians "savages" and try to convert them, or to call the Christlike analogy in the poem "as inept as Lampman's moose" in the light of seventeenth-century Catholic persecution of the Huguenots in France,[66] is surely to beg the question. Pratt knows his history only too well, but his vision here extends beyond its dark ages to a deity who is not the Panjandrum of a perfect universe but an incarnate God who works through and in spite of fallen but redeemed human nature.

Pratt's Jesuits strengthen their wills for the task ahead in the Pauline spirit of asceticism (*PE* 61–2). Brébeuf makes use of a year's delay "by hardening his body and his will" (2.50); Garnier is resolved

> To seek and to accept a post that would
> Transmit his nurture through a discipline
> That multiplied the living martyrdoms
> Before the casual incident of death. (2.56)

In the case of Chaumonot (2.57), Pratt illustrates the thin line that can distinguish Christian asceticism from that of a stoic or Essenic nature (*PE* 61–2), which is so severe that it breaks down the body.[67] In *Pauline Eschatology*, Pratt remarks that the real asceticism which Paul preaches is to be effected "by the exercise of the volitions which constitute, in the truest sense, the service of Christ" (*PE* 64). In this thesis Pratt's stress on the role of the will approaches that semi-Pelagianism which has been attributed to the Methodists.[68] There is little doubt that he saw in "the Jesuit will and courage" (2.109), also associated in the past with semi-Pelagianism,[69] an echo of his own emphasis. But in Pratt's sources, as well as in his thesis and his poem, asceticism as a discipline of the will is acceptable only in so far as it leads to closer union with Christ in charity.

Through fidelity to the vision that motivates them, and through lives of asceticism and charity, Pratt's Jesuits "put on Christ" (Gal 3:27; Rom 13:14). But it is in their relationship with the Body of Christ in its eucharistic sense that Pratt shows them to be incorporated most fully into the Mystical Body. In *Pauline Eschatology*, Pratt touches upon the role of the sacraments in general only to refute Schweitzer's claim that Paul saw them as part of a "magical process" (*PE* 183). He makes no mention of the Eucharist, even in its specific context in Paul's eschatology (1 Cor 10:16; 1 Cor 11:20). Although rejection of the doctrine of transubstantiation had been specifically enjoined on the Methodist church, which in doctrine if not always in practice still held fast to the main elements of John Wesley's Anglican birthright, the Eucharist, more than a simple memorial or token of the Lord's Supper, was to be accepted as "a sacrament of our redemption by Christ's blood." However, it was to be received only "after a heavenly or spiritual manner" and to be "fed on in the heart by faith."[70] This concept preserves intact the teaching on the Eucharist embodied in the Thirty-Nine Articles of 1571. While the connection between the Eucharist and the Mystical Body of Christ is more implicit in the Anglican form of the sacrament than in the Methodist, there is a sense that Pratt's grasp of the essential relationship between the sacrificial banquet of the Eucharist and the Mystical Body of Christ, which is explicit in Catholic doctrine, must have constituted for him more than an intellectual understanding, a moment of apocalyptic insight such as he himself had described (*PE* 92).

Pratt's attitude towards the Eucharist in the early poetry is best expressed in "Before an Altar" (1.110). In the wartime setting, Pratt implies that there is little time for that faith which could see in the bread and wine anything more than a token or simple memorial of Christ's passion and death, and their significance, even in this respect, pales before the reality of the human "blood ... on the brow / And the frail body broken." Here, the human situation appears to eclipse the ritual and to become the sacrament. But Pratt also suggests that before there can be another meaningful celebration of the Eucharist there must be Shrovetide, the time for men and women to be reconciled with their brothers and sisters (Mt 5:24), to purge themselves of "the old leaven of malice and wickedness," and to prepare to "feed on the unleavened bread of sincerity and truth" (1 Cor 5:8).

In a later poem, "The Depression Ends" (1.261), Pratt uses the image of the Eucharist as an eschatological symbol. The apocalyptic dinner which redeems humankind from "a world predestinate" and ushers in "a golden era" is more than the traditional Methodist *agape* or love-feast with its usual menu of bread and water.[71] It has its analogues in the saving feast of Isaiah (25:6), the marriage feast of Luke (14:12–24), and the eschatological feast of the Lamb (Rev 7:16–17; 19:9). In this dream the miseries of the economic order and the attendant psychological and spiritual depression are left far behind. The guest list is truly universal, extending to the four corners of the earth, but "the faithful and the elect" invited are neither ticket-holders nor church members, much less the proud, "the well-groomed and the sleeked." They are "the shabby ones of earth's despite," even "the starved, the maimed, the deaf and dumb" (Lk 12:13), all "misfits in a world of evil" (1.266). At this feast, the like of which has not been seen "since Galilean days," the dichotomy between the "Lord of Love" and "the Lord of the planets and the suns" has disappeared (1.266–7). This banquet, which like the redeeming act in *The Iron Door* is also "vouched for by a sacred precedent" (1.209), drowns "all memories of earth" and quenches "the midnight chimes" (1.267). With the eschatological feast, it ushers in the dawn (2 Peter 2:19). Like the Christmas gifts "as real as bread / Something to touch and taste and eat" (1 Jn 1:1) which are bestowed by loving hands in *Magic in Everything* (2.197), this feast is by nature purely gratuitous. Having "no logic beyond a dream," it transcends both space and time, and like the experience portrayed in *The Iron Door*, it provides the dreamer with hope for salvation.

The concepts of the Eucharist as memorial of the past ("Before an Altar"), and as eschatological feast or future hope ("The Depression Ends"), are brought together and charged with greater depth in *Brébeuf and His Brethren* by the sacramentalism which was inherent, to a certain extent, in Pratt's primary sources. In keeping with the *Relations*, he pictures the Jesuits as men whose apostolic lives centre around the daily celebration of the Eucharist. All of their visions and vows are related to Christ's body and blood (2.54–7). By the words of Brébeuf's first vow, *"I shall be broken first before I break them"* (2.49), Pratt associates him with the eucharistic body that is broken. After his first experience in the New World, he finds himself swung between two nostalgic fires, two homes. In one there was

> The daily and vicarious offering
> On which no hand might dare lay sacrilege:
> But in the other would be broken altars
> And broken bodies of both Host and priest. (2.55)

The altar-stone and the necessities for Mass which the priests carry with them are described in terms of a cross (2.76). The availability of wheat and grapes (2.72), or of bread and wine (2.81) for the sacrifice, is related to the availability of their daily substantial bread. The priests dispense "the Bread of Life to all," feeding both souls and bodies (2.98). Ironically, the "Bread of Life" is a sign of contradiction to the Indians, who see "Death following hard upon each offered Host" (2.78), and who want to kill the priests and eat their white flesh (2.80, 108). They associate the sights and sounds of the Mass not with salvation but with judgment (2.74). In time, all the missionaries, by their association with the Eucharist, are like the Christ of Brébeuf's first vision, "bleeding and broken, though not in will" (2.59).

For the final and climactic sections of his poem Pratt found his historical sources scanty in detail. It is here that he exercised most fully his powers of invention. In presenting Brébeuf's actual *Via Dolorosa* (2.104–8), the fulfilment of his early vision (2.48), Pratt gives it greater dramatic intensity and depth of meaning by having his hero remember the details of the Mass which he sensed would be his last. Each of the vestments which he puts on with its appropriate prayer assumes its full symbolic meaning (2.103). By virtue of its victim, the rude altar is no less hallowed than that of St Peter's in Rome. In directing attention to its stone, Pratt is able to suggest much. With its

> relic of a charred or broken body
> Which perhaps a thousand years ago or more
> Was offered as a sacrifice to Him
> Whose crucifix stood there between the candles (2.104)

the stone recalls the prologue where "the sound of bugles from the Roman catacombs," heard by seventeenth-century men and women, is associated with the animating Spirit of God (2.46). The mention of the "broken body" echoes Brébeuf's first vow (2.49) and foreshadows his death. It refers not only to the early martyr who gave his life for the faith, but also to the broken body of Christ, whose sacrifice (which Brébeuf helps to re-enact) is an eternal one. As he pronounces the words of consecration with which the book ends, the mystical exchange of life for Life is consummated. United with the Son in that obedience which extends even to the cross, Brébeuf goes out from the sacrificial meal to his passion and death. The "little tributaries of wayward wish" (2.105), memories of his home and past that intrude upon his consciousness, are reminders of his humanity, and occasions for him, once more, to confirm his choice. In this section, Pratt changes minor details provided by the *Relations*[72] so that the hours of Brébeuf's passion correspond more closely to those of Christ (2.106).

It has been suggested that Brébeuf's "thundering reproof to his foes / Half-rebuke, half-defiance" (2.107) is less than Christlike and may, in fact, undercut the image of his hero that Pratt has taken pains to construct.[73] The account in the *Relations* mentions that during his agony Brébeuf was silent, except when he spoke to encourage Lalemant and the other Christian captives, and to beg his torturers to change their hearts.[74] The attitude that Pratt attributes to his hero is derived, it seems, from Francis Parkman's rephrasing of the description in the *Relations* of the torture of Jogues: "a derisive word against his faith would change the lamb into the lion, and the lips that seemed so tame would speak in sharp, bold tones of menace or reproof."[75] Parkman, who is not always sympathetic in his treatment of the Jesuits, nevertheless admires Jogues for this attitude.[76] In applying these terms to Brébeuf, Pratt suggests that his hero is a man pushed beyond the limits of endurance by the sacrilegious actions of his torturers. He thereby counteracts any suggestion that Brébeuf's end is the simple fulfilment of a death-wish,[77] or that his close union with Christ, especially in his last Mass, is part of a magical process once associated with the mystery cults (*PE* 170–1). It does not deify him, or make him perfect. Pratt also indicates that the ultimate victor in whose triumph Brébeuf shared is more than a "pale Galilean." On this occasion, as a result of Pratt's liberty in the handling of less important details in his source material Brébeuf should be seen as no less honourable for his outcry – only stronger and more human.

In his passion Brébeuf is made to endure the ironic "baptism into death" (Col 2:12) and the collar of hatchets that he saw the Hurons use on the captive Iroquois (2.65–6) in "a mixture of aboriginal instinct with sophisticated mockery" (MS 3:24).[78] His courageous endurance holds the Indians in awe just as it angers them. Their brutal dismemberment of his body fails to reveal its source. As Pratt has presented his hero, there is only one explanation:

> But not in these was the valour or stamina lodged;
> Nor in the symbol of Richelieu's robes or the seals

> Of Mazarin's charters, nor in the stir of the *lilies*
> Upon the Imperial folds; nor yet in the words
> Loyola wrote upon a table of lava-stone
> In the cave of Manresa – not in these the source –
> But in the sound of invisible trumpets blowing
> Around two slabs of board, right-angled, hammered
> By Roman nails and hung on a Jewish hill. (2.108)

This is the intangible secret in the heart of Echon (2.60).[79] It links the prologue to the first vision of the Cross, to the final Mass and to the conclusion. These are the sections of the poem which Pratt considered to be of major importance and for which he could find little help from his sources. They are also the sections of the poem which best reveal Pratt's personal attitude towards his subjects, and his interpretation of their historical situation.

The final example in the poem of Pratt's invention is the epilogue. Coming as it does after the dramatic intensity of Brébeuf's death and Ragueneau's writing the final chapter of the history of Sainte Marie by setting the mission on fire, its tone does appear subdued. However, to call it an "almost wearied comment on the illusion which the shrine perpetuates"[80] is surely an unjust criticism.

Three hundred years have passed since the burning of Sainte Marie, and Pratt brings his work to a close by looking at the historical events in their current perspective. There may be little to admire in the modern highways that lead to the top of the hill, but Pratt cannot advocate a return to the seventeenth century. In drawing together the central images of the poem, he suggests that if the martyrs and their achievements "went into the soil," or died, it was only like the grain of wheat, to rise again, "to come back at the turn / Of the spade with the carbon and calcium char of the bodies" (2.110). As long as the prayers ascend, and "the holy bread is broken" (2.110) on the site of Sainte Marie, the martyrs have not died in vain. Their sacrifice is seen as part of an eternal sacrifice which is eschatological by its very nature, for it proclaims "the death of the Lord until He comes" (1 Cor 11:26). If contemporary humanity is unable to share the faith of the martyrs, or their zeal, Pratt implies that it may perhaps be heartened in its darkest hour by the example of their endurance and heroism,[81] or share in their "triumph of the spirit over failure" (2.77).

The last lines of *Brébeuf and His Brethren* express the broader sense of the doctrine of the Atonement towards which Pratt has moved in the course of this poem. In adopting the point of view of his Jesuit heroes, Pratt found the problematic or unbalanced theories reflected in some of his earlier poems subsumed by a theology embodied in the liturgy.

This understanding of the Atonement reaches out until it includes the whole universe in space and time (Rom 8:21; *PE* 97, 156–7) and "the whole mundane creation made for God, by God is drawn back into union with [God]."[82] God is no longer far off and detached but present in all things, and Pratt finds himself free like his Jesuits to indulge, on occasion (2.54–5, 93–6), in the real delight in nature that is his by instinct but which he seldom expresses poetically elsewhere.[83]

The strain of Christian imagery running through Pratt's poetry from the beginning, although it often contributes to his fundamentally ironic vision, is in many places flat and two-dimensional. But the eucharistic and incarnational symbolism of *Brébeuf and His Brethren* lends to the texture of the poem a structural coherence, a complexity, and that "greater range of suggestiveness"[84] that Pratt struggled towards elsewhere but often failed to achieve. There is a vertical dimension to this poem which penetrates through the finely woven historical narrative and finds its roots in the rich subsoil of *Pauline Eschatology* and in the years of theological and religious development that preceded and followed it. As a result, in the epilogue of the poem, with its wedding of the historical and the transcendent, Pratt is able to see Christianity and evolution not as two irreconcilable visions but once more as George Blewett and Teilhard de Chardin see them, as two complementary perspectives destined in the end to converge.[85]

Had Pratt held consistently to this synthesis, which he touched upon in "The Highway," he might have seen it not as solving but as embracing and illuminating some of the mysteries which confronted him during his lifetime – the relationship between humankind and nature, between evolution and creation, and more significantly between men and women and God. He achieved the synthesis, objectively and temporarily at least, in *Brébeuf and His Brethren*.

Conclusion

> We shall not cease from exploration
> And the end of all our exploring
> Will be to arrive where we started
> And know the place for the first time.
>
> T.S. Eliot, *The Four Quartets*

There is a sense in which, with journey completed, the reader as explorer may feel that he or she does indeed know Pratt and his poetry for the first time. The degrees of longitude and latitude have been recorded; the coastlines have been charted; the main physical features surveyed and put on the map; climate, prevailing winds, and precipitation noted; flora and fauna identified and photographed. The mists of myth have been gradually dispelled, and some of the assumptions have given way to certitude, yet for all the knowledge, as the explorer withdraws and surveys the whole, much of the mystery remains.

What can we ascertain at the end of this journey? No doubt we have a truer sense of the degree to which the poetic imagination of E.J. Pratt was formed by the experiences of his childhood, youth, early education, and years as teacher and local preacher on the circuit in Newfoundland. These experiences provided him, too, with a rich heritage of language, rhetoric, myth, and metaphor in which to express this imagination. Studies in philosophy, psychology, and theology, and years of teaching English at Victoria College in Toronto, together with travels and summer appointments first as a student preacher in rural

Ontario, Saskatchewan, Alberta, and British Columbia, and later as a teacher at summer schools in Ontario and Nova Scotia, while they provided no simple fulfilment of what was to be his ultimate quest, further nourished and then helped to liberate the imagination that Newfoundland had formed.

What may be said of the religious crisis that Pratt is reputed to have undergone? In the first place, it is fairly clear that E.J. Pratt, while remaining a religious man and a Christian throughout his life, never experienced a personal call to the ordained ministry. His lack of self-confidence, shyness about speaking in public, artistic temperament, and personality made him ill equipped to follow in the footsteps of "fiery" John Pratt. Yet, feeling indebted to his dying father for allowing him to resume his education at the Methodist College in St John's after three unsuccessful years as a clerk in a dry-goods shop, he promised his parents that he would submit his name as a candidate for the ministry. He would never go back on his word.

It is equally clear, if we do not have Pratt's words for it, that the greatest test came not so much in terms of "the primary Victorian dilemma" – the challenge which the Darwinian theory of evolution offered to religious faith – as in terms of the shadow cast over his life by the cruel suffering and untimely death of so many people, including many he had known and loved. In 1898, his first year out of school, he witnessed the return of the *Greenland* with its cargo of frozen bodies; in September 1916, newspapers reported almost seven hundred members of the Royal Newfoundland Regiment dead or wounded in a single day at Beaumont-Hamel;[1] friends and former classmates went down with the *Florizel* off Cape Race in 1918.[2] To these were added the more personal blows – the sudden illness and death in 1912 of his fiancée, Lydia Trimble, and, three months later, the accidental drowning of his teacher and mentor, George Blewett. Within the next fifteen years he lost his close friend Robert LeDrew (1919);[3] student and athlete Langford Rowell (1923);[4] his brother Will (1924); and his mother (1926). The serious illness (1925) and consequent suffering of his only child, Claire, was almost more than he could bear. For one who was by nature or by nurture uncomfortable with the expression of powerful personal feelings, the depression must surely have been great. Rather than jettison religious faith and succumb to despair, Pratt chose to wrestle with his God.

In an age when postmodernism and deconstruction are still in vogue, the prophetic stance of E.J. Pratt, his belief in the creative power of the imagination, his celebration of the potential for heroism in the anonymous individual or "the beleaguered group," his apophatic Christian faith and unquenchable hope may often appear to be embarrassingly out of fashion.

201 Conclusion

Nevertheless, the past fifteen years have seen the quiet but steady establishment of a solid foundation from which to undertake a fresh critical approach to the poetry of Pratt and a reassessment of his contribution to Canadian literature. David Pitt's long-awaited and painstakingly detailed biography has been instrumental in establishing or confirming the facts, in setting Pratt's poetry in the context of his life and times, and in helping us appreciate the complexity of the man and of his particular response to the world in which he lived. The publication of the two-volume *Complete Poems* edited by Sandra Djwa and R.G. Moyles has provided access to the whole canon of Pratt's poetry, including "Clay," and made possible a serious study of the development of his major themes and poetic technique. The best of Pratt's shorter prose – essays, introductions to readings of his poetry, occasional talks, and radio interviews – has been collected, edited and included in Susan Gingell's *E.J. Pratt on His Life and Poetry*, and in *Pursuits Amateur and Academic*, while Lila Laakso's comprehensive and descriptive bibliography provides a compass and a guide for anyone who feels encouraged to undertake further exploration.[6] In addition, collections of manuscripts in the libraries of Victoria University, Toronto; Queen's University, Kingston; and McMaster University, Hamilton, have been catalogued and made accessible, as has much of Pratt's correspondence with friends and contemporaries such as W.A. Deacon, Lorne Pierce, and Earle Birney.

Research and publication in related fields of scholarship, particularly in Canadian church and social history,[7] and in the history of education not only in the arts and sciences but also in theology, philosophy, and psychology,[8] have illuminated one or more facets of Pratt's life and work and by doing so have shed light on others. A CD ROM containing Pratt's most important works together with relevant background and illustrative materials is under preparation by Zailig Pollock of Trent University. Significantly, apart from one good but general overview by Robert Collins,[9] a critical introduction to the *Collected Poems* by Sandra Djwa,[10] and a light scattering of theses, articles, and monographs, there has been little or no new criticism of note.

What remains to be done? The time is ripe, if the fashion is not, for a reassessment of Pratt's place in the emergence of a distinctively Canadian voice and point of view, if one cannot yet say identity. Pratt deserves to be read, enjoyed, and appreciated. He also deserves to be taken seriously by critics whose knowledge of his poetry is extensive but who will bring to their investigation of his work a knowledge of theology, philosophy, history, psychology, science, technology, and the arts, and whose experience of life is a match for his. Such a re-evaluation could well lead to a task that has not yet been undertaken – a major study of Pratt's notion of irony as "the convergence of the manifold" with specific reference to its place in the Canadian tradition.

It is time, too, for a serious study of Pratt as narrative poet, of the persona of the storyteller, of his use of myth and metaphor, language and rhetoric. While poems such as "Come Away, Death," "Erosion," "Cycles," "From Stone to Steel," and "The Highway" provide evidence of Pratt's mastery of shorter stanzaic forms, his shrinking from the expression of personal emotion prevented him from becoming a great lyric poet.[11] At the same time, his need for a "large screen" on which to depict the vastness of the natural environment, celebrate heroic action, and display the importance of "the deed" drew him more and more frequently to the narrative, despite the fact that by 1925 the genre had been long outdated.

But all of this could create the image of a tendentious moralist rather than a genial host of stag parties and apocalyptic dinners, or a highly original poet who was able to relate within these narrative forms the language, terminology, and technical details of science, the insights of modern psychology, and the many and complex theories of history to events of contemporary national and international significance.

That a measure of Pratt's predilection for the narrative may be attributed to the native Newfoundland-Irish love of storytelling there is little doubt. Moreover, earlier centuries such as that of Chaucer were aware of the affinity between the roles of the preacher and the entertainer. One might ask how many of Pratt's poems, notably the longer ones, despite his quest for objectivity and his painstaking documentation of facts, are not related in some way to the parable, the fable, the saint's tale, and even the exemplum. How frequently does he indulge in the devices of the pulpit rhetoric in which he was trained, even to achieve a comic or ironic effect?

For a son of the parsonage whose faith was real and whose nature was sensitive and artistic, the tradition and the environment in which Pratt was raised, nurtured, and educated and the experiences of childhood, adolescence, and early adulthood tended to foster a particular and problematic image of God as the "good Lord" with the "glittering monocle," omnipotent, transcendent, and aloof – if not uncaring – in the early poems; a concomitant image of nature as ambivalent, unpredictable, and, often, unevangelical, and of human beings as frail and powerless yet intelligent creatures at the mercy of both. Apart from *Brébeuf and His Brethren* and some of the shorter poems that followed it, Pratt never seems to have resolved entirely for himself what appears in the poetry as the breach between the God of the Old Testament and the Christ of the New. There is a sense in which throughout his life he continued to search for humanity behind the divine log, for the human face of God.

In spite of his studies in philosophy, theology, and the psychology of religion, which he undertook in preparation for the ministry, Pratt would never have laid claim to being a theologian. For him, religion would always be a way of life rather than a system of beliefs – and it is always possible that a failure to integrate these facets satisfactorily (one that was inherent in his tradition) may have compounded his problem. Nevertheless, Pratt claimed that in Christianity, human beings might find all the elements that give meaning to life. There, he claimed:

The realist, the stoic, the prophet [may] at the end of their climb find a common ground. The desperate cruelty of existence may be seen in the lament over Jerusalem, and in that cry of abandonment on the Cross, but with that was [Christ's] belief in love, human and divine, stubbornly held, sublimely contrasted with the ignorance of his enemies. It is a hard faith as everyone knows who has tried to maintain it when failure, suffering and death crawl like shadows over the hopes. (MS 9.70:2)

The same inheritance contributed to Pratt's vision of humankind, a vision basically religious and essentially Christian which sees little genus *homo, simul peccator et justus*, with an indestructible spirit walking the narrow path between "the temple and the cave." Without generalizing from the tendency to absolutize that characteristerizes the apocalypse, Pratt plumbed in imagination the deep morasses into which humanity can fall as well as the heights of mystic union to which it may be called. He never lost his belief that, no matter how great the odds against them, human beings are capable, individually and communally, of breaking the regressive silence, speaking the creative word, choosing freely, and performing deeds of selfless and heroic love.

No matter how frequently he may have been tempted to adopt a fatalistic attitude – by the influences of his early environment, the experiences of his life, his studies in philosophy, psychology, and history, the authors that he read, or even his own temperament – Pratt's ironic vision enabled him to look on the human scene with compassion and humour and saved him from despair:

It is not just a matter of complete pessimism or of unqualified optimism. Both are lines of least resistance. The problem is an honest facing of the two realities, two groups of challenging facts. We deplore the debris in the wake of a storm, a flood, a fire. But [men and women] do get to work to clear up the rubble, to rebuild demolished homes, to assuage stricken souls. (MS 9.70:2)

In the end, it is probably this ironic vision, one that is much more challenging and sophisticated than many wish to ascribe to him, that best expresses Pratt's religious attitude. This gift, not unrelated to the irony of that kingdom as small and obscure in its origin as a mustard seed, where the first shall be last and the last first, where the tares are allowed to grow along with the wheat, where the rich are sent away empty and the poor are blessed, he recognized and cultivated. It was this that enabled him to see and to face with equanimity all the apparent contrarieties of life and death, wrestling at times with one or the other, but always allowing them to coexist, because he saw through them that the ultimate reality, the paradoxical sign of contradiction, far transcends all these limited aspects of truth.

Notes

CHAPTER ONE

1 Lench, *Methodism in Bonavista*, 153.
2 Inglis, *Churches and the Working Class*, 10–11; Semple, *The Lord's Dominion*, 28–30, 100–103, 179–180, 192–210.
3 Wesley, *Journal*, 10 June 1784.
4 21st Sessions Newfoundland Conference, *Minutes*, 13–14, 422.
5 Elliott-Binns, *Religion*, 457–8; M.C. Pratt, *The Silent Ancestors*, 95–6; Pitt, *The Truant Years*, 7–8.
6 21st Sessions Newfoundland Conference, *Minutes*, 14.
7 Semple, *The Lord's Dominion*, 29–30, 179; Walsh, *Christian Church*, 216.
8 Semple, *The Lord's Dominion*, 6–7, 254–75.
9 United Church Archives Biography File: John Pratt 1840–1904; Pitt, *The Truant Years*, 12–13; Semple, *The Lord's Dominion*, 232–8.
10 Skevington Wood, *The Burning Heart*, 265.
11 A. Lloyd Smith, "Victoria and a Century of Theological and Religious Life," 75; Hughes, "Wesleyan Roots of Christian Socialism," 49–53; Semple, *The Lord's Dominion*, 56.
12 Johnson, *History of Methodism*, 260–95.
13 Lench, *Methodism in Bonavista*, 91.
14 21st Sessions Newfoundland Conference, *Minutes*, 2.
15 Wakefield, *Methodist Devotion*, 20, 80; Davies, *Worship and Theology*, 4:282–348.
16 Frye in "Letters in Canada," 272, calls Pratt "a poet unusually aware of the traditional connection between poetry and oratory."

17 20th Sessions Newfoundland Conference, *Minutes*, 2.
18 21st Sessions Newfoundland Conference, *Minutes*, 9.
19 *Methodist Monthly Greeting* (June 1904): 12.
20 21st Sessions Newfoundland Conference, *Minutes*, 9.
    The deathbed witness of a fervent Methodist was considered of great value in fortifying the faith and the hope of others. See Semple, *The Lord's Dominion*, 60–1.
21 St John's *Daily News*.
22 25th Sessions Newfoundland Conference, *Minutes*, 8.
23 Pitt, *The Truant Years*, 12.
24 Semple, *The Lord's Dominion*, 18–23, 232–5.
25 Semple, *The Lord's Dominion*, 63.
26 Semple, *The Lord's Dominion*, 64. The childhood conversion of E.J. Pratt at the age of ten was recorded at Blackhead Church. See Twillingate District, *Minutes*, May 1904.
27 Semple, *The Lord's Dominion*, 64–5.
28 Pitt, *The Truant Years*, 51; M.C. Pratt, *The Silent Ancestors*, 144. In a private interview, Claire Pratt said that her parents were aware of the circumstances of Will's death, as was her Aunt Nellie, who identified the body.
29 *Doctrine and Discipline of the Methodist Church*, 16–19; Semple, *The Lord's Dominion*, 225.
30 Mrs H.G. Puddester to A. McAuliffe, personal letter, 3 December 1974.
31 Pitt, *The Truant Years*, 23–4.
32 Questioned after her parents' death about the veracity of these rumours, Claire Pratt acknowledged that she and her mother had been aware of them and had welcomed the opportunity to deny them.
33 Pitt, *The Truant Years*, 56, 60, 39; M.C. Pratt, *The Silent Ancestors*, 19–23.
34 *Doctrine and Discipline of the Methodist Church*, 141, 274, 530.
35 *Methodist Monthly Greeting* (February 1894): 20. John Pratt had given his coat to someone needier than he.
36 Quoted in M.C. Pratt, *The Silent Ancestors*, 16–19.
37 Johnson, *History of Methodism*, 256.
38 Pitt, *The Truant Years*, 53–7.
39 An exhortation to reading and education was a regular feature of the Pastoral Address read at each session of the General Conference. See 20th Sessions, General Conference, *Minutes*, 9–13.
40 Rupp, *Methodism*, 13; Dimond, *Psychology of Methodist Revival*, 80; Whaling, Introduction to *John and Charles Wesley*, 10–12; D.W. Johnson, *History of Methodism*, 262; United Church Archives, St John's, Newfoundland.
41 Rupp, *Methodism*, 29; Chapman, *The Victorian Debate*, 56. The United Church Archives, St John's, contains collections of books from the small libraries of Methodist ministers of John Pratt's time.
42 *Methodist Monthly Greeting* (June 1895): 85. This bias was characteristic,

too, of Nathanael Burwash, president and chancellor of Victoria College. See Van Die, *An Evangelical Mind*, 131.
43 Ronald A. Knox in his *Enthusiasm*, 447, remarks that Wesley too was "a complete Philistine about literature, a utilitarian concentrated on 'the one thing necessary.' He wrote for the utility, not for the pleasure of mankind."
44 Pitt, *The Truant Years*, 59–60.
45 *Methodist Monthly Greeting* (September 1888): 2.
46 McNeill in *The History and Character of Calvinism*, 395, comments on the stress placed upon the teaching of science in the Nonconformist schools and its later effect upon attitudes towards religion and theology.
47 21st Sessions Newfoundland Conference, *Minutes*, 72.
48 21st Sessions Newfoundland Conference, *Minutes*, 73.
49 20th Sessions Newfoundland Conference, *Minutes*, 77; D.W. Johnson, *History of Methodism*, 256.
50 Pitt, *The Truant Years*, 64–70.
51 This promise would also defer any prospects of marriage until after ordination. Pitt, *The Truant Years*, 114–15.
52 *Doctrine and Discipline*, 345–6.
53 21st Sessions Newfoundland Conference, *Minutes*, 84.
54 *Doctrine and Discipline*, 530.
55 *Doctrine and Discipline*, 84–5.
56 *Doctrine and Discipline*, 346–7.
57 *Methodist Monthly Greeting*, (May 1905): 12.
58 24th Sessions Newfoundland Conference, *Minutes*, 48.
59 Pitt, *The Truant Years*, 59–60. Peter Buitenhuis's assumption that "evolutionary theory came into conflict ... with the Christian belief in which Pratt had been brought up, and it probably had a good deal to do with his decision to leave the ministry," appears to lack foundation in fact. See his "E.J. Pratt," *The Canadian Imagination*, 50–1.
60 Walsh, *The Christian Church*, 214; Semple, *The Lord's Dominion*, 7.
61 G.W. Brown, "The Founding of Victoria College," 76; John Webster Grant in "Asking Questions of the Canadian Past," 98–104, as he draws attention to the need for an investigation of the place of theological education in Canadian churches, remarks perceptively, "When Thomas McCulloch modelled his seminary on the log Colleges of American Presbyterianism and on the University of Edinburgh, he began an equivocal tradition that is distinctly Canadian, and so familiar that we tend to take it for granted."
62 Walter T. Brown, "Victoria and a Century of Education," 109, 115–16.
63 Van Die, *An Evangelical Mind*, 45–6.
64 Weir, "Religious Thought and Evolutionary Ideas," 77.
65 Sissons, *A History of Victoria University*, 249.

66 Pitt, *The Truant Years*, 104–10.
67 *Doctrine and Discipline*, 297.
68 *Victoria College Bulletin* (1911–12): 42.
69 Paterson, "The Mind of a Methodist," 6–8; Van Die, *An Evangelical Mind*, 57.
70 Van Die, *An Evangelical Mind*, 57.
71 Van Die, *An Evangelical Mind*, 57; A. Lloyd Smith, "Victoria and a Century of Theological and Religious Life," 141–2.
72 A. Lloyd Smith, "Victoria and a Century of Theological and Religious Life," 137; Burwash, *History of Victoria College*, 470.
73 Hook, *From Hegel to Marx*, 79.
74 Van Die, *An Evangelical Mind*, 57.
75 Paterson, "The Mind of a Methodist," 6–8.
76 *Victoria College Bulletin* (1909–10): 24; (1911–12): 35, 42.
77 Many members of the Faculty of Theology at Victoria College had begun their teaching careers in the sciences. Among those whom Pratt remembered fondly was J.F. McLaughlin, who taught oriental languages and Old Testament exegesis and who presided at his marriage to Viola Whitney. Pitt, *The Truant Years*, 175.
78 Van Die, *An Evangelical Mind*, 104–5.
79 Van Die, *An Evangelical Mind*, 102.
80 Van Die, *An Evangelical Mind*, 96, 99–100.
81 Van Die, *An Evangelical Mind*, 105.
82 Van Die, *An Evangelical Mind*, 147.
83 Reardon, *From Coleridge to Gore*, 346–59; Rupp, *Methodism*, 10.
84 Van Die, *An Evangelical Mind*, 104.
85 Van Die, *An Evangelical Mind*, 104.
86 Van Die, *An Evangelical Mind*, 108.
87 Sissons, *A History of Victoria University*, 233–40.
88 Paterson, "The Mind of a Methodist," 5–41.
89 Blewett, *The Christian View*, vii, 309–10.
90 For the fullest available discussion of Blewett's contribution to philosophy see Armour and Trott, *The Faces of Reason*, 321–53.
91 *Doctrine and Discipline*, 543–4.
92 Victoria University Library, E.J. Pratt Collection, MS 61. All further references to this thesis, hereafter designated as DS, will appear in parentheses in the text. The title page reads "The Demonology of the New Testament," while the heading on the first page is "The Demonology of the Synoptics." It appears from the text that the latter title is the correct one.
93 Demonology, especially with relation to Christ's miracles of healing, was a central issue of nineteenth-century religious controversy. For a concise summary of the issues involved, see Irvine, *Apes, Angels and Victorians*, 381–405. The topic fascinated John Wesley, who attributed to demonic

powers "many disorders seemingly natural." See his *Notes on the New Testament*: Mt 12:22; Mt 10:8.

94 While Pratt does not cite as one of his sources Wrede's *The Messianic Secret*, a work which displayed the futility of the liberal Protestant quest for the Jesus of history and which prepared the way for form criticism, here, as in *Studies in Pauline Eschatology*, Wrede's influence on Pratt's interpretation can be sensed.

95 In *Studies in Pauline Eschatology*, 73, Pratt attributes a similar attitude to Paul. On the two previous pages he explores Paul's demonology.

96 Pratt's handling of Strauss and of other critics runs contrary to Sandra Djwa's assumptions in *E.J. Pratt: The Evolutionary Vision*, 24–7.

97 Pratt's evaluation of the miracles of healing approaches that of more recent Catholic scholars. See Donahue, "Miracles, Mysteries and Parables," and Stanley, "Believe the Works," 272–86.

98 Special Committee of Newfoundland Conference, *Minutes* (January 1912); Pitt, *The Truant Years*, 115–17.

99 9th Sessions Alberta Conference, *Minutes*, 66.

100 Pitt, *The Truant Years*, 115–17.

101 On the same occasion Pratt was awarded the Wallbridge Prize (New Testament Exegesis); the Cox Bursary (New Testament Theology); and the Frederick Langford Scholarship (Homiletics). In 1912, he had been granted the T.H. Bull, KC, Scholarship (Old Testament Introductions). *Victoria College Bulletin* (1912): 41.

102 10th Sessions Alberta Conference, *Minutes*, 137, 178, 182; 30th Sessions Toronto Conference, *Minutes*, 7. This year was extended annually according to the minutes of subsequent sessions. That it was not an unusual arrangement for those engaged in teaching is evident in the example of Blewett and others before him.

103 Further references to this thesis, hereafter designated as *PE*, will appear in parentheses in the text.

104 Pratt's interest in the dream as a source of insight into the nature of immortality, evident also in DS 10, is reflected later in poems such as *The Iron Door*.

105 Fitzmyer, "The Letter to the Romans," 9:5. There is general consensus among biblical scholars that Paul used the title only once. Pratt's view does not differ from it to any extent.

106 While in this section of the thesis Pratt reflects the influence of Harnack, especially with regard to the relationship between Gnosticism and Christianity (*History of Dogma*, 1:300ff), here as elsewhere he remains independent of Harnack's conclusions.

107 Once again the influence of Harnack's *History of Dogma* is evident, but Pratt sees Harnack's conclusion as one of many possible explanations.

108 John Wesley, *Notes on the New Testament* 1 Thess 23, explores the rela-

tionship between these terms: "Of the three mentioned here, only the two last are the natural constituent parts of man. The first is adventitious, and the supernatural gift of God to be found in Christians only." There is a real dichotomy in Wesley's concept of human nature, perhaps owing to the strong Augustinian influence in his thought.

109 In DS, Pratt notes that the paraphernalia of the professional exorcist and all the startling accompaniments of his rites become unnecessary as authority is vested in Christ, "whose word alone is sufficient."

110 Fernand Christian Baur (1792–1860), a disciple of Hegel and founder of the Tübingen school of theology, to whom Pratt refers in both theses, but more frequently in the second, tried to apply Hegelian concepts to the early development of Christianity, especially to the teaching of Paul. See Tillich, *Perspectives on Nineteenth and Twentieth-Century Protestant Theology*, 138–9. While the terms of Pratt's dialectic are quite different, he learned much from Baur about the historical development of biblical writings.

111 Pitt, *The Truant Years*, 154–5.
112 Bouyer, *The Spirit and Forms of Protestantism*, 168–9.
113 Walsh, *Christian Church*, 124; Knox, *Enthusiasm*, 586.
114 John Sutherland, *The Poetry of E.J. Pratt*, 29.
115 Sharman, "Illusion and an Atonement," 21–2.
116 Skevington Wood, *The Burning Heart*, 270–2; Knox, *Enthusiasm*, 515–18.
117 Bouyer, *The Spirit and Forms of Protestantism*, 168–9; Marty, *Protestantism*, 109–10; Semmel, *The Methodist Revolution*, 13, 86–7.
118 For example, *Acta Victoriana* (1913): 300–1; *Canadian Journal of Mental Hygiene* 3 (1921): 95–116; *Public Health Journal* 12 (1921): 148–55. The latter article records observations on the application of the Binet-Simon (Stanford) Tests to children in Western Avenue School, Toronto.
119 Sissons, *A History of Victoria College*, 253.
120 Pitt, *The Truant Years*, 152.
121 Burwash, *The History of Victoria College*, 245.
122 Sissons, *A History of Victoria College*, 230.
123 Van Die, *An Evangelical Mind*, 130.
124 Pitt states that "a 'serious illness' some time before [Pratt's] sixth year – undiagnosed...but probably rheumatic fever – had left him a reputed heart murmur. To aggravate his case, he was highly susceptible to respiratory infections.... His need to be very careful about himself and what he did," Pitt claims, resulted in "important psychological consequences." He records that Pratt suffered a number of "physical and nervous" breakdowns: see *The Truant Years*, 23–4, 72–3, 103–9; 115–16, 227–30; *The Master Years*, 300.
125 Sissons, *A History of Victoria College*, 277.
126 *Victoria College Bulletin* (1920–1): 10; (1933–4): 31.

127 Pacey, "E.J. Pratt," 173.
128 36th Meeting Alberta Conference, *Minutes*, 70.
129 "Ned Pratt," *CBC Times*, 4–10 February 1961: 4.
130 Viola Pratt, personal interview, Toronto, 19 July 1977. Viola Pratt stated that by 1960 she was doing her husband's correspondence as he directed, and that she wrote no letter expressing this request or that of resignation. The Archives of the United Church, Alberta and Toronto Conferences, have failed to uncover any letter to this effect, although it is possible that a verbal request could have been made. See also Pitt, *The Master Years*, 487–8.
131 Pratt cashed in his pension to pay for the medical expenses of his daughter, Claire. Viola Pratt, personal interview, Toronto, 19 July 1977.
132 "E.J. Pratt," *Globe and Mail*, 27 April 1964: 8.

CHAPTER TWO

1 These four different religious attitudes attributed to Pratt are found in Sharman, "Illusion and an Atonement," 21–2; Buitenhuis, Introduction to *Selected Poems of E.J. Pratt*, xvi; Birney, "E.J. Pratt and His Critics," 143; and Frye, Introduction, xiii, xiv–xv, respectively. John Sutherland in the preface to his *The Poetry of E.J. Pratt*, viii, finds "orthodox Christian thought implicit in the narratives," but does not, he says, attribute to Pratt "an orthodox Christian position."
2 Djwa, *The Evolutionary Vision*, 26–7.
3 Augustine, *Ennarationes in Psalmos* 84:10–12; Owst, *Literature and Pulpit in Mediaeval England*, 90–2.
4 Hodges, *The Pattern of Atonement*, 10.
5 H.G. Wood, *Belief and Unbelief since 1850*, 28; Davies, *The Vigilant God*, 2–7; Tracy, *The God Who Acts*, 2–3, 7.
6 Bouyer, *The Spirit and Forms of Protestantism*, 168–9.
7 Lench, *An Account of the Rise and Progress of Methodism*, 59.
8 Calvin, *Institutes*, 1:5.1; 3:23.2.
9 Bouyer, *The Spirit and Forms of Protestantism*, 66. Probably the most positive image of Calvin's God may be found in his *Sermons sur la Nativité, la Passion, la Resurrection, et le dernier Avènement de Notre Seigneur, Jesus Christ*.
10 Bouyer, *The Spirit and Forms of Protestantism*, 152.
11 This interpretation, held by Julian in Pratt's "Clay" (2.319, 334–5), leads him to reject belief in God.
12 Marty, *Protestantism*, 86–97.
13 Dillenberger and Welch, *Protestant Christianity Interpreted through Its Development*, 20.
14 Dillenberger and Welch, *Protestant Christianity Interpreted through Its Development*, 200.

15 Dillenberger and Welch, *Protestant Christianity Interpreted through Its Development*, 200.
16 McNeill, *The History and Character of Calvinism*, 35. See also 9, 14, above.
17 Chapman, *The Victorian Debate*, 49.
18 Semmel, *The Methodist Revolution*, 13.
19 Wesley, *The Nature, Design and General Rules of the United Societies*, 270.
20 The remainder of the quotation is taken from the typescript of this interview, which was later edited and abridged for presentation on CBC Radio.
21 Rupp, *Methodism in Relation to the Protestant Tradition*, 16.
22 Lawton, *John Wesley's English*, 20.
23 Wesley, "The Great Assize," *Sermons on Several Occasions*, 238. All further references to the sermons in this series will be included in parentheses in the text.
24 Lawton, *John Wesley's English*, 20.
25 Wesley as quoted by Shaw, *Digest of the Doctrinal Standards*, 129.
26 This sermon, "The Righteousness of Faith," provides a fine illustration of Wesley's sermon technique and psychological orientation, and might with interesting results be compared to the Ignatian method of prayer called "the application of the senses." See *Spiritual Exercises of St. Ignatius*, 65–70.
27 To describe this remedy, Wesley elsewhere uses the term "therapeiea psyches," the healing of the soul (44:64).
28 A. Skevington Wood, *The Burning Heart*, 238.
29 A. Skevington Wood, *The Burning Heart*, 269; Knox, *Enthusiasm*, 583–5.
30 Bouyer, *The Spirit and Forms of Protestantism*, 184.
31 *Methodist Monthly Greeting* (June 1890): 100.
32 Bouyer, *The Spirit and Forms of Protestantism*, 184.
33 The Twenty-Five Articles of Religion were abridged from the Thirty-Nine Articles by Wesley in 1784 in an attempt to eliminate what he considered to be the extreme influences of Calvinism and Arminianism on the one hand and Sacramentarianism on the other (Shaw, *Digest of the Doctrinal Standards*, 14). However, these Articles belonged to the discipline of the Methodist Episcopal Church. They were not part of the British Wesleyan tradition of John Pratt, and did not apply to Methodism in Newfoundland until the formation of the Methodist church in Canada in 1884. Until then, Wesley's *Notes on the New Testament* and the four volumes of his *Sermons* were the sole source of the doctrine preached by the British Wesleyan Connexion in Canada, and remained the sole source in Britain.
34 Emphasis mine.
35 Bouyer, *The Spirit and Forms of Protestantism*, 174; Dillenberger and Welch, *Protestant Christianity Interpreted through Its Development*, 213; McNeill, *The History and Character of Calvinism*, 395.

36 Dillenberger and Welch, *Protestant Christianity Interpreted through Its Development*, 213–14; Marty, *Protestantism*, 110.
37 H.G. Wood, *Belief and Unbelief since 1850*, 52.
38 Chapman, *The Victorian Debate*, 40.
39 Marty, *Protestantism*, 110; McNeill, *The History and Character of Calvinism*, 406.
40 Marty, *Protestantism*, 110.
41 Marty, *Protestantism*, 110.
42 Marty, *Protestantism*, 110.
43 Marty, *Protestantism*, 28.
44 Davies, *Worship and Theology in England*, 5:83.
45 Djwa, *The Evolutionary Vision*, 11, 17, 92.
46 On this topic see also John Wesley, *Sermons*, 9:108; 10:11–122; 41:259.
47 The "hollow of God's hand" was also a recurring image in certain lyrics in John Wesley's *A Collection of Hymns for the Use of the People Called Methodists*, notably in hymns "For Going on Shipboard" and "On Going to Sea," nos 762–4.
48 Magoun, ed., *Anglo-Saxon Poems*, 21. While there is no evidence that Pratt had any knowledge of Anglo-Saxon, he may have read such poems in translation.
49 An interesting study of the cosmic irony in this early work is Gibbs' "A Knocking in the Clay," 56–64.
50 "Clay" abounds in the "O-thouing" which Pratt later took pains to expunge from his poetry. It also contains some fine examples of his ear for clear and colloquial twentieth-century language suited to his subjects.
51 Klinck and Wells, *Edwin J. Pratt*, 16.
52 See Fitzgerald, lxxix–xcvii; Browning, "Rabbi Ben Ezra," lines 145–92, and "Caliban upon Setebos," lines 75–9. Clay is a common biblical term for the flesh or the body or the material out of which it is fashioned: see Is 29:16; Job 4:19; Jer 18:4; Rom 9:20. It was one of John Wesley's favourite terms for the body and suggests a dualism inherited from Augustine and from Neoplatonic philosophy: see *Sermons* 3:348; *Letters* 1:29; *A Collection of Hymns*, 718–19. In the cancelled fragment usually appended to the end of Shelley's "Julian and Maddalo," the dead are seen as "dust and clay and nothing more" (618). The image is also significant in Francis Thompson's *The Hound of Heaven*, believed by Pratt to be the finest religious poem written (MS 72); see chapter 5, 169, below.
53 It is interesting to compare Pratt's "Clay" with Archibald MacLeish's contemporary adaptation of Job, *J.B.: A Play in Verse*. J.B., too, attempts to reconcile belief in Divine Providence with the problem of human suffering. Like Job he suffers directly, but like Julian, the only answer that he can find is in human terms.
54 The refinement of this theme in terms of the relationship between bar-

barism and civilization, or nature and grace, recurs throughout Pratt's poetry and may be seen in condensed form in poems such as "From Stone to Steel" (1.260) and *They Are Returning* (2.140).
55 Lewis, *The Problem of Pain*, 3, 25; Murray, *The Problem of God*, 104.
56 Pratt uses the same metaphor in *The Fable of the Goats* (2.12).
57 Murray, *The Problem of God*, 108.
58 For other echoes of *King Lear* see "Clay," 2.308, 316, 322–3.
59 Or what C.S. Lewis calls "the concept of plurality." In *The Problem of Pain*, 23, Lewis discusses the notion of a perfect world in terms of its consequences for human freedom: "Try to exclude the possibility of suffering which the order of nature and the existence of free wills involve and you will find that you have excluded life itself."
60 Just as in *The "Roosevelt" and the "Antinoe"* (1.235–8), the prayers of clergyman and priest appear to be lost in the fury of the storm.
61 Lewis, *The Problem of Pain*, 14.
62 The most common New Testament titles of God, and those most frequently used in Wesley's *Sermons* (see 43, above).
63 Pratt explores the response of stoicism to suffering in *The Iron Door* (1.209) and in "The Stoics" (2.131). The only answer that he finds to the question that he poses in "The Stoics" is not a "stoic" answer at all. It is that of "The Truant" (2.131), or of Paul (*PE* 62–7, 162).
64 Lewis, *The Problem of Pain*, 30. It should be noted, however, that this same analogy is used by Isaiah (64:8) to express the close relationship between the Creator, who is no less the Father for being the potter, and his creature. It is also used by Paul (Rom 9:21) to refute the argument that God's designs are unjust.
65 Lewis, *The Problem of Pain*, 36.
66 Wilfred Owen, *War Poems and Others*, 88, 95–6.
67 Hardy, *The Collected Poems*, 78–91.
68 Joyce, *Dubliners*, 223–4.
69 Lynch, *Images of Hope*, 105–25.
70 J.T. Forrestell, "The Letter to the Thessalonians" 48:14, and Joseph Grassi, "The Letter to the Colossians" 55:10, in *The Jerome Biblical Commentary* 2:229, 336, discuss the relationship of the virtues in Paul in terms similar to those used by Pratt.
71 See 71–2, below, for a more detailed examination of this question.
72 27 August 1927, W.A. Deacon Correspondence, Thomas Fisher Rare Book Library, Toronto. Pratt's interest in spiritualism after the writing of *The Iron Door* is documented by David Pitt in his *E.J. Pratt: The Master Years 1927–1964*, 8–11.
73 For A.J.M. Smith's use in *The Book of Canadian Poetry*, Pratt offers him "The Truant" as "the only good thing I have done this past summer" (20 October 1942). Later Pratt expressed bewilderment at adverse criticism

of *Still Life* (1943), and especially of "The Truant" on the grounds of obscurity: "I thought it was clear that I was making an indictment of power by humanity." (28 January 1944, A.J.M. Smith Correspondence, Thomas Fisher Rare Book Library, Toronto).

74 Lucretius, *De rerum natura*, 2.646ff; 5.55–234; 6.1–96; Eliot, "The Hollow Men," *Collected Poems*, 90.

75 The "absolutizing instinct magnifies. In its presence each thing loses its true perspective ... The small becomes the big ... The absolutizing instinct is the father of the hopeless, and adds that special feeling of weight that hopelessness attaches to everything it touches. It is, in general, the creator of hopeless projects, the creator of idols" (Lynch, *Images of Hope*, 106).

76 Personal interviews with Northrop Frye, Victoria College, 22 May 1974; E.J. McCorkell, CSB, St Michael's College, 16 May 1974; J.S. McGivern, SJ, archivist, Martyrs' Shrine, 15 July 1974; Viola Pratt, 15 June 1974 and 19 July 1977; Claire Pratt, 15 June 1974.

77 Murray, *The Problem of God*, 18.

CHAPTER THREE

1 For example: Djwa, *The Evolutionary Vision* 27, 55, 76; Frye, *Silence in the Sea*, 193; Horwood "E.J. Pratt and William Blake," 197–207; King, "The Mind of E.J. Pratt," 10–11; Macpherson, *Pratt's Romantic Mythology*, 5, 12; John Sutherland, *The Poetry of E.J. Pratt*, 22, 25, 36–7; West, "E.J. Pratt's Four-Ton Gulliver," 13–20; Wilson, *E.J. Pratt*, 5, 8, 33–6.

2 For example, Robert Gibbs in his "Poet of the Apocalypse" 32–41, provides an interesting study of *The Witches' Brew* and "The Great Feud" in relation to Pratt's imagination, yet he fails to associate the poet's use of the apocalyptic genre and style with Pratt's familiarity with biblical literature.

3 Grelot, "Apocalyptic," 17–18.

4 In *Brébeuf and His Brethren* (2.46), the members of the Petun and Neutral tribes associate the black-robed missionaries with the spirits of disease and famine, and exorcise them from their villages.

5 McKenzie, *Dictionary of the Bible*, 39, 41–2; Cantley, "Introduction to Apocalyptic," 501.

6 Rahner and Vorgrimler, *Theological Dictionary*, 149–50.

7 "The stony" was John Wesley's favourite term for the core of evil which he saw in the human personality. See Lawton, *John Wesley's English*, 161.

8 Gibbs, "Poet of the Apocalypse," 41.

9 Luther, *Lectures on Romans*, 5:4; 6:6; 8:3.

10 William Shaw in his *Digest of the Doctrinal Standards of the Methodist Church*, 51, comments that Traducianism, a theory adopted by Tertullian in the

third century that accounts for all the phenomena of heredity including moral depravity and death, has been made to do service for the erroneous conception of hereditary guilt. Properly understood, he adds, Traducianism is the theory most widely accepted, "especially as co-ordinating with the results of the scientific study of heredity."

11 Piet Smulders, "Evolution and Original Sin," 74, remarks that "original sin frequently appears as the weight of evil that burdens every man by his birth and by his solidarity with all mankind prior to all his sins."
12 Shaw, *The Doctrine and Discipline of the Methodist Church*, 61.
13 27 August 1927, W.A. Deacon Correspondence.
14 In a similar way Christ's answer to the question posed by the Pharisees with which Pratt ends his first thesis, "The Demonology of the Synoptics," indicates how, in all their legal arguments and in their rationalization of the case, they have completely misunderstood the issue.
15 Vawter, "Missing the Mark," 19–20; Barclay, *New Testament Words*, 118–20.
16 Barclay, *New Testament Words*, 132–3.
17 Lynch, *Images of Hope*, 177.
18 A.J.M. Smith, *Some Poems of E.J. Pratt*, 13.
19 Sandra Djwa in "E.J. Pratt and Evolutionary Thought," 417, attributes "the life and death impulse" in Pratt's poetry to Darwinism alone. While Pratt was aware of its presence in Darwin's thought, he gives ample evidence in *Pauline Eschatology* (63–4, 76–7, 80–1, 128, 141) that this impulse antedates the nineteenth century.
20 McKenzie, *Dictionary of the Bible*, 39, 41–2.
21 Atwood, *Survival*, 93.
22 Excellent examples of John Wesley's apocalyptic vision of nature may be found in Sermon 15, "The Great Assize," and in Sermon 56, "God's Approbation of His Works."
23 Atwood, *Survival*, 73.
24 Darwin, *On the Origin of Species*, 73.
25 This poem, first published in *Poetry* 58 (1941): 1–4, probably refers to the Battle of Britain, which reached its climax in September 1940.
26 A.J.M. Smith, *Some Poems of E.J. Pratt*, 5.
27 In *Towards the Last Spike*, Pratt describes the Rockies, which exemplify his concept of the sublime (MS 63), in a similar fashion: "Terror and beauty like twin signal flags / Flew on the peaks" (2.231).
28 A.J.M. Smith, *Some Poems of E.J. Pratt*, 5.
29 There is evidence throughout the poem that Pratt had in mind the notion that "the blood of the martyrs is seed" (Tertullian, *Apology*, 50:13).
30 Harriott, "The Last Enemy," 100.
31 Vulcan, a symbol of the corrupt or weak soul, bears a family resemblance to the traditional Christian concept of the devil. See Cirlot, *A Dictionary of Symbols*, 342.

32 Pratt's "silent underwater kill" suggests Albany's line from *King Lear* 4.2.55, "Humanity must perforce prey on itself / Like monsters of the deep."
33 Shaw, *Doctrine and Discipline*, 118–19. "It [Hades] is without any disciplinary or purgatorial action."
34 Macpherson, *Pratt's Romantic Mythology*, 7–10, 16–17.
35 X.W.P. Corcoran, "Celtic Mythology," 232–6.
36 Cirlot, *A Dictionary of Symbols*, 348.
37 Adler, *The Living Symbol*, 260.
38 Djwa, *The Evolutionary Vision*, 37.
39 Lorne Pierce to E.J. Pratt, 1 December 1923.
40 From the inscription on Tom's head in the manuscript copy of "The Witches' Brew or The Immortals' Night Off: A Pot-Pourri in Verse" in the Lorne Pierce Collection of Manuscripts.
41 Séan O'Súilleabhain, "The Sea," 403. For the appearance of the sea-cat as a symbol in contemporary Irish literature, see Flann O'Brien, *The Poor Mouth*.
42 Tennyson's kraken is to remain in its lair "until the latter fire shall heat the deep; / Then once by man and angels to be seen / In roaring he shall rise and on the surface die." See Tennyson, *Poems and Plays*, 15.
43 E.J. Pratt to Earle Birney, February 1950.
44 Cantley, "Introduction to Apocalyptic," 501; Grelot, "Apocalyptic," 17–18.
45 Greene, *The Wooden Walls among the Ice-Floes*, 63–4; John Melendy, survivor of the SS *Greenland* as quoted by Mowat in *In the Wake of the Great Sealers*, 95–8. Pratt refers to this incident again in *Rachel*, 7.
46 Darwin, *On the Origin of Species*, 73–5.
47 Darwin, *On the Origin of Species*, 68–9.
48 A common symbol of immensity in apocalyptic literature. See McKenzie, *Dictionary of the Bible*, 39.
49 Pratt's comments on seals and sealing in "The Great Seal Hunt" (MS 68.5) should be read for their bearing on the interpretation of this poem. They reveal both his reverence for the beauty of the seal pups and his consciousness of the place of sealing in the economy of nature as well as in the economy of the people of Newfoundland. In MS 2:15 he notes that in 1910 the price brought by seals was $5.00 for a young harp, and $3.70 for an old one.
50 "The mass slaughter of the seals and the mass starving and freezing of the hunters unite them in a common sacrifice, and at times even in a common grave." Wilson, *E.J. Pratt*, 11.
51 In "Call and Answer on the Sea" (MS 68:6, p. 3) Pratt elaborates on the asdic and radar as conductors leading "to life or to death."
52 Frye, *Silence in the Sea*, 193.

53 Cantley, "Introduction to Apocalyptic," 501.
54 Horwood, "E.J. Pratt and William Blake," 198.
55 Livesay, "The Documentary Poem," 277–80.
56 Dodd, *The Parables of the Kingdom*, 16–21.
57 Darwin, *The Descent of Man and Selection in Relation to Sex*, 1: 161–3. Darwin describes the emergence of the instincts in the apelike progenitors of the human race.
58 In *E.J. Pratt: The Evolutionary Vision*, 61ff, Sandra Djwa has perceptively indicated Pratt's possible debt to Sir Charles G.D. Roberts's prehistoric romance, *In the Morning of Time* (1922). She does not, however, mention the probable debt of both to Darwin's *Descent of Man*.
59 Darwin, *Descent of Man*, 1:238–40.
60 Darwin *On the Origin of Species*, 71–2; George Blewett, *The Christian View of the World*, 280–1 These passages speculate upon the way in which the moral sense, or conscience, emerged in animals.
61 Darwin, *Descent of Man*, 74.
62 Darwin, *Descent of Man*, 81.
63 John Sutherland, *The Poetry of E.J. Pratt*, 105–6.
64 McKenzie, *Dictionary of the Bible*, 39.
65 Darwin, *The Emotions in Man and in Animals*, 13.
66 John Sutherland, "E.J. Pratt: A Major Contemporary Poet," 47–8. In a letter to Dorothy Doyle, 21 July 1957, Pratt wrote of Sutherland's criticism in this article and in his book: "Sutherland brought out many facets of my work of which I was unaware (or but *dimly* conscious) at the time of writing, out of which I could see the partial truths after re-reading his book. He did plough back into the past to uncover the unconscious processes, and I was amazed at the skill with which he did his microscopic analysis. It is true that the microscope was unduly active when it played upon the squid and the cachalot."
67 Freud, *Civilization and Its Discontents*, 122.

CHAPTER FOUR

1 Pratt's admiration for Hardy is expressed in his article "Thomas Hardy," 239–47.
2 Nor does St Thomas Aquinas, provided that fate is understood to be in the disposition of Providence, which "does not deprive things of contingency and changeableness" (*Contra Gentiles* xciii; *Summa Theologiae* I, q 22, 1.4). In general agreement are Boethius, *De consolatione philosophiae*, ii, p 2; and Dante, *Inferno*, vii, 49–98.
3 Calvin, *Institutes* 3.21.5, 3.21.7.
4 This passage recalls the description of the deceptive beauty of the muskeg in *Towards the Last Spike* (2.239–40).

5 It is possible, but not likely, that by the time of writing "Clay" Pratt had read Oswald Spengler's *Der Untergang des Abendlandes*, translated as *The Decline of the West*. Spengler acknowledges his debt to Hegel (1:377; 2:47).
6 Schweitzer, *The Quest of the Historical Jesus*, 368–9.
7 In his letter to Dorothy Doyle, 21 July 1957, Pratt later adds, "The poem is a *dream* of an Armageddon. I think John Sutherland forced the religious issue in this allegory, though his treatment was superb."
8 Huxley, *Evolution and Ethics*, 32.
9 Northrop Frye in his "The Narrative Tradition in English-Canadian Poetry," 145–55, places Pratt in the proper perspective of the development of the literary forms to which he found himself best adapted.
10 John Sutherland, "E.J. Pratt: A Major Contemporary Poet," 51–2.
11 John Sutherland, "E.J. Pratt: A Major Contemporary Poet," 55–6.
12 John Sutherland, *The Poetry of E.J. Pratt*. A similar misunderstanding of Pratt's point of view is evident in Frank Birbalsingh's "The Tension of His Time," 77–8.
13 Though Pratt's is "a hundred feet or thereabout" (1.152), the *Encyclopedia Britannica* (1964 ed) reports that the sperm whale (*Physeter catodon*) measures up to sixty-three feet in length, weighs from seventy-five to one hundred tons, and has ten to sixteen teeth on each side of the jaw and vestigial upper teeth which enable it to feed on squid (1.155) and to break up the boat (1.163). The Bowhead or Greenland whale (*Balaena mysticetus*) belongs to a less developed species, is toothless, feeds upon plankton only, and is not as well equipped in the battle against the human race.
14 For good general treatments of Pratt's use of diction, metre, and rhyme in "The Cachalot," see E.K. Brown, *On Canadian Poetry*, 139–41, and Gibbs, "The Living Contour," 17–25.
15 Scott, *The Poems of Duncan Campbell Scott*, 35–40
16 Pratt wrote the introduction to a textbook edition of *Moby-Dick* that was published by Macmillan in 1929.
17 Djwa, *The Evolutionary Vision*, 70–1, 147, 151.
18 E.K. Brown, *On Canadian Poetry*, 138.
19 Hardy, *Collected Poems*, 1:288–9.
20 E.J. Pratt to W.A. Deacon, 8 April 1935, W.A. Deacon Correspondence.
21 For interest, compare the christening of the *Titanic* with Pratt's lyric "The Ritual" (1.129).
22 Pratt discusses the double function of such means of communication, "like a human hand that might be extended in a friendly grasp or closed like a fist" (MS 3:18:6).
23 Hardy, *Collected Poems*, 1:288–9.
24 Pratt compares the mountain peaks to cathedral spires in *Towards the Last Spike* (2.214).

25 Pratt uses this term in a context of fear in "The Great Feud" (1.171).
26 Pratt may have had in mind Milton's analogy between Satan sleeping on the burning lake (*Paradise Lost*, 1:355) and Leviathan "slumbering on the Norway foam," whom sailors sometimes mistook for an island. Later in the same book Milton mentions Gibraltar (1:355). He also associates the Titans, who were thrown out of heaven into the underworld for their pride and their rebellion against Jupiter, with the fallen angels. A Titan was among the first to arrive at Milton's "Great Consult" (1:510).
27 In various introductions to readings of the poem, Pratt remarked upon the irony implicit in the *Titanic*'s silence: "The announcement of the presence of a radio on board recalls the sense of conquest over nature which visited the world, the trust in science for the prevention of grosser human calamities ... It was there as a voice with a call the radius of 500 miles and more" (MS 68:6). When it did cry out, "the call was met by silence" (MS 2:12).
28 Six of the stars and constellations mentioned by Pratt appear also in Hardy's description, including "red Aldebaran" (see also "The Highway," 1.256).
29 This image recalls that of the "great daffodil" in Isabella Valancy Crawford's "Malcolm's Katie," *Collected Poems*, 203.
30 E.J. Pratt to Dorothy Doyle, 21 July 1957.
31 In a discussion of The *"Titanic"* (MS 3:18), Pratt remarks on the behaviour of Ida Strauss as an incident which he cannot forget. "It was a magnificent gesture backed up by a sacrifice. Such actions are made for poetry ... It shows the fine stuff which has entered into the composition of human nature, something so fine, so durable, that we have no descriptive terms adequate to its worth."
32 Genuine pride has nothing to do with haughtiness, which is a caricature of it. It is perfectly compatible with humility, and is related to liberty. See Xavier Léon-Dufour, *Dictionary of Biblical Theology*, 404–5.
33 Pratt uses this phrase also in "The Mirage" (1.282).
34 Hardy, *Collected Poems*, 288.
35 Atwood, *Survival*, 58.
36 Germaine Warkentin in "The Aesthetics of E.J. Pratt's Shorter Poems," 18, indicated the relationship between "aesthetic units," incidents or images such as this one, which, recurring in Pratt's poetry, sometimes take on a different form, function, or tone, as they appear in lyric or in narrative context.
37 West, "E.J. Pratt's Four-Ton Gulliver," 13–20.
38 Djwa, *The Evolutionary Vision*, 107.
39 *Canadian Forum* (1942), 264–5; see ch 2, note 77, above.
40 Thomas Aquinas, *Summa Theologiae* I, q.2, a.3.
41 *Queen's Quarterly* 41 (1934): 255.

42 Ronald Knox in his *Enthusiasm*, 585–9, discusses the typical distrust of human thought processes on the part of the enthusiast or mystic. Pratt may have been rebelling, to a certain extent, against the strong influence in his earlier philosophical and theological studies of the thought of Hegel, for whom "the real" was limited to the rational.
43 John Sutherland, "A Major Contemporary Poet," 48.
44 Davey, "E.J. Pratt: Rationalist Technician," 70.
45 Lynch, *Images of Faith*, 88.

CHAPTER FIVE

1 United Church of Canada/Victoria University Archives, Toronto.
2 United Church of Canada/Victoria University Archives, Toronto
3 These lines may recall phrases from John Henry Newman's "Praise to the Holiest in the Height" from "The Dream of Gerontius" in *Verses on Various Occasions*, 363. It is possible that Pratt's admiration of Newman (MS 72) owes something to the influence of George Blewett. See Blewett, "The Scientist and the Vision of God."
4 "God of All Children of the Earth," *One Family*, inside back cover.
5 See for example the "First Contemplation of the Fourth Week," *The Spiritual Exercises of St. Ignatius Loyola*, nos 101–9, nos 218–25.
6 This poem first appeared in *Canadian Forum* 14 (1933): 14. It was reprinted in *The Fable of the Goats and Other Poems*, 27–31.
7 Livesay, *Collected Poems*, 120–5.
8 The last line of "A Prayer-Medley" as it appears in *The Fable of the Goats and Other Poems* is "Give us this day our daily bread and forgive us our trespasses" (1.297). In the version which appeared in the *Canadian Forum* an additional line follows: "For we do not forgive those who trespass against us" (93).
9 F.R. Scott, "All the Spikes But the Last," *Selected Poems*, 64.
10 E.J. Pratt in response to Dorothy Doyle, 21 July 1957.
11 Davey, "Rationalist Technician," 65–78.
12 Dudek, "Poet of the Machine Age," 75–80.
13 E.J. Pratt to W.A. Deacon, 27 August 1927; E.J. Pratt to Lorne Pierce, 29 September 1927, 5 March 1928; E.J. Pratt to Dorothy Doyle, 21 July 1957.
14 Thompson, *The Collected Poetry of Francis Thompson*, 52–7. All further references in this text to "The Hound of Heaven" will be designated HH.
15 James, *The Varieties of Religious Experience*, 380.
16 Underhill, *Mysticism*, 137–8.
17 James, *The Varieties of Religious Experience*, 381.
18 Underhill, *Mysticism*, 380.
19 Underhill, *Mysticism*, 340.

20 Underhill, *Mysticism*, 137–8.
21 Underhill, *Mysticism*, 340.
22 See Teresa of Avila, *Life*, 28, 5–8: "In comparison [with the vision] the brightness of the sun seems to be so obscure that no one would ever wish to open his eyes again." Quoted by Underhill, *Mysticism*, 347.
23 Horwood, "E.J. Pratt and William Blake," 197.
24 Sharman, "Illusion and an Atonement," 24.
25 Clever, *On E.J. Pratt*, 66.
26 E.J. Pratt in response to Dorothy Doyle, 21 July 1957.
27 Pratt's daughter, Claire, though gravely ill at the time, was later to make a partial recovery.
28 Djwa, *The Evolutionary Vision*, 6.
29 Huxley, *Evolution and Ethics*, 3. Further references to this work, hereafter designated EE will be included in parentheses in the text.
30 Djwa, *The Evolutionary Vision*, 26–7, 105.
31 John Wesley in "The Great Assize," *Sermons* 15, identifies the "Son of Man" with the "Son of God" in full eschatological context, as does George Blewett in *The Christian View of the World*, 309–11.
32 Bernard Delfgaauw, *Evolution*, 92–3. See also George Blewett, "The Scientist and the Vision of God," 323.
33 In "Clay," Penrose remarks about Julian that one mark of his cynicism is that he saw "the ape ... grinning through men's eyes and teeth" (2.307–8). A similar telescoping of the evolutionary process is evident in *They Are Returning* (2.141).
34 Teilhard de Chardin, *The Phenomenon of Man*, 26. Robert Faricy in *Teilhard de Chardin's Theology of the Christian in the World*, 15, discusses Teilhard's insight into modern man's fear that there may be no way out of what appears to be a blind alley. Teilhard uses the figure of miners trapped underground to uphold the argument that human beings will make no effort to emerge if they believe there is no opening or way out. There is a startling similarity between Teilhard's image and one used by Pratt in a speech, "In Quest of the Humanities." Pratt states, "there is a mental therapy in hope, in the expression of a positive faith that a tunnel, however dark the passageway, has an exit into some measure of sunlight. To believe otherwise means inertia, frustration, and continuous darkness" (MS 70:2).
35 Northrop Frye, *Silence in the Sea*, 16; John Sutherland in "E.J. Pratt: A Major Contemporary Poet," 41, remarks that Pratt frequently stresses Gethsemane rather than the Cross, but rather than pursue this observation in the poems in which it is obvious, he turns instead to *Titans* and *The "Titanic"*.
36 The fountain of life is a recurring image in Wesleyan hymnody. For examples see *A Collection of Hymns for the Use of People Called Methodists*, nos. 4, 10.

37 Wilson, *E.J. Pratt*, 12.
38 A.J.M. Smith in *Some Poems of E.J. Pratt*, 20, remarks that "Pratt's would seem a meaningless universe were it not for the one inexplicable (or if you prefer, miraculous) intervention symbolized by the Rood." See also Lynch, *Images of Faith*, 166–70.
39 E.J. Pratt to Dorothy Doyle, 21 July 1957.
40 Faulkner, "On Receiving the Nobel Prize," 120.
43 Lynch, *Images of Faith*, 101.
44 This poem first appeared in *Here and Now* 4 (1949): 77.
45 Freud, *The Origin and Development of Psychoanalysis*, 11–12.
46 Arnold, *Poetry and Criticism of Matthew Arnold*, 161–2.
47 The present situation in Bosnia, Pakistan, or Israel lends a contemporaneity to this poem. In 1948, the year in which it was written, Mahatma Gandhi, a Hindu pacifist trying to negotiate between Hindus and Moslems in India, was assassinated by a Hindu fanatic on his way home from a prayer meeting. The state of Israel was founded, and Count Folke Bernadotte, the United Nations' Representative for Palestine, was assassinated by Israeli terrorists.
48 John Wesley, presented with a life of Ignatius Loyola, read it with interest, and found it "surprising." He concluded that Ignatius was "surely one of the greatest men that was ever engaged in the support of so bad a cause." (*Journal*, 16/8/42).
49 Milton Wilson, *E.J. Pratt*, 54.
50 See Blewett, *The Christian View* 156; Wesley, *Sermons* 8:88, 13:152, 74:396–406; *Minutes of the Conference of the United Societies*; "Form of Ordaining Ministers" and "Form of Receiving Persons into the Church after Probation," *Doctrine and Discipline of the Methodist Church*, 534, 538; Rupp, *Methodism in Relation to the Protestant Tradition*, 6.
51 See Wynne, *The Jesuit Martyrs of North America*, 1–10. This was, in all likelihood, Pratt's source for the historical details in this section of the poem. It is sadly lacking in the sense of vitality that Pratt was able to infuse into his work. Another source is the *Jesuit Relations*. See Thwaite's edition, 8:1, 237–43.
52 For further development of these signs of the presence of the Holy Spirit, see Wesley, *Sermons*, 8, 9, 10, 16, 18.
53 Critics have associated the trumpet call, a prominent image in Pratt's poetry, with both martial imagery and the stimulus of Wundtian psychology. In *PE*, 75, Pratt traces Paul's use of the image to its roots in the Old Testament. In Ex 19, "the voice of the trumpet exceeding loud" summons the people to Sinai where they ratify the covenant with God; in Is 27:3 it recalls the dispersed of Israel from their exile; in 1 Thess 4:16 it summons those who have died in Christ to rise and return to him. In these texts it symbolizes the voice of God. In *The*

Hound of Heaven the trumpet sounds "from the hid battlements of eternity."

54 Wesley, *Sermons*, 60:248; Teilhard de Chardin, *The Divine Milieu*, 124–6; Blewett, *The Christian View*, 309–10.
55 Pratt quotes from Wesley (*Sermons*, 3. 434) to describe these experiences which "Turned ... a brand / Of shame into the ultimate boast of time" (2.71).
56 Wesley's stress on "the discernment of spirits," which Ignatius also emphasized (*Exercises*, 313–36), is found in *Sermons* 9, 10, 11, 21, 22, 23.
57 See Thomas à Kempis, *Of the Imitation of Christ*, 12, 80.
58 M. Desjardins in "A Study of E.J. Pratt's 'Brébeuf and His Brethren,'" 73, remarks that Pratt is "concerned with the courage and force displayed by the priests, much more than with their deep motivation for the love of God ... He does not worry much about the inner quality of their faith." Desjardins suggests that since Pratt's theology is beclouded, the poet "falls back on a form of visionary Christianity, or private revelations which he handles more or less skilfully." It would appear, on the contrary, from the poem and from his comments on its sources, that Pratt was deeply concerned with the priests' motivation, which he saw to be rooted in prayer. All "visions" except Brébeuf's first one are accounted for in the *Relations* and should be interpreted in the light of the Ignatian concept of prayer. Excellent discussions of its implications may be found in Joseph de Guibert's *The Jesuits, Their Spiritual Doctrine and Practice*, 544–68; Lynch, *Christ and Apollo*, 53–61.
59 In the *Rules for the Discernment of Spirits Appropriate to the Second Week of the Spiritual Exercises*, no 330, Ignatius defines consolation without previous cause as the experience of being drawn to the love of God "without any preceding perception or knowledge of any subject by which a soul might be led to such a consolation through its own acts of intellect or will."
60 In Brébeuf's experience Pratt may have found, too, an analogue to Wesley's doctrine of "perceptible inspiration," the experience of faith, or the inner perception that God, in Christ, is graciously disposed. Wesley held that this perception, wrought inwardly by the Holy Spirit, is as indubitable a perception as sight, sound, or self–consciousness (*Sermons* 10:11–22). The analogy between faith and sight is illustrated in *Letters* 1:255; 2:24, 48, 50; 4:116, 126, 176. See also Outler, ed., *John Wesley*, 39.
61 For example, Paul on the road to Damascus (*PE* 92, 188), Ignatius at Manresa, and Wesley at Aldergate.
62 Wolman, *Historical Roots of Contemporary Psychology*, 27.
63 G. Stanley Hall, *Founders of Modern Psychology*, 107.
64 In an introduction to a reading of the poem (MS 3:24, 3) Pratt remarked that "this drama ran for thirty years and more ... I was struck by the number of times the priests in the Huron country renewed their vows. It

could mean only one thing – that the strain of labour, exposure and constant irritation, must have so strenuously tested the will that it needed the refuge and the fortress of prayer and pledge." The custom of the renewal of vows, especially in writing, may have reminded Pratt of the Methodist practice of renewing the Covenant which the minister was accustomed to lead on his first tour of the Circuit each January. See *Doctrine and Discipline of the Methodist Church*, 540.

65 Clever, *On E.J. Pratt*, 43; Atwood, *Survival*, 93–5.
66 Clever, *On E.J. Pratt*, 42
67 It is this type of asceticism that Ignatius, as a result of his own experience, warned against. See *Constitutions of the Society of Jesus*, 6:3; 582. John Wesley in *Sermons*, 10:359, seems to echo Ignatius's words.
68 Bouyer, *The Spirit and Forms of Protestantism*, 168, 211.
69 de Guibert, *Constitutions of the Society of Jesus*, 171, 570–1.
70 *Doctrine and Discipline of the Methodist Church*, 19.
71 The love-feast was to be held in each Circuit and Mission at least once a quarter, and was to last no longer than an hour and a half. See *Doctrine and Discipline of the Methodist Church*, 84, 117. Adapted by Wesley from the Moravians, and based on a reference to Jude 12, the *agape* was a gathering at which prayer and praise were mingled with testimonies to the goodness of God, and during which the congregation was fed on bread and water. It was intended to promote piety, mutual affection, and zeal. See Davies, *Worship and Theology in England*, 3:261–2. For an interesting parallel to "The Depression Ends," see "Come Sinners to the Gospel Feast" in *A Collection of Hymns for the Use of the People Called Methodists*, 8.
72 Kenton, ed., *The Jesuit Relations and Other Allied Documents*, 223.
73 Jones, *Butterfly on Rock*, 65–6; Djwa, "The Civil Polish of the Horn," 97.
74 Kenton, *Jesuit Relations*, 222.
75 Parkman, *The Jesuits in North America in the Seventeenth Century*, 403; Kenton, ed., *The Jesuit Relations and Other Allied Documents*, 195.
76 Brébeuf's attitude is not inconsistent with John Wesley's notion of meekness. The meek "do not desire to extinguish any of their passions which God has, for wise ends, implanted in their nature, but they have mastery of all. They hold them all in subjection, and employ them only in subservience to those ends. And thus even the harsher and more unpleasing passions are applicable to the noblest purposes, even anger and hatred and fear when engaged against sin, and regulated by faith and love, are as bulwarks to the soul" (*Sermons*, 22:263).
77 Sharman, "Illusion and an Atonement," 27–8; Djwa, *The Evolutionary Vision*, 97–8.
78 Pratt later remarked about his sources, "a most dramatic feature of the story is the disclosure of one facet of the Indian mind, ... the sense of irony ... the sarcasm, and the sense of *double-entendre* ... Torture is charac-

teristically a human process implying a development in self-consciousness. In one respect it is an art with a sense of design and elaboration, a feeling for effect. Its [irony's] presence in the Indian nature, Huron and Iroquois alike, shows that an injustice has been done to them by the Romantics who would strip them of all amenities of civilization" (MS 70:3).

79 Of his use of this image Pratt wrote, "the central idea to me was to get hold of a symbol which at the time of the Crucifixion represented the very limit of shame in the eyes of the pagan world, but later became the transcendent glory of Christian theology and experience, namely the Cross. I had to end on that note." E.J. Pratt to Dorothy Doyle, 21 July 1957; Wakefield in *Methodist Devotion*, 18, remarks that "the object [of Methodist devotion] is eternally Christ crucified."

80 Sharman, "Illusion and an Atonement," 29; equally unfounded is Glenn Clever's contention that "rhetoric and plot ... inconsistent with the narrative imperatives of the topic ... result in an impropriety, a melodrama and a sentimentality which preclude the development of the tragic potential inherent in the context of the story material" (*On E.J. Pratt*, 43).

81 E.K. Brown discusses the patriotic implications of this poem in his *On Canadian Poetry*, 147.

82 Hodges, *The Pattern of Atonement*, 12.

83 There are exceptions in prose, notably in Pratt's letters. See, for example, those to W.A. Deacon, August 1922, and to Dorothy Doyle, 21 July 1957.

84 Frye, "The Narrative Tradition in English–Canadian Poetry," 153.

85 Blewett, *The Christian View*, ix, 216–17.

CONCLUSION

1 Careless, *Canada, a Story of Challenge*, 398.
2 Pitt, *The Truant Years*, 206, 262.
3 Pitt, *The Truant Years*, 196.
4 Pitt, *The Truant Years*, 260.
5 Pitt, *The Truant Years*, 309–10.
6 Laakso et al, *E.J. Pratt: An Annotated Bibliography*.
7 Semple, *The Lord's Dominion*.
8 Dowbiggin, *Keeping America Sane*.
9 Collins, *E.J. Pratt*, 193.
10 Djwa, Introduction to *Complete Poems of E.J. Pratt*, xi–xlvii.
11 Froese, "E.J. Pratt as Lyricist," 20.

Bibliography

PRIMARY SOURCES

Pratt's Poetic Works

Rachel: A Sea Story of Newfoundland in Verse. New York: privately printed 1917
Newfoundland Verse. Toronto: Ryerson 1923
The Witches' Brew. London: Selwyn and Blount 1925; Macmillan 1926
Titans: Two Poems. Toronto: Macmillan 1926
The Iron Door (An Ode). Toronto: Macmillan 1927
The "Roosevelt" and the "Antinoe". New York: Macmillan 1930
Verses of the Sea. Toronto: Macmillan 1930
Many Moods. Toronto: Macmillan 1932
The "Titanic". Toronto: Macmillan 1935
The Fable of the Goats and Other Poems. Toronto: Macmillan 1937
Brébeuf and His Brethren. Toronto: Macmillan 1940
Brébeuf and His Brethren. 2nd revised edition. Toronto: Macmillan 1940
Dunkirk. Toronto: Macmillan 1941
Brébeuf and His Brethren: The North American Martyrs. Detroit: Basilian Press 1942
Still Life and Other Verse. Toronto: Macmillan 1943
Collected Poems. Toronto: Macmillan 1944
Collected Poems. With an introduction by William Rose Benét. New York: Knopf 1945
They Are Returning. Toronto: Macmillan 1945
Behind the Log. Toronto: Macmillan 1947
Ten Selected Poems. With notes by E.J. Pratt. Toronto: Macmillan 1947

Towards the Last Spike. Toronto: Macmillan 1952

Magic in Everything. Toronto: Macmillan 1955

A Club's Inventory of Hades. Toronto: privately printed 1958

The Collected Poems of E.J. Pratt. Edited with an introduction by Northrop Frye. 2nd edition. Toronto: Macmillan, 1958

Lines on the Occasion of Her Majesty's Visit to Canada, 1959. Toronto: CBC Information Services, 1959

Here the Tides Flow. Edited with an introduction and questions by David G. Pitt. Toronto: Macmillan, 1962

"Eight Poems." *Tamarack Review* 41 (1966): 74–81

Selected Poems of E.J. Pratt. Edited with an introduction and notes by Peter Buitenhuis. Toronto: Macmillan 1968

E.J. Pratt: Complete Poems. 2 vols. Edited with an introduction by S. Djwa and R.G. Moyles. Toronto: University of Toronto Press 1989

Some of Pratt's Contributions to Anthologies

Klinck, Carl F., and Reginald E. Watters, eds. *Canadian Anthology.* Revised edition. Toronto: Gage 1955

Pratt, E.J., Robert Finch, Leo Kennedy, A.M. Klein, F.R. Scott, and A.J.M. Smith. *New Provinces: Poems of Several Authors.* Toronto: Macmillan 1936

Scott, F.R. and A.J.M. Smith, eds *The Blasted Pine: An Anthology of Satire, Invective, and Disrespectful Verse Chiefly by Canadian Writers.* Revised and enlarged edition. Toronto: Macmillan 1957

Smith, A.J.M., ed. *The Book of Canadian Poetry: A Critical and Historical Anthology.* 2nd edition, revised and enlarged. Chicago: University of Chicago Press 1948

Wilson, Milton, ed. *Poets between the Wars: New Canadian Library Original.* Toronto: McClelland and Stewart 1967

Some Prose Writings by E.J. Pratt

"The Scientific Character of Psychology." *Acta Victoriana* 37 (1913): 300–4

"The Demonology of the Synoptics in Relation to Earlier Developments and to the Mind of Christ." MA thesis. University of Toronto 1913

Studies in Pauline Eschatology and Its Background. Ph.D. thesis. Toronto: William Briggs 1917

"Mental Measurements as Applied to a Toronto Public School." *Public Health Journal* 12 (1921): 148–55

"The Application of the Binet-Simon Tests (Stanford Revision) to a Toronto Public School." *Canadian Journal of Mental Hygiene* 3 (1921): 95–116

"Thomas Hardy." *Canadian Journal of Religious Thought* 1 (1924): 239–47

Introduction and notes to *Moby-Dick* by Herman Melville. Toronto: Macmillan 1929

"Canadian Poetry – Past and Present." *University of Toronto Quarterly* 8 (1938): 1–10

Introduction to *Under the Greenwood Tree* by Thomas Hardy. St Martin's Classics. Toronto: Macmillan 1943

Foreword to *St. Ignace, Canadian Altar of Martyrdom* by W.S. Fox and Wilfred Jury. Toronto: McClelland and Stewart 1949

Gingell, Susan, ed. *E.J. Pratt on His Life and Poetry*. Toronto: University of Toronto Press 1983

– *E.J. Pratt: Pursuits Amateur and Academic*. Toronto: University of Toronto Press 1995

Manuscript Collections and Correspondence

Kingston

Queen's University, Douglas Library. E.J. Pratt Manuscripts

Queen's University Archives. Lorne Pierce Correspondence with E.J. Pratt, 1920–56

Toronto

Thomas Fisher Rare Book Library
 Earle Birney Correspondence, 1938–58
 W.A. Deacon Correspondence, 1925–46
 A.J.M. Smith Correspondence, 1941–60

Victoria University Library
 Pelham Edgar Papers. Correspondence with E.J. Pratt, 1930–48 and undated
 Claire Pratt Correspondence
 E.J. Pratt Collection of Manuscripts
 Viola Pratt Correspondence
 Acta Victoriana, 1909–33
 Victoria College Bulletin, 1909–64

Church Documents

The Doctrine and Discipline of the Methodist Church. Edited by a committee appointed by the General Conference. Toronto: William Briggs 1900–24

Methodist Monthly Greeting. St John's, Newfoundland, 1888–1924

Missionary Monthly. Toronto; United Church of Canada 1925–61

One Family. Toronto: United Church of Canada Women's Missionary Society 1937

Shaw, William I. *Digest of the Doctrinal Standards of the Methodist Church*. Toronto: William Briggs 1895

United Church of Canada Archives
Minutes of the Annual Conferences from the First, Held in London. London: Conference Office 1812
Edmonton, Alberta. *Minutes of the Proceedings of the 9th and 10th Sessions of the Alberta Conference of the Methodist Church.* Edmonton: Methodist Publishing House 1912–13
St John's, Newfoundland. *Minutes of the Proceedings of the 1st–25th Sessions of the Newfoundland Conference of the Methodist Church.* St John's: Methodist Publishing House 1874–1912
– Report of the Executive Board of the Methodist College, 1916–17
– Newfoundland Conference, Special Committee, *Minutes,* January 1912
– Twillingate District Meetings, *Minutes,* May 1904
Toronto, Ontario. Biography File: Reverend John Pratt 1840–1907
– The Great Appeal and Final Triumph. Pictorial Pageant presented in Massey Hall, Toronto. Epilogue by Edwin John Pratt
– *Minutes of the Proceedings of the 20th Sessions of the Toronto Conference of the Methodist Church.* Toronto: William Briggs 1913
– *Minutes of the 42nd and the 53rd Meetings of the Toronto Conference of the United Church of Canada.* Toronto: United Church of Canada 1925, 1936
– Triumphs of the Faith. A pictorial presentation produced by Denzil G. Ridout, 1954. Hymns by E.J. Pratt
– *World Friends.* Toronto: United Church of Canada. January 1932–December 1938

SECONDARY SOURCES

Adler, Gerhard. *The Living Symbol.* New York: Pantheon 1961
Amiot, Francois. *The Key Concepts of St. Paul.* Translated by John Dingle. New York: Herder and Herder 1962
Armour, Leslie, and Elizabeth Trott. *The Faces of Reason.* Waterloo: Wilfrid Laurier University Press 1981
Arnold, Matthew. *Poetry and Criticism of Matthew Arnold.* Edited by A. Dwight Culler. Boston: Houghton Mifflin 1961
Atwood, Margaret. *Survival: A Thematic Guide to Canadian Literature.* Toronto: Anansi 1972
Aulen, Gustaf. *Christus Victor: An Historical Study of the Three Main Types of the Idea of the Atonement.* Translated by A.G. Herbert. London: SPCK 1950
Barclay, William. *New Testament Words.* London: SCM 1964
Barrow, Logie. *Independent Spirits: Spiritualism and English Plebeians 1850–1910.* London: Routledge and Kegan Paul 1986
Barth, Karl. *Protestant Theology in the Nineteenth Century.* Valley Forge, Ind: Judson Press 1973

Batstone, H.A. "Methodism in Newfoundland: A Study of Its Social Impact." STM thesis. Montreal: McGill University 1967

Beattie, Munro. "E.J. Pratt." In *A Literary History of Canada*. General editor, Carl F. Klinck. Toronto: University of Toronto Press 1965

Bednar, Gerald J. *Faith as Imagination: The Contribution of William F. Lynch, SJ*. Kansas City: Sheed and Ward 1996

Beesley, Lawrence. *The Loss of the Titanic*. New York: Nautilus Library 1912

Benét, William Rose. Introduction to *Collected Poems* by E.J. Pratt. 1st American edition. New York: Knopf 1945

Birbalsingh, Frank. "The Tension of His Time." *Canadian Literature* 64 (1975): 75–82

Birney, Earle. "E.J. Pratt and His Critics." In *Our Living Tradition*. Edited by Robert L. McDougall. 2nd ser. Toronto: University of Toronto Press 1959

Blacker, C.P. *Eugenics, Galton and After*. Cambridge: Harvard University Press 1952

Blake, William. *The Complete Writings of William Blake with Variant Readings*. Edited by Geoffrey Keynes. London: Oxford University Press 1966

Blewett, George John. *The Christian View of the World*. Toronto: William Briggs 1912

– "The Scientist and the Vision of God." *Acta Victoriana* 21 (1898): 316–18

– *The Study of Nature and the Vision of God: With Other Essays in Philosophy*. Toronto, William Briggs 1907

Bouyer, Louis. *The Spirit and Forms of Protestantism*. Translated by A.V. Littledale. Westminster, Maryland: Newman Press 1956

Bowles, R.P. "The Spirit of Victoria." In *On the Old Ontario Strand: Victoria's Hundred Years*. Toronto: Victoria University 1936

Brewster, Elizabeth. "Aftermath of 'The Titanic.'" *The E.J. Pratt Symposium*. Edited by Glenn Clever. Ottawa: University of Ottawa Press 1977

Brown, E.K. *On Canadian Poetry*. Toronto: Ryerson 1943

Brown, George W. "The Founding of Victoria College." In *On the Old Ontario Strand: Victoria's Hundred Years*. Toronto: Victoria University 1936

Brown, Raymond E., Joseph A. Fitzmyer, and Roland E. Murphy, eds. *The New Jerome Biblical Commentary*. Englewood Cliffs, NJ: Prentice Hall 1990

Brown, Thomas E. "Dr Ernest Jones, Psychoanalysis and the Canadian Medical Profession." In *Medicine in Canadian Society: Historical Perspectives*. Edited by S.E.D. Shortt. Montreal: McGill-Queen's University Press 1981: 315–60

Brown, Walter T. "Victoria and a Century of Education." In *On the Old Ontario Strand: Victoria's Hundred Years*. Toronto: Victoria University 1936

Browning, Robert. *Poems of Robert Browning*. Edited by Donald Smalley. Boston: Houghton Mifflin 1956

Buechner, Frederick. *Telling the Truth: The Gospel as Tragedy, Comedy, and Fairy Tale*. New York: Harper and Row 1977

Buitenhuis, Peter. "E.J. Pratt." In *The Canadian Imagination: Dimensions of a Literary Culture*. Edited by David Staines. Cambridge, Mass: Harvard University Press 1977
- "E.J. Pratt: Poet of the Seas." In *The E.J. Pratt Symposium*. Edited by Glenn Clever. Ottawa: Ottawa University Press 1977
- Introduction to *Selected Poems of E.J. Pratt*. Toronto: Macmillan 1968

Burwash, Nathanael. *The History of Victoria College*. Toronto: Victoria College 1927

Butler, Samuel. *Erewhon or Over the Range*. London: Jonathan Cape 1933

Caldecott, Randolph, illus. *The Panjandrum Picture Book*. London: Routledge 1885

Calvin, John. *Institutes of the Christian Religion*. Edited by John T. McNeill, translated by Ford L. Battles. 2 vols. Philadelphia: Westminster Press 1960
- "Sermon du dernier avènement de N.S. Jésus Christ: 2 Thess 1." In *Sermons sur la nativité, la passion, la résurrection, et le dernier avènement de N.S. Jésus Christ*. Edited with notes by Albert Marie Schmidt; preface by Jean de Saussure. Paris: Editions "Je Sers" 1936

Campbell, Roy. *The Collected Poems of Roy Campbell*. Vol. 1. London: Bodley Head 1949

Cantley, Michael J. "Introduction to Apocalyptic." *Bible Today* 1 (1963): 500–5

Careless, J.M.S. *Canada, a Story of Challenge*. Toronto: Macmillan 1970

Cerfaux, Lucien. *Christ in the Theology of St Paul*. Translated by Geoffrey Webb and Adrian Walker. Freiberg: Herder 1958

Chapman, Raymond. *The Victorian Debate: English Literature and Society, 1832–1901*. New York: Basic Books 1968

Cirlot, J.E. *A Dictionary of Symbols*. Translated by J. Sage. New York: Philosophical Library 1962

Clever, Glenn. *On E.J. Pratt*. Ottawa: Borealis 1977
- "Pratt as War Poet." *The E.J. Pratt Symposium*. Ottawa: Ottawa University Press 1977

Clever, Glenn, ed. *The E.J. Pratt Symposium*. Reappraisals: Canadian Writers, vol 4. Ottawa: University of Ottawa Press 1977

Collin, W.E. "Pleiocene Heroics." In his *The White Savannahs*. Toronto: Macmillan 1936

Collins, Robert G. *E.J. Pratt*. Boston: Twayne 1988
- Introduction to *Selected Poems of E.J. Pratt*. Toronto: Macmillan 1968

Corcoran, X.W.P. "Celtic Mythology." *New Larousse Encyclopedia of Mythology*. London: Paul Hamlyn 1956

Cox, Leo G. *John Wesley's Concept of Perfection*. Kansas City, Mo: Beacon Hill Press 1964

Crawford, Isabella Valancy. *The Collected Poems of Isabella Valancy Crawford*. Edited by J.W. Garvin with introduction by Ethelwyn Wetherals. Toronto: William Briggs 1905

Crowther, M.A. *Church Embattled: Religious Controversy in Mid-Victorian England*. Newton Abbot, Devon: David and Charles 1970

Darwin, Charles. *The Descent of Man and Selection in Relation to Sex.* 2 vols. London 1871
- *The Emotions in Man and in Animals.* London 1872
- *On the Origin of Species.* Facsimile of 1st edition (1859) with introduction by Ernst Mawr. Cambridge: Harvard University Press 1964

Davey, Frank. "E.J. Pratt: Apostle of Corporate Man." *Canadian Literature* 43 (1970): 54–66
- "E.J. Pratt: Rationalist Technician." *Canadian Literature* 61 (1974): 65–78

Davies, Horton. *The Vigilant God: Providence in the Thought of Augustine, Aquinas, Calvin, and Barth.* New York and San Francisco: Peter Lang 1992
- *Worship and Theology in England.* 5 vols. Princeton: Princeton University Press 1961–65

Deacon, William Arthur. "Laureate Takes Leave." *Canadian Author and Bookman* 39 (1964): 2

de Guibert, Joseph. *The Jesuits, Their Spiritual Doctrine and Practice: A Historical Study.* Translated by W.J. Young, edited by George E. Ganss. Chicago: Loyola University Press, Institute of Jesuit Sources 1964

Delfgaauw, Bernard. *Evolution: The Theory of Teilhard de Chardin.* Translated by Hubert Hoskins, introduction by Bernard Towers. New York: Harper and Row 1969

de Lubac, Henri. *Teilhard Explained.* Translated by Anthony Buono. Glen Rock: Paulist Press 1968

Desjardins, Maurice. "A Study of E.J. Pratt's 'Brébeuf and His Brethren.'" M.Phil. thesis, University of Toronto 1968

Dillenberger, John, and Claude Welch. *Protestant Christianity Interpreted through Its Development.* New York: Charles Scribner's Sons 1954

Dimond, Sydney G. *The Psychology of the Methodist Revival: An Empirical and Descriptive Study.* London: Oxford University Press 1926

Djwa, Sandra. "Canadian Poetry and the Computer." *Canadian Literature* 46 (1970): 43–54
- "Canadian Poets and the Great Tradition." *Canadian Literature* 65 (1975): 42–52
- "The Civil Polish of the Horn." *Ariel* 4 (1973): 82–103
- *E.J. Pratt: The Evolutionary Vision.* Studies in Canadian Literature. Toronto: Copp Clark 1974
- "E.J. Pratt and Evolutionary Thought: Towards an Eschatology." *Dalhousie Review* 52 (Autumn 1972): 414–26
- "Milton and the Canadian Folk Tradition: Some Aspects of E.J. Pratt's 'The Witches' Brew.'" *Literary Half-Yearly* 13 (1972): 56–71
- "The 1920's: E.J. Pratt, Transitional Modern." In *The E.J. Pratt Symposium.* Edited by Glenn Clever. Ottawa: Ottawa University Press 1977
- Introduction to *E.J. Pratt: Complete Poems.* 2 vols. Toronto: University of Toronto Press 1989

Dodd, Charles Harold. *The Parables of the Kingdom.* London: Collins 1961

Donahue, John R. "Miracles, Mysteries and Parables." *The Way* 18 (1978): 252–62.

Dowbiggin, Ian Robert. *Keeping America Sane: Psychiatry and Eugenics in the United States and Canada 1880–1940.* Ithaca: Cornell University Press 1997

Dudek, Louis. "Poet of the Machine Age." *Tamarack Review* 6 (1958): 74–80

– "E.J. Pratt." *Globe and Mail,* 27 April 1967, 1: 8

Dudek, Louis, and Michael Gnarowski. *The Making of Modern Poetry in Canada.* Toronto: Ryerson 1967

Edgeworth, Maria. *Harry and Lucy Concluded.* 4 vols. London: Routledge 1825

Edinger, Edward F. *Ego and Archetype.* New York: Putnam 1972

Eliot, T.S. *Collected Poems: 1909–1935.* London: Faber and Faber 1959

Elliott-Binns, Leonard. *The Development of English Theology in the Later Nineteenth Century.* London: Longmans Green 1952

– *English Thought 1860–1900: The Theological Aspect.* London: Longmans Green 1956

– *Religion in the Victorian Era.* London: Lutterworth Press 1936

Encyclopedia of Ireland. Dublin: Allen Figgis 1971

Faricy, Robert. *Teilhard de Chardin's Theology of the Christian in the World.* New York: Sheed and Ward 1967

Faulkner, William. "On Receiving the Nobel Prize." In *Essays, Speeches and Public Letters of William Faulkner.* Edited by James B. Meriwether. New York: Random House 1965

Fischer, Kathleen R. *The Inner Rainbow: The Imagination in Christian Life.* Ramsey, NJ: Paulist Press 1983

Fischlin, Daniel T. "A Critical Appraisal of 'The Parable of Puffsky.'" *Studies in Canadian Literature* 14:2 (1989): 84–104

Fitzgerald, Edward. *Variorum and Definitive Edition of Poetical and Prose Writings.* Edited by George Bentham. 7 vols. New York: Phaeton Press 1902

Fitzmyer, Joseph A. *Pauline Theology: A Brief Sketch.* Englewood Cliffs, NJ: Prentice Hall 1966

– "The Letter to the Romans." *The New Jerome Bibliocal Commentary.* Edited by R. Brown ss, J. Fitmyer sj, Roland Murphy O. Carm. Englewood Cliffs: Prentice Hall, 1990

Fowler, James W. *Stages of Faith: The Psychology of Human Development and the Quest for Meaning.* New York: HarperCollins 1981

Freud, Sigmund. *Civilization and Its Discontents.* London: Hogarth Press 1930

– *The Origin and Development of Psychoanalysis.* Chicago: Regnery 1955

Froese, Edna. "E.J. Pratt as Lyricist." *Canadian Poetry: Studies, Documents, Reviews* 30 (Spring 1992): 18–29

Frye, Northrop. *Anatomy of Criticism: Four Essays.* Princeton: Princeton University Press 1957

– *The Bush Garden: Essays in the Canadian Imagination.* Toronto: Anansi 1971

- "Edwin J. Pratt: 1882–1964. *Proceedings of the Royal Society of Canada* 4th ser, 3 (1965): 161–5
- "E.J. Pratt: The Personal Legend." *Canadian Literature* 21 (1964): 6–9.
- "Haunted by the Lack of Ghosts: Some Patterns in the Imagery of Canadian Poetry." In *The Canadian Imagination: Dimensions of a Literary Culture*. Edited by David Staines. Cambridge: Harvard University Press 1977
- Introduction to *The Collected Poems of E.J. Pratt*. 2nd edition. Toronto: Macmillan 1958
- "Letters in Canada: Poetry 1952." *University of Toronto Quarterly* 22 (1953): 269–73
- "The Narrative Tradition in English-Canadian Poetry." In *Canadian Anthology*. Edited by Carl F. Klinck and Reginald E. Watters. Rev. ed. Toronto: Gage 1966
- "The Road of Excess." In *Myth and Symbol: Critical Approaches and Applications*. Edited by Bernice Slote. Lincoln: University of Nebraska Press 1963
- *The Modern Century: The Whidden Lectures, 1967*. Toronto: Oxford University Press 1967
- *Silence in the Sea*. Pratt Memorial Lecture. St John's: Memorial University of Newfoundland 1968

Gibbs, Robert J. "Aspects of Irony in the Poetry of Edwin John Pratt." Ph. D. dissertation, University of New Brunswick, 1970
- "A Knocking in the Clay." *Canadian Literature* 55 (1973): 50–64
- "The Living Contour: The Whale Symbol in Melville and Pratt." *Canadian Literature* 40 (1969): 17–25
- "Poet of the Apocalypse." *Canadian Literature* 70 (1976): 32–41
- "A True Voice: Pratt as Lyric Poet." In *The E.J. Pratt Symposium*. Edited by Glenn Clever. Ottawa: Ottawa University Press 1977

Grant, John Webster. "Asking Questions of the Canadian Past." *Canadian Journal of Theology* 1 (1955): 98–104
- *Moon of Wintertime: Missionaries and the Indians of Canada in Encounter since 1534*. Toronto: University of Toronto Press 1984

Greene, William Howe. *The Wooden Walls among the Ice Floes: Telling the Romance of the Newfoundland Seal Fishery*. London: Hutchinson 1933

Grelot, Pierre. "Apocalyptic." In *The Encyclopedia of Theology: The Concise Sacramentum Mundi*. Edited by Karl Rahner. New York: Seabury Press 1975

Hall, Calvin S. *A Primer of Freudian Psychology*. London: George Allen and Unwin 1954

Hall, G. Stanley. *Founders of Modern Psychology*. New York: Appleton Century Crofts 1924

Hambleton, Ronald. "An Experience of Life." *CBC Times*, 6 March 1955: 3; 20 March 1955: 3

Hanson, Paul D. *The Dawn of Apocalyptic: The Historical and Sociological Roots of Jewish Apocalyptic Eschatology*. Philadelphia: Fortress Press 1975

Hardy, Thomas. *The Collected Poems of Thomas Hardy*. London: Macmillan 1932
- *The Dynasts: A Drama of the Napoleonic Wars*. London: Macmillan 1904–8
- *Far from the Madding Crowd*. London: Macmillan 1932

Harnack, Adolf. *History of Dogma*. Translated by Neil Buchanan. 7 vols in 4. New York: Peter Smith 1961

Harriott, John. "The Last Enemy." *The Way* 16 (1976): 97–106

Hodges, H.A. *The Pattern of Atonement*. London: SCM Press 1955

Hook, Sidney. *From Hegel to Marx: Studies in the Intellectual Development of Karl Marx*. New York: Humanities Press 1958

Horwood, Harold. "E.J. Pratt and William Blake: An Analysis." *Dalhousie Review* 39 (1959): 197–207

Hughes, Robert D. "Wesleyan Roots of Christian Socialism." *Ecumenist* 13 (1975): 49–53

Hunt, Peter R. "E.J. Pratt's 'Brebeuf and His Brethren' – The Critics and the Sources." In *The E.J. Pratt Symposium*. Edited by Glenn Clever. Ottawa: Ottawa University Press 1977
- "Two Catholic Epics of the Twentieth Century, James McAuley's *Captain Quiros* and E.J. Pratt's *Brébeuf and His Brethren*." MA thesis, University of New Brunswick 1975

Huxley, Thomas Henry. *Evolution and Ethics*. The Romanes Lecture. London: Macmillan 1893
- *Science and the Christian Tradition*. Authorized edition. New York: D. Appleton 1897

Inglis, Kenneth S. *Churches and the Working Class in Victorian England*. London: Routledge and Kegan Paul 1963

Innis, Harold A. *The Bias of Communication*. 2nd edition. Toronto: University of Toronto Press 1964
- *Empire and Communication*. Edited by Mary Quayle Innis, introduction by H.M. McLuhan. Toronto: University of Toronto Press 1972
- *The Fur Trade in Canada: An Introduction to Canadian Economic History*. Revised edition. Toronto: University of Toronto Press 1956
- *The History of the Canadian Pacific Railway*. Reprint of 1923 edition. Toronto: University of Toronto Press 1970.

Irvine, William. *Apes, Angels and Victorians: Darwin, Huxley and Evolution*. Introduction by Julian Huxley. New York: McGraw Hill 1955

James, William. *The Varieties of Religious Experience*. London: Longmans Green 1902

Johnson, D.W. *The History of Methodism in Eastern British America ... from the Beginning till the Consummation of Union with the Presbyterian and Congregational churches in 1925*. Sackville, NB: Tribune Publishing Co [1927]

Johnson, James F. "'Brébeuf and His Brethren' and 'Towards the Last Spike': The Two Halves of Pratt's National Epic." *ECW* 29 (1984): 142–51

Jones, Douglas G. *Butterfly on Rock: A Study of Themes and Images in Canadian Literature.* Toronto: University of Toronto Press 1970

Jones, Ernest, ed. *The Life and Works of Sigmund Freud.* New York: Basic Books 1953–1957

Joyce, James. *Dubliners.* New York: Viking Books 1961

Jung, Carl G., ed. *Man and His Symbols.* New York: Doubleday 1964

à Kempis, Thomas. *Of the Imitation of Christ in Four Books.* Oxford: James Parker and Co [n.d.]

Kenton, Edna, ed. *The Jesuit Relations and Other Allied Documents.* Introduction by Reuben Gold Thwaites. New York: Burrows 1896

Kewley, Arthur E. "The Influence of Isolation on the Theology of Methodism in Newfoundland, 1874–1924." Paper presented to the Canadian Society of Church History, Toronto, 29 May 1971

King, Carlyle. "The Mind of E.J. Pratt." *Canadian Forum* 36 (1965): 9–10

Kipling, Rudyard. *Rudyard Kipling's Verse: Inclusive Edition: 1885–1926.* Toronto: Copp Clark 1927

Klinck, Carl F., and Henry W. Wells. *Edwin J. Pratt: The Man and His Poetry.* Toronto: Ryerson 1947

– "Thoughts on E.J. Pratt." In *The E.J. Pratt Symposium.* Edited by Glenn Clever. Ottawa: Ottawa University Press 1977

Knox, Ronald A. *Enthusiasm: A Chapter in the History of Religion.* Oxford: Clarendon Press 1950

Kopp, Joseph V. *Teilhard de Chardin: A New Synthesis of Evolution.* New York: Mercier Press 1964

Laakso, Lila, comp. "E.J. Pratt: A Preliminary Checklist of Publications by and About Him with a Short List of Manuscript Collections." In *The E.J. Pratt Symposium.* Edited by Glenn Clever. Ottawa: Ottawa University Press 1977

Laakso, Lila, Raymond Laakso, Moira Allen, and Marjorie Linden. *E.J. Pratt: An Annotated Bibliography.* In *The Annotated Bibliography of Canada's Major Authors,* vol 2. Downsview: ECW Press 1980

Langland, William. *Piers Plowman.* Edited by Elizabeth Salter and Derek Pearsall. York Mediaeval Texts. London: Edward Arnold 1967

Lawton, George. *John Wesley's English: A Study of His Literary Style.* London: Allen and Unwin 1962

Lench, Charles. *An Account of the Rise and Progress of Methodism, Grand Bank and Fortune Circuits, 1816–1916.* St John's: Barnes 1916

– *The Story of Methodism in Bonavista, and of the Settlements Visited by the Early Preachers.* St John's: Robinson 1919

Léon-Dufour, Xavier, ed. *Dictionary of Biblical Theology.* Translated by P.J. Cahill. New York: Desclée 1967

Lewis, C.S. *The Problem of Pain.* London: Geoffrey Bles 1940

Livesay, Dorothy. *Collected Poems: The Two Seasons.* Toronto: McGraw Hill Ryerson 1972

- "The Documentary Poem: A Canadian Genre." In *Contexts of Canadian Criticism*. Edited by Eli Mandel. Toronto: University of Toronto Press 1971
- "The Polished Lens: Poetic Techniques of Pratt and Klein." *Canadian Literature* 25 (1965): 33–42

Loyola, Ignatius de. *The Spiritual Exercises of St. Ignatius Loyola: A New Translation Based on Studies in the Language of the Autograph.* Translated by Louis Puhl. Chicago: Loyola University Press 1951
- *Constitutions of the Society of Jesus.* Translated with introduction and commentary by George E. Ganss SJ. St Louis: Institute of Jesuit Sources 1970

Lucretius, Carus Titus. *De rerum natura.* With an English translation by W.H.D. Rouse. 3rd edition, revised. Loeb Classical Library of Latin Authors. London: Wm Heinemann 1943

Luther, Martin. *Lectures on Romans: Glosses and Scholia.* Vol 15 of *Luther's Works.* Edited by Helmut T. Lehmann and Jaroslav Pelikan. St Louis: Concordia 1972

Lynch, William F., SJ. *Christ and Apollo: The Dimensions of the Literary Imagination.* New York: Sheed and Ward 1960
- *Images of Faith: An Exploration of the Ironic Imagination.* Notre Dame, Ind: University of Notre Dame Press 1973
- *Images of Hope: Imagination as Healer of the Hopeless.* Montreal: Palm Publishers 1965

MacDonald, R.D. "E.J. Pratt: Apostle of the Techno/Corporate Culture?" *Canadian Poetry* 37 (1995): 17–41

Mackay, Louis A. "The Poetry of E.J. Pratt." *Canadian Forum* 24 (1944): 208–9

Mackendrick, Louis K. "Disjecta Membra: The Uncollected Pratt." In *The E.J. Pratt Symposium.* Edited by Glenn Clever. Ottawa: Ottawa University Press 1977

MacLeish, Archibald. *J.B.: A Play in Verse.* Boston: Houghton Mifflin 1956

Macpherson, Jay. *Pratt's Romantic Mythology: "The Witches' Brew".* Pratt Memorial Lecture. St John's: Memorial University of Newfoundland 1972

Magoun, Francis P., ed. *Anglo-Saxon Poems Represented in Bright's Anglo-Saxon Reader Done in a Normalized Orthography.* Cambridge, Mass: Harvard University Press 1956

Maly, Eugene. *Sin: Biblical Perspectives.* Cincinnati: Pflaum Publishers 1973

Mandel, Eli, ed. *Contexts of Canadian Criticism.* Patterns of Literary Criticism. Chicago: University of Chicago Press 1971

Maritain, Jacques. *Creative Intuition in Art and Poetry.* New York: Pantheon 1953

Marshall, Tom. "The Major Canadian Poets: E.J. Pratt." *Canadian Forum* 57 (1977): 19–21

Marty, Martin E. *Protestantism.* History of Religion Series. Edited by E.O. James. New York: Morehouse-Barlow 1966

Mascall, Eric. *The Christian Universe*. New York: Morehouse-Barlow 1966
Masefield, John. *Poems, Complete in One Volume*. New York: Macmillan 1929
McConnachie, Kathleen Janet Anne. "Science and Ideology: The Mental Hygiene and Eugenics Movements in the Inter-War Years, 1919–1939." Ph.D. thesis, University of Toronto, 1987
McDowell, Franklin Davey. *The Champlain Road*. Toronto: Macmillan 1939
McKenzie, John L. *Dictionary of the Bible*. London: Chapman 1966
McLaren, Angus. "Birth Control and Abortion in Canada 1870–1920." *Medicine in Canadian Society: Historical Perspectives*. Edited by S.E.D. Shortt. Montreal: McGill-Queen's University Press, 1981: 285–313
– *Our Own Master Race: Eugenics in Canada 1885–1945*. Toronto: McClelland and Stewart 1990
McNeill, John T. *The History and Character of Calvinism*. New York: Oxford University Press 1962
Monden, Louis. *Sin, Liberty and Law*. Translated by Joseph Donceel. New York: Sheed and Ward 1965
Mooney, Christopher. *Teilhard de Chardin and the Mystery of Christ*. New York: Harper and Row 1964
Mowat, Farley. *In the Wake of the Great Sealers*. Toronto: Little Brown 1974
Murray, John Courtney, SJ. *The Problem of God: Yesterday and Today*. New Haven and London: Yale University Press 1964
"Ned Pratt." *CBC Times*. 4–10 February 1961: 4.
Nelson, Geoffrey K. *Spiritualism and Society*. London: Routledge and Kegan Paul 1969
New, William H. "The Identity of Articulation: Pratt's 'Towards the Last Spike.'" In *Articulating West: Essays on Purpose and Form in Modern Canadian Literature*. Toronto: New Press 1972
The New Jerome Biblical Commentary. Edited by Raymond Brown, Joseph Fitzmyer, and Roland Murphy. Englewood Cliffs, NJ: Prentice Hall 1990
Newman, John Henry. *An Essay on the Development of Christian Doctrine*. 1878 edition. London: Longmans Green 1914
– *Verses on Various Occasions*. London: Longmans Green 1903
Nyland, Agnes. "Pratt and History." In *The E.J. Pratt Symposium*. Edited by Glenn Clever. Ottawa: Ottawa University Press 1977
O'Brien, Flann. *The Poor Mouth: A Bad Story about the Poor Life*. Translated by Patrick C. Power. Dublin: Richard Seaver 1974
Oppenheim, Janet. *The Other World: Spiritualism and Psychical Research in England 1850–1914*. London and New York: Cambridge University Press 1985
O'Súilleabhain, Séan. "The Sea." In *The Encyclopedia of Ireland*. Dublin: Allen Figgis 1971
Outler, Albert Cook. *Evangelism in the Wesleyan Spirit*. Nashville: Tidings Press 1971

Outler, Albert Cook, ed. *John Wesley*. New York: Oxford University Press 1964

Owen, Alex. *The Darkened Room: Women, Power and Spiritualism in Late Victorian England*. Philadelphia: University of Pennsylvania Press 1990

Owen, Wilfred. *War Poems and Others*. Edited with an introduction and notes by Dominic Hibberd. London: Chatto and Windus 1973

Owst, G.R. *Literature and Pulpit in Mediaeval England*. 2nd edition, revised. Oxford: Basil Blackwell 1961

Pacey, Desmond. *Creative Writing in Canada: A Short History of English-Canadian Literature*. 2nd edition. Toronto: Ryerson 1961

– "E.J. Pratt," in his *Ten Canadian Poets*. Toronto: Ryerson 1958

Paisley, Alixe Catherine. "Epic Features of *Brébeuf and His Brethren* by E.J. Pratt." MA thesis, Assumption University of Windsor 1960

Parkman, Francis. *The Jesuits in North America in the Seventeenth Century*. Vol 2 of *France and England in North America*. Toronto: George N. Morang 1899

Paterson, Morton. "The Mind of a Methodist: The Personalist Theology of George John Blewett." *Bulletin* 27 (1978): 94–103

Pitt, David G. *E.J. Pratt: The Truant Years 1882–1927*. Toronto: University of Toronto Press 1984

– *E.J. Pratt: The Master Years 1927–1964*. Toronto: University of Toronto Press 1987

Pitt, David G., ed. *E.J. Pratt: Critical Views on Canadian Writers*. Toronto: Ryerson 1969

Polkinghorne, John. *Science and Providence: God's Interaction with the World*. Boston: Shambhala 1989

Pratt, Mildred Claire. *The Silent Ancestors: The Forebears of E.J. Pratt*. Toronto: McClelland and Stewart 1973

Progoff, Ira. *Jung, Synchronicity, and Human Destiny: Noncausal Dimensions of Human Experience*. New York: Dell 1973

Rahner, Karl, ed. *Encyclopedia of Theology: The Complete Sacramentum Mundi*. New York: Seabury Press 1975

Rahner, Karl, and Herbert Vorgrimler. *Theological Dictionary*. Edited by Cornelius Ernst, translated by Richard Strachan. New York: Herder and Herder 1965

Rashley, R.E. *Poetry in Canada: The First Three Steps*. Toronto: Ryerson 1958

Rattenbury, J. Ernest. *The Evangelical Doctrine of Charles Wesley's Hymns*. London: Epworth Press 1941

Reaney, James. "'Towards the Last Spike': The Treatment of A Western Subject." *Northern Review* 7 (1955): 18–25

Reardon, Bernard M.G. *From Coleridge to Gore: A Century of Religious Thought in Britain*. London: Longmans 1971

– *Religious Thought in the Nineteenth Century*. Cambridge: Cambridge University Press 1966

Reynolds, Quentin. *The Battle of Britain*. New York: Random House 1953.
Roberts, Sir Charles G.D. *In the Morning of Time*. Toronto: McClelland and Stewart 1922
- Introduction. *Verses of the Sea* by E.J. Pratt. Toronto: Macmillan 1930
Rupp, E. Gordon. *Methodism in Relation to the Protestant Tradition*. London: Epworth Press 1954
Sanderson, J.E. *The First Century of Methodism in Canada*. 2 vols. Toronto: William Gibbs 1908, 1910
Schweitzer, Albert. *The Quest of the Historical Jesus: A Critical Study of Its Progress from Reimarus to Wrede*. London: A. and C. Black 1910
Scott, Duncan Campbell. *The Poems of Duncan Campbell Scott*. Toronto: McClelland and Stewart, 1926
Scott, F.R. *Selected Poems*. Toronto: Oxford University Press 1966
Semmel, Bernard. *The Methodist Revolution*. New York: Basic Books 1973
Semple, Neil. *The Lord's Dominion: The History of Canadian Methodism*. Montreal and Kingston: McGill-Queen's University Press 1996
Sharman, Vincent D. "Illusion and an Atonement: E.J. Pratt and Christianity." *Canadian Literature* 19 (1964): 21–32
- Patterns of Imagery and Symbolism in the Poetry of E.J. Pratt." MA thesis, University of British Columbia 1963
Shaw, William I. *Digest of the Doctrinal Standards of the Methodist Church*. Toronto: William Briggs 1895
- *The Doctrine and Discipline of the Methodist Church*. Edited by a Committee appointed by General Conference. Toronto: William Briggs 1900–13
Shelley, Percy Bysshe. *The Complete Poetical Works of P.B. Shelley*. Edited by Thomas Hutchinson. London; Oxford University Press 1956
Shirer, William. *The Rise and Fall of the Third Reich*. New York: Simon and Schuster 1960
Siebert, Rudolf. "Hegel and Theology." *Ecumenist* 12 (1973): 1–6
- Hegel's Political Theology: Liberation." *Ecumenist* 12 (1974): 33–41
Sissons, C.B. *A History of Victoria University*. Toronto: University of Toronto Press 1936
Slote, Bernice, ed. *Myth and Symbol: Critical Approaches and Applications by Northrop Frye, L.C. Knights and Others*. Lincoln: University of Nebraska Press 1963
Smith, A.J.M., ed. *Masks of Poetry: Canadian Critics on Canadian Verse*. New Canadian Library Original. Toronto: McClelland and Stewart 1962
- "Review of 'Towards the Last Spike.'" *Critically Speaking*. Typescript, CBC Press and Information Services, 10 August 1952
- *Some Poems of E.J. Pratt: Aspects of Imagery and Theme*. Pratt Memorial Lecture. St John's: Memorial University of Newfoundland 1969
- *Towards a View of Canadian Letters: Selected Critical Essays, 1928–1971*. Vancouver: University of British Columbia Press 1973

Smith, A. Lloyd. "Victoria and a Century of Theological and Religious Life." *On the Old Ontario Strand: Victoria's Hundred Years.* Toronto: Victoria University, 1936.

Smith, T.W. *A History of the Methodist Church within the Territories Embraced by the Late Conference of Eastern British America including Nova Scotia, New Brunswick, and Bermuda.* 2 vols. Halifax: Methodist Book Room 1877

Smulders, Piet. "Evolution and Original Sin." *The Mystery of Sin and Forgiveness.* Edited by M.J. Taylor. Staten Island: Alba House 1971

Smuts, Jan Christian. *Holism and Evolution* Reprint of 1926 edition. Westport, Conn: Greenwood Press 1973

Spengler, Oswald. *The Decline of the West.* 2 vols. Revised edition. Authorized translation with notes by Charles Francis Atkinson. London: George Allen and Unwin 1926–28

Staines, David, ed. *The Canadian Imagination: Dimensions of a Literary Culture.* Cambridge, Mass: Harvard University Press 1977

Stanley, David. "Believe the Works." *The Way* 18 (1978): 272–86

Starkloff, Carl. "Mission: Jesuits and Native Canadians – Learning the Meaning of Universalism." *Compass* (July/August 1991): 17–19

Stevens, Peter. "Language and Man in the Poetry of E.J. Pratt." In *The E.J. Pratt Symposium.* Edited by Glenn Clever. Ottawa: Ottawa University Press 1977

Stevenson, Lionel. *Appraisals of Canadian Literature.* Toronto: Macmillan 1926

Strauss, David Friedrich. *The Life of Jesus Critically Examined.* Translated from the 4th German edition by George Eliot. 2nd edition. London: Swann Sonnenschein 1892

Stogre, Michael. "Ministry to Indigenous People: The Search for a Balanced Critique." *Compass* (March/April 1994): 33–5

Story, Norah. *The Oxford Companion to Canadian History and Literature.* Toronto: Oxford University Press 1967

Sulzberger, C.L. *World War II.* New York: Simon and Schuster 1966

Sutherland, Alex. *The Methodist Church and Its Missions in Canada and in Newfoundland.* Toronto: Methodist Book Room 1906

Sutherland, John. "E.J. Pratt: A Major Contemporary Poet." *Northern Review* 5 (1952): 36–64

– "The Poetry of E.J. Pratt." *First Statement* 2 (1945): 27–30

– *The Poetry of E.J. Pratt: A New Interpretation.* Toronto: Ryerson 1956

Sutherland, Neil. "'To Create a Strong and Healthy Race': School Children in the Public Health Movement 1880–1914." In *Medicine in Canadian Society: Historical Perspectives.* Edited by S.E.D. Shortt. Montreal: McGill-Queens University Press 1981

Teilhard de Chardin, Pierre. *The Divine Milieu.* New York: Harper, 1960

– *The Phenomenon of Man.* New York: Harper, 1959

Tennyson, Alfred Lord. *Poems and Plays.* Edited by T. Herbert Warren, revised and enlarged by Frederick Page. London: Oxford University Press 1965

Thompson, Francis. *The Collected Poetry of Francis Thompson.* London: Hodder and Stoughton 1913
Thwaites, Reuben Gold, ed. *The Jesuit Relations and Allied Documents.* 73 vols. Cleveland: Burrows, 1896–1901.
Tillich, Paul. *Morality and Beyond.* Religious Perspectives, 9. New York: Harper and Row 1963
– *Perspectives on Nineteenth and Twentieth-Century Protestant Theology.* Edited with an introduction by Carl E. Braaten. New York: Harper and Row 1967
Tracy, Thomas F., ed. *The God Who Acts: Philosophical and Theological Explorations.* University Park: Pennsylvania State University Press 1994
Tschachler, Heinz. "The Cost of Story: Ideology and Ambivalence in the Verse Narrative of E.J. Pratt." *Canadian Literature* (Autumn–Winter 1989): 93–106.
Underhill, Evelyn. *Mysticism: A Study in the Nature and Development of Man's Spiritual Consciousness.* 4th edition. London: Methuen 1912
Vallins, George Henry. *The Wesleys and the English Language.* London: Epworth Press 1957
Van Die, Marguerite. *An Evangelical Mind: Nathanael Burwash and the Methodist Tradition in Canada, 1839–1918.* Kingston, Montreal, London: McGill-Queen's University Press 1989
Vawter, Bruce. "Missing the Mark." *The Way* 2 (1962): 19–27
Victoria College Bulletin. Toronto: Victoria University 1909–65
Victoria University. *On the Old Ontario Strand: Victoria's Hundred Years.* Addresses at the Centenary of Victoria University and the Burwash Memorial Lectures of the Centennial Year. Toronto: Victoria University 1936
von Gernet, Alexander. "Culture Contact in the Canadian Wilderness." *Compass* (July/August 1991): 19–22
Wakefield, Gordon S. *Methodist Devotion: The Spiritual Life in the Methodist Tradition.* London: Epworth Press 1966
Walsh, H.H. *The Christian Church in Canada.* Toronto: Ryerson Press 1956
Warkentin, Germaine. "The Aesthetics of E.J. Pratt's Shorter Poems." In *The E.J. Pratt Symposium.* Edited by Glenn Clever. Ottawa: Ottawa University Press 1977
Watt, Frank. "Edwin J. Pratt." *University of Toronto Quarterly* 29 (1959): 77–84
Welch, Claude. *Protestant Thought in the Nineteenth Century.* New Haven: Yale University Press 1972
Wesley, Charles, and John Wesley. *A Collection of Hymns for the Use of the People Called Methodists: with a Supplement.* London [1874]
Wesley, John. *The Journal of the Reverend John Wesley,* A.M. Edited by Nehemiah Curnock. 8 vols. London: Robert Culley 1909
– *The Nature, Design and General Rules of the United Societies in London, Bristol, Kingswood, Newcastle-upon-Tyne etc.* London: Epworth 1743
– *Notes On the New Testament.* 4 vols. Wakefield: William Nicholson n.d.

- *Sermons on Several Occasions.* Vols 5 and 6 of *The Works of the Reverend John Wesley,* A.M. 3rd edition. London 1829
- *Letters of the Reverend John Wesley.* Edited by John Telford. 8 vols. London: Epworth Press 1931

West, Paul. "E.J. Pratt's Four-Ton Gulliver." *Canadian Literature* 19 (1964): 13–20

Whaling, Frank. Introduction to John and Charles Wesley, *Selected Writings and Hymns.* New York: Paulist Press 1981

Whalley, George. "Birthright to the Sea: Some Poems of E.J. Pratt." *Queen's Quarterly* 85 (1979): 578–94.

Willey, Basil. *More Nineteenth-Century Studies: A Group of Honest Doubters.* London: Chatto and Windus 1956

- *Nineteenth-Century Studies: Coleridge to Matthew Arnold.* London: Chatto and Windus 1949

Wilson, Milton. *E.J. Pratt.* Canadian Writers. New Canadian Library Original. Toronto: McClelland and Stewart 1969

- "Pratt's Comedy." *Journal of Canadian Studies* 3 (1968): 21–30

Wolf, William J. *No Cross, No Crown.* New York: Doubleday 1957

Wolman, B.B. *Historical Roots of Contemporary Psychology.* New York: Harper and Row 1968

Wood, A. Skevington. *The Burning Heart: John Wesley, Evangelist.* London: Paternoster 1967

Wood, H.G. *Belief and Unbelief since 1850.* Cambridge: Cambridge University Press 1953

Woodcock, George, ed. *A Choice of Critics: Selections from "Canadian Literature".* Toronto: Oxford University Press 1966

Wrede, W. *The Messianic Secret in the Gospels.* London: James Clarke 1971

Wynne, John J. *The Jesuit Martyrs of North America.* New York: Universal Language Foundation 1925

Young, Kenneth. *Chapel.* London: Eyre Methuen 1972

Index

Acta Victoriana, 13
agnostic, 36, 39; agnosticism, 55
angelology, 24, 67; angels, 26; angels, fallen, 104, 114
Apocalypse, 4–5, 67, 84, 115, 118, 123; the beast of, 100, 107, 110; as expression of cosmological perspectives, 65, 107; of eschatological concerns, 65, 76, 79; as flash of insight, 24–5, 68, 126, 145, 150, 171–2, 193; as literary form, 24, 65, 67–8, 107, 113; of the synoptics, 116–17; traditional accompaniments of, 24, 31, 68, 84, 93, 169
apologetics, 12–13, 17
apperception, theory of, 50, 191
apprenticeship, 8
Armageddon, 57, 70, 108, 113, 119
Arminianism, 42
Arnold, Matthew, 149, 182
asceticism, 7, 24, 192–3; ascetical practices, 114
atheism, 36, 54–5
Atonement, doctrine of, 40–4, 175–9, 187, 197–8; vicarious, 72
Auden, W.H., 188

Baur, Fernand Christian, 20, 31, 210n110
baroque, 188

beauty, 133, 134–5, 139
Bengel, Johannes, 46
Birney, Earle, 201
Blewett, George John, 14, 17, 36, 177, 187, 198; Chair of Ethics and Apologetics at Victoria, 17–18; "oecumenical" and "catholic" world view, 18; in education, 32–6; *The Christian View of the World*, 32, 48; sudden death, 22, 35; influence on E.J. Pratt, 47, 177–8, 187, 198
blindness. *See* infirmity, physical
Body of Christ: eucharistic, 193–4; mystical, 185, 187, 188–90, 193, 197
Browning, Robert, 53; "Caliban upon Setebos," 53; "Rabbi Ben Ezra," 53
Bullen, Frank, 136; *The Cruise of the "Cachalot"*, 136
Burns, Robert, 92, 100; reason for E.J. Pratt's admiration of, 92, 100, 187–8
Burwash, Nathanael: as first head of Department of Theology at Victoria, 15; as president and chancellor of Victoria College, 15; influence on Canadian Methodism, 15–17
Byron, Lord, 133; "The Prisoner of Chillon," 133

Calvary, 59, 158–9
Calvin, John, 41, 43–4; image of God,

40, 41, 43, 52; double predestination, 125; decree of reprobation, 125
Calvinism: influence on religion of E.J. Pratt's childhood, 40, 48; on his image of God, 40, 52; on Methodism in Newfoundland, 41; on John Pratt's preaching, 40
Campbell, Roy, 136; "The Flaming Terrapin," 136
Canadian Broadcasting Corporation, 37
Canadian Forum, 163
Canadian National Committee for Mental Hygiene, 35
Canadian Poetry, 36
Carman, Albert, 15, 17
Chaucer, Geoffrey, 169, 202; "The Book of the Duchess," 169
children, place of in Methodist Church, 6–7
Christ, 41, 44–5, 48, 59, 175; Christology, 27, 157–8
Churchill, Winston, 66; the Churchillian pause, 180
church union, 12, 16, 36
Clarke, Dr C.F., as head of psychiatric clinic at Toronto General Hospital, 35
Coleridge, Samuel Taylor, 136; "The Rime of the Ancient Mariner," 136
conversion (Wesleyan) 44, 47
cosmology, 65, 107–22
criticism, higher, 15, 16–18, 42, 46–7
Cross, the, 18, 44, 158, 179; the Crucifixion, 24, 26, 32

Dante Alighieri, 50, 191
Darwin, Charles, 31; read by Pratt under Holloway's guidance, 9, 12; theory of evolution, 12, 15, 47, 125; publication of *On the Origin of Species*, 15, 46–7, 31; theme of adaptation and survival, 107, 117; of web of life and death, 82; E.J. Pratt's debt to, 88, 107, 125, 127, 176
Deacon, William Arthur: literary critic for *Saturday Night*, 62, 137, 201
death, 66, 74–91, 95–107, 113, 200; death as birth, 88–91; double stroke of, 135; death the leveller, 84
deism, 42, 43, 52
demons, 20, 99, 104, 124; demonic power, 20–1

"The Demonology of the [New Testament] Synoptics." *See* Pratt, E.J.
determinism, 127; biological, 126–7; historical, 125, 127; moral, 124, 125; natural, 124–5; philosophical, 14–15, 123; psychological, 14–15, 124, 127, 129
Devotio Moderna, 187
devotion, Methodist, 32, 168, 226n79
Dewey, John, 35
Djwa, Sandra, 176
documentary, 112
Dodd, C.H., 112–13
dream: as literary form, 113, 168; as romantic dream, 167–8; psychological interpretation of, 62, 165, 167; "The Great Feud" as dream, 117; as source of religious insight, 167–9, 170–1

Edgar, Pelham: chairman of Department of English at Victoria College, 36; faculty advisor of *Acta Victoriana*, 13
education, 3, 4, 8–11, 15
elements, conflict with, 80
Eliot, T.S., 188
eschatology, 33–4, 65, 66, 67, 79, 194, 197
evangelical religion, 9, 33, 42–3
evangelism, 4–5, 33
evil, 40; moral evil, 57, 72; natural evil, 71; evil spirit, 18, 19, 34
evolution, 13, 66, 68, 117, 178

fable, 117; "The Cachalot," 132; "The Fable of the Goats," 129
faith, 156; crisis of, 35, 49, 159, 200; evangelical, 77, 188; false faith, 138, 143
Fall, the, 69–70, 74
fate, 123–5, 127–9, 137, 151; fatalism, 123
Faulkner, William, 180
Fitzgerald, Edward: "The Rubáiyát of Omar Khayyám," 53
fountain of life, 180–1
Four Daughters of God, the, 40, 184
freedom, 48, 54, 70, 124–5, 144, 191
Freud, Sigmund, 35, 40, 118, 167; Freudian psychology, 167
Frye, Northrop, 38

Gehenna, 92

Gethsemane, 178, 180, 182, 191
God, image of, 41, 157, 173
Greenland, return of the, 8

Hardy, Thomas, 15, 57, 123, 127, 138; fate as "convergence of the twain," 127, 137; 138; *The Dynasts*, 53; *Far from the Madding Crowd* 141, 145, 183; *War Poems*, 57
Harnack, Adolf von, 31
Harris, Rev. William, 10
heaven, 169, 170, 192; as exclusive club, 167–8; as geographical location, 51
Hegel, Georg Wilhelm, 14, 30, 46; Hegelian idealism, 13
hell, 94–9, 167
Henley, W.E., 50
Hincks, Clarence, 35, 46
higher criticism, 42
history, 9
Holloway, R.A., 9, 12
Hopkins, Gerard Manley, 188
Horwood, Harold, 173
hubris, 128, 137, 141, 144
humanism, 39
Huxley, Thomas Henry, 9, 131, 176; *Evolution and Ethics*, 176

imagination, 5, 40, 42, 65, 75, 76, 78, 98–9, 101, 113, 128, 133, 188, 199–200
immortality, 79, 124, 161, 166
Incarnation, the, 18, 158, 184, 189
infirmity, physical, 86–8; blindness, 174
irony, 21, 39, 48, 62, 132, 141, 147, 192; of Christ, 180; of circumstance, 145; as "convergence of the manifold," 35, 137, 138

Jackson, Rev. George, 17
James, William, 32, 35
Jesuits, the, 187, 198
Joan, Saint, 66, 191
Jones, Ernest, 167–8
Joyce, James, 57
judgment, 91–4
Jung, Carl, 167
justice: divine, 161, 166; social, 166

Kant, Immanuel, 14, 46
kardia, 50
Kingsley, Charles, 50

Kirschmann, August, 14
Knight, Fanny, 5, 6, 7
Knight, Captain William, skipper of sealing vessel, 5

Lawrence, Joseph, 3
LeDrew, Robert, 200
Lench, Rev. Charles, 4
Leviathan, 136
Lewis, C.S., 55–6
lex talionis, 163
liberalism, 48
life, 79, 173, 175; life and death, 79, 107, 113–14, 166; life for life, 111, 184–5, 196; light and life, 173
Livesay, Dorothy, 112, 164
Loyola, Saint Ignatius, 187
Lucretius, Titus Carus, 63–4
Lyell, Sir Charles: *Principles of Geology, Geological Evidences of the Antiquity of Man*, 13

MacLeish, Archibald, *J.B.*, 75, 77
McLaughlin, J.F. Rev., 208n77
Marconi, Guglielmo, 137; first transatlantic cable message, 8, 66, 137
Melville, Herman: *Moby-Dick*, 136
Methodism: doctrinal flexibility of, 46; relieving philosophy of repentance, 43; weakness of, 45
Methodism, British: conservative nature, 4, 12; education of clergy, 10–11; missionary thrust, 3
Methodist Church of Canada: Boarding Home for Ministers' Children, 8; foundation, 4; Methodist College in St John's, 8; schools supported by Methodist Board, 8
Methodist Monthly Greeting, 9
Milton, John, 114, 187
Moore, Dr A.B.B., 37
Murray, John Courtney, 54, 64
mysticism, 17, 65, 124, 168, 173, 188, 190–2; "The Mystic," 154; mystics, 176, 187; mystical experiences, 191; mystical state, 172

narrative point of view, 132
nature, 47, 80, 123, 130, 137–46, 151; E.J. Pratt's enjoyment of, 198; evolving nature, 82; "quirkiness" of, 131; Wesley's view of, 43, 82

Nelles, Dr Samuel, 14, 16
Newman, John Henry Cardinal, 31

Owen, Wilfred, 57

Paley, William: *View of the Evidences of Christianity*, 13
Panjandrum, 52, 63, 164
parable, 112–13, 129
paradox, 35
Parousia, 65, 84, 158
parresia (pride), 144
Pelagianism, 34, 193
philosophy, 15, 124; idealism, 13–14; Scottish common-sense philosophy, 14; spiritual philosophy, 14
Pierce, Lorne, 201, 217n39, 217n40
Pike, W.H., 11, 206n28
Pratt, E.J.: ancestry and birth, 3; family life, 5–7; childhood illness, 7–8; elementary education, 9; childhood conversion, 206n26, as apprentice, 8; reading, 8, 9; secondary education, 9–10; as teacher and local preacher, 10; as probationer on circuit, 10–11; as undergraduate at Victoria College, 12–18; as graduate student in philosophy (psychology) 18; MA thesis, "The Demonology of the [New Testament] Synoptics in [Its] Relation to Earlier Developments and to the Mind of Christ," 30–5, 39, 88, 124, (summary) 18–22; relationship with Lydia Trimble, 22; transfer to Alberta Conference, 22; death of Lydia Trimble, 22; death of George Blewett, 22; B.Div. degree and ordination in Toronto, 22; further studies, 23; summary of doctoral thesis, *Studies in Pauline Eschatology and Its Background*, 23–31; both theses, 31–5; work as a psychologist, 35; failure to take up ministerial charge, 35–6; acceptance of Pelham Edgar's invitation to teach English, 36; marriage to Viola Whitney, 36; professional life, 36; "crisis of faith," 36, 200; "general modification of religious views," 36; membership in United Church of Canada, 36–7; Governor-General's Literary Award, 162; as "pacifist," 166; interviewed by J. Frank Willis, 37; three years of failing health, 37; death, 26 April 1964, 37; memorial service in Convocation Hall, 37

– books of poetry: *Collected Poems*, 163; *The Fable of the Goats and Other Poems*, 162; *Titans*, 112

– individual poems: "Armistice Silence," 85; "The Baritone," 71, 100; "Before an Altar," 194; *Behind the Log*, 85–6, 108–12, 120–1, 186–7; "Blind," 87, 174; "Blind from Singapore," 87; *Brébeuf and His Brethren*, 49, 71, 78, 94–5, 187–98; "But Mary Kept All These Things and Pondered Them in Her Heart," 161; "The Cachalot," 73, 89, 103, 112, 132–9; "Carlo," 49, 92, 95, 149, 150, 167, 173; "Clay," 50, 52–61, 75–9, 146–58, 175–6; "Come Away, Death," 51, 83–4, 110; "Come Not the Seasons Here," 80; "Comrades," 71–85; "Convict Holocaust," 71, 82, 85, 93, 110, 152; "Cycles," 52, 71, 87, 127, 152, 181–2; "The Decision," 52, 173; "The Deed," 83, 185; "The Depression Ends," 49–50, 88, 98, 107, 119, 154, 175, 194; "Displaced," 182–4; "The Doctor in the Boat," 51; "Doors," 174; "Dunkirk," 49, 97, 104–6, 120, 185; "The Dying Eagle," 104–5; "The Empty Room," 174; "The Fable of the Goats," 129, 154, 162–3; "Fire," 82; "From Stone to Steel," 71, 107, 127, 178; "The Good Earth," 73, 82, 91; "The Great Appeal and Final Triumph," 160; "The Great Feud," 69, 71, 86, 88, 96, 102–3, 104, 112–18, 119, 127, 129–31, 150–2; "The Great Tides," 82, 129; "The Ground Swell," 51; "The Highway," 49, 73, 171, 175, 198; "The History of John Jones," 167; "Horizons," 174; "The Ice-Floes," 73, 87, 96, 107–8, 110, 119, 127; "The Impatient Earth," 78, 84; "In Absentia," 82; "The Invaded Field," 90; "The Iron Door," 53, 59, 61–2, 63–4, 88, 96, 107, 127, 146–7, 154, 159, 167–73, 184, 194; "January the First," 161; "Jock o' the Links," 52; "A Legacy," 174; "The Lost Cause," 87, 174; "Magic," 177; "Magic in Everything," 185, 194; "The Manger under the Star," 161; "The Mirage," 139; "Mother and Child," 161; "The Mystic," 154;

249 Index

"Myth and Fact," 106; "Newfoundland," 81; "Newfoundland Seamen," 78, 185; "A November Landscape," 82; "Old Age," 87, 173–4; "Old Harry," 99, 104; "The Old Organon," 152; "Out of Step," 52, 92, 107; "The Parable of Puffsky," 52, 92–3, 95, 99, 104, 151, 167; "A Prayer-Medley," 163–5; "Putting Winter to Bed," 86; *Rachel*, 74, 79, 88, 127–9, 195; "The Radio in the Ivory Tower," 52, 97, 107; *The "Roosevelt" and the "Antinoe"*, 51, 62, 64, 74, 80–1, 87, 88, 93, 94, 96, 111, 112, 119, 120, 127, 130, 181, 184, 185–6; "The Sea-Cathedral," 139; "Silences," 66, 71, 97, 167; "The 6000," 96, 105; "Still Life," 83; "The Stoics," 148; "The Submarine," 89–90, 100, 105; "Summit Meetings," 107; "Thanksgiving," 161–2; "They Are Returning," 105, 120, 122, 181, 185; *The "Titanic"*, 49, 71, 73–4, 87, 93–4, 145, 107, 120, 127, 137–46, 151, 152, 153. 184; "To an Enemy," 70, 78, 179, 181; "To Angelina, an Old Nurse," 167; "The Toll of the Bells," 51, 186; *Towards the Last Spike*, 52, 62, 86, 93, 102–4; "Triumphs of the Faith," 161; "The Truant," 52, 59, 62–4, 83, 87, 93, 104, 107, 119, 149, 180–1, 182; "Under the Lens," 51; "The Unromantic Moon," 107; "The Witches' Brew," 58, 85, 97, 98–9, 100–1, 107, 127, 150
– prose works: "The Demonology of the [New Testament] Synoptics in [Its] Relation to Earlier Developments and to the Mind of Christ," 67, 88, 106, 124, 157, 168; *Studies in Pauline Eschatology and Its Background*, 65, 67, 98, 99, 124, 57, 168, 177, 188, 189, 193, 198
Pratt, Fanny Knight (mother), 5–7, 61–2, 173–4, 200
Pratt, James Spurgeon (brother), 5
Pratt, Rev. John (father): "fiery John Pratt," 3–4, 5, 6, 8–9, 10, 40; sermon at meeting of theological union, 45; preaches at Metropolitan Tabernacle, London, 4; death and burial, 5, 206n20
Pratt, Mildred Claire (daughter), 174, 200

Pratt, Viola Whitney (wife), 36, 161
Pratt, William (Will) (brother), 6–7, 200
preaching (Methodist), 4–5, 11, 15, 45, 66
predestination, 69, 114, 125, 149
probationer, 4, 10–11, 13, 22
problem of God, 40, 49, 52, 158
Protestantism, 40, 41, 45, 46, 48
providence, 40, 125
psychiatric clinic, Toronto General Hospital, 35
psychology, 14, 23, 35

rationalism, 16, 42, 149–56
reading, 9
realism, 83
Rebel (precursor of *Canadian Forum*), 13
Relations, Jesuit, 187, 194, 196
remnant, the, 118–22
Resurrection, the, 76, 174, 186
Ritschl, Albrecht, 32
romanticism, 83, 128
Ryerson, Egerton, 12–13

Sabatier, Auguste, 32
Satan, 19, 21, 99–100
Schleiermacher, David Friedrich, 32, 34, 47
Schopenhauer, Arthur, 58, 125
Schweitzer, Albert, 31, 126, 193
science, 9, 12, 16, 207n46
Sclater, W.A., 8
Scott, Duncan Campbell: "The Piper of Arll," 136
Scott, Frank, 166
sea, the, 80, 81; sea-shepherding, 118–22, 185
Shakespeare, William: *King Lear*, 53, 55, 77; *Macbeth*, 53; *The Tempest*, 54; *Twelfth Night*, 83; *The Winter's Tale*, 77
Shaw, William I., 46
Shelley, Percy Bysshe: *Julian and Maddalo*, 53, 79; *Prometheus Unbound*, 53
shrine in the ruins, the, 159
silence, 97
sin: as "Faustian clamour," 73; as *hamartanein* or *hamartia*, 72; as *hubris*, 73; as "the loathsome leprosy," 44; as narcissism, 70–1, 84; as a "taint in the blood," 71; as transformation of the heart to stone, 70; as "deep malaise in the communal heart of the world," 34

Smith, A.J.M., 79
Smith, W.G., 35
socialism, 166
Soper, S.H. (Sam), 11
soteriology, 29, 33, 185
Spengler, Oswald, 32, 148
spirituality, Ignatian, 187; incarnational, 187; Wesleyan, 187
Spurgeon, Charles Haddon, 4
stoicism, 54, 79, 125, 146–9
Strauss, David Friedrich, 22, 177, 209n96
Sutherland, John, 133

Teilhard de Chardin, Pierre, 18, 177–8, 198
theology, 40; natural, 42, 60, 158; theological education, 188
Thompson, Francis, 169; "The Hound of Heaven," 188
Titchener, E.B., 14, 35

Toynbee, Arnold, 32
tragedy, 75, 123
Trimble, Lydia, 22, 36

Underhill, Evelyn, 173
United Church of Canada: foundation of, 48, 160
universalism, 27, 33, 43, 47, 161
University of Toronto, 11, 12–14

Victoria College/University, 12–18, 35–6, 207n61
Volkmar, G., 20

war, 82–4, 89–90, 108–11
Wesley, John, 3, 43–4, 47–8, 50, 187, 191; debt to Bengel, 46; interest in study of psychology, 32
Whitney, Viola. *See* Pratt, Viola Whitney
Workman, Dr George, 17
Wundt, Wilhelm, 14, 17, 32, 35, 50